Science and the construction of women

Science and the construction of women

Edited by

Mary Maynard

UCL
PRESS

First published in 1997 by UCL Press

UCL Press Limited
1 Gunpowder Square
London EC4A 3DE
UK

and

1900 Frost Road, Suite 101
Bristol
Pennsylvania 19007-1598
USA

The name of University College London (UCL) is a registered
trade mark used by UCL Press with the consent of the owner.

British Library Cataloguing-in-Publication Data
A CIP catalogue record for this book is available from the British Library.

Library of Congress Cataloging-in-Publication Data are available

ISBNs: 1-85728-786-X HB
       1-85728-787-8 PB

Typeset in 10/12pt Times by Best-set Typesetter Ltd, Hong Kong

Printed and bound in Great Britain by SRP Ltd, Exeter

Contents

Contents

Acknowledgements

The editor is grateful to Elsevier Science Limited for permission to reprint the article by Jean Barr and Lynda Birke, 'Women, science and adult education: Towards a feminist curriculum?', which first appeared in *Women's Studies International Forum*, **17**, 5, 1994, pp. 473–83, and to the editors of the *Journal of Gender Studies* for permission to reprint the article by Cecilia Ng Choon Sim and Rohini Hensman, 'Science and technology: Friends or enemies of women?', which first appeared in the *Journal of Gender Studies*, **3**, 3, 1994, pp. 277–87.

Chapter 1

Revolutionizing the Subject: Women's Studies and the Sciences

Mary Maynard

Introduction

Amidst the boom in publishing, teaching and research which has accompanied the growth of western women's studies,[1] it seems that less attention has been afforded to the natural sciences or technology than to other disciplinary areas. This is not to say, of course, that there has not been some significant work in these fields. Writers such as Donna Haraway, Sandra Harding and Evelyn Fox Keller, for example, have developed sustained philosophical and epistemological critiques of scientific rationality, while others, Cynthia Enloe and Cynthia Cockburn, for instance, have examined the patriarchal and manipulative usages of technology (Cockburn, 1983, 1985; Cockburn and Fürst-Dilić, 1994; Cockburn and Ormrod, 1993; Enloe, 1989; Haraway, 1989, 1991; Harding, 1986, 1991, 1993; Keller, 1985, 1993). Further areas which have attracted attention are those of reproductive technology and genetic engineering (Arditti, Duelli Klein and Minden, 1984; Spallone, 1988, 1992; Stanworth, 1987). This is especially in relation to the ways in which women are objectified into body parts and reduced to the carriers of male genetic material. In addition to research and publications emanating from the US, Australia and Britain, important analytical and critical work on science has also emerged from European networks, such as the Danish Gender–Nature–Culture group and the feminism and science cluster of the Network of Inderdisciplinary Women's Studies in Europe (NOI ♀ SE) (Lykke and Braidotti, 1996; Lykke, Bryld and Markussen, 1992). In general, however, most western women's studies courses, whether undergraduate or graduate, have tended to focus their concerns on the humanities or social sciences. Science seems to have been able to maintain a stronger resistance to feminist influences and has featured less prominently on the women's studies agenda (Harding, 1986).

Recently, two British feminists, Linda Birke and Hilary Rose, both of whom have published extensively on matters to do with feminism and science and who are also both contributors to this volume, have commented upon the anti-science feeling that seems to exist in women's studies and in feminism more generally. Birke, for instance, points out that, compared to some subjects, there is relatively little interest in science within the women's movement or women's studies, except around specific issues such as women's health, and comparatively few women's studies books or courses that explicitly address science and technology (1994). She refers to science as hostile territory, not just in terms of her experiences in the laboratories of academia, but in the women's movement as well. Discussing this hostility, Birke remarks: 'I remember when I was surrounded by several women who wanted to know how I could possibly be doing research in science because it was so heavily patriarchal. I did wonder at the time and I'm still wondering since why science gets singled out. Can you name one area of the academy that isn't patriarchal?' (1994: 187).

Rose also identifies an anti-science tendency within feminism. Focusing, in particular, on what she refers to as the 'postmodern deluge', Rose is critical of this development because, she argues, an over-emphasis on language and discourse leads to a refusal to distinguish between *true* and *false* knowledge and *good* and *bad* science (1994: 23). She suggests that postmodernism's relegation of the contest between more and less truthful accounts, to one about different stories that we may choose to believe or not, is immensely politically damaging. Crucially, such an anti-science position denies the possibilities of either developing empowering knowledge or of making practical social interventions.

It is the argument of this book that women's studies stands aloof from the sciences at its peril. More specifically, this collection of interdisciplinary essays aims to explore some of the major questions and topics with which feminist scholars of science are currently engaging. It is concerned with what constitutes science, how feminists have investigated it, the ways in which science is able to construct women, the possibilities of generating new feminist discourses of science and the extent to which current developments might be to the advantage or disadvantage of women. In this, the text draws on material and utilizes examples from a wide range of natural scientific, humanities and social science sources. It employs feminist methods derived from history, sociology, deconstruction, discourse analysis and literary criticism. It also critically examines the usefulness to feminists of postmodern, materialist, cyborgian and standpoint theory. Overall, the book indicates that to present the relationship between women and science in polarized terms is too simplistic. There has been a tendency for some writers to see the sciences *either* as inherently oppressive of women *or* as their salvation (Jordanova, 1995). Yet, as the contributions collected here indicate, not only are the very terms *women* and *science* problematic, since they imply the existence of homogeneous, static and ahistorical categories, neither can the relationship between them be taken for granted. Not only do differences between women position them differentially to take advantage of whatever potential science might offer, but different aspects of scientific endeavour may be more or less coercive or empowering of women. For these reasons various contributors present their arguments in relation to issues of class, race and sexuality, as well as geographical location.

Some of the chapters in the book were originally presented as public lectures in the highly successful series on Women and Science organized by the

Centre for Women's Studies at the University of York, UK, as part of its tenth anniversary celebrations. The theme was specifically chosen in order to raise the profile of questions about science for women, although it was acknowledged that the title itself, selected in an attempt to maximize the potential audience, was deeply problematic. Other material has been commissioned or included to widen the book's scope.

It is the aim of this chapter to provide a context for those which follow. It begins by outlining some of the characteristic features of the women and science literature, considering why science might have generated so much negativity and the reasons which might be bringing about change. The chapter then pays attention to issues concerning science, technology and power and the ways these are addressed in this volume. It concludes by suggesting feminist debates on science and technology need to pay more attention to race and racism and to environmentalism and ecology in relation to science, especially as they relate to non-western contexts.

Women's Studies and the Study of Science

There are several possible reasons why women's studies has paid less attention to the sciences than to other disciplines. As Nancy Lane (Chapter 3), Ailsa Swarbrick (Chapter 4) and Jean Barr and Linda Birke (Chapter 5) indicate, for instance, science tends to be regarded as a male preserve. Lane shows how, despite marked improvements in the number of young women taking and succeeding in examinations in some science subjects, their presence still decreases dramatically the higher up the student, academic and professional hierarchy one travels. Further, despite rhetoric to the contrary, there have been difficulties in persuading the British government to take this problem seriously. Swarbrick discusses the difficulties faced by women wishing to pursue a career in technology, particularly if they have families. She argues that, in striving to counter gendered constraints, such women demonstrate considerable commitment to technology as a career, although this is not often recognized or valued. Barr and Birke's research suggested that women feel excluded from science and that this is rooted in the distinction they make between commonsense, perceived as owned knowledge, and science, which is treated as alienated knowledge and, therefore, has nothing to do with them. In the accounts collected from interviews, Barr and Birke found that women portrayed the activities of science as 'boring, tedious, mathematical' (this volume, p. 82). The attribution of a form of knowledge as being 'scientific' tended to be reserved for something which, by definition, they could not, or did not expect to, understand.

It is tempting to suggest, then, that the relative disinterest in the sciences, often found within women's studies, is to do with the fact that many of those involved in it have not studied science to any great extent and feel that they have a rather ambiguous relationship to the subject. Interestingly, the terms of the debate have changed over the years, so that it is now the nature of science, rather than the deficiencies of women, which are seen as the problem (Birke, 1994). Yet, this ambivalence within women's studies furthers women's general marginalization from both understanding and generating powerful knowledge forms. After all, scientists hold privileged and prestigious positions as creators of knowledge in western societies. The work which they produce is still, despite the supposed advent of the postmodern and 'risk' society, afforded a high degree of legitimacy and is used to justify all kinds of social decisions and interventions (Beck, 1992; Crook, Pakulski and Waters, 1992). As Rose points out, not only is women's exclusion part of the general sexual division of labour in a society where most roles are deeply gendered, but the nature of the science subjects themselves is unlikely to change until women are in a position to make more realistic challenges to them (1994; Chapter 2). Additionally, in a world which is becoming increasingly technologized, women will be severely penalized if they are not able to operate and benefit from the new developments, as they take place. This is particularly the case when the acquisition of knowledge enhances control over use (Cockburn and Fürst-Dilić, 1994; Gray, 1992).

Another reason for women's studies' disenchantment with the practices of science can be linked to early feminist critiques of male knowledge, particularly the philosophical stance of positivism which scientific practices are said to embody (Mackinnon, 1982; Smith, 1974; Stanley and Wise, 1983; 1993). Bryman has outlined how positivism might be regarded as comprising at least five components (1988). First, it entails a belief that the methods and procedures of the natural sciences can be applied in the social sciences. Second, it holds that only those phenomena which are observable directly, or indirectly through the aid of instruments, can be legitimately researched. This largely excludes emotions, feelings and the notion of subjective experience. A third tenet suggests that scientific knowledge is produced through the accumulation of verified facts. These aid the formulation and generation of theoretical understandings, so that theory expresses and reflects the findings of empirical research. Fourth, scientific theories are regarded by positivists as providing an underpinning for empirical research, in the sense that it is the hypotheses derived from them which are then submitted to empirical test. Finally, positivism requires the researcher to be purged of all values, thereby adopting an objective, value free and politically neutral stance towards all aspects of the research process.

Now, it is not difficult to see why feminists, alongside others, might have problems with all of the above defining characteristics of science. For instance, feminists have been critical of the idea that researchers can stand back and remove themselves from personal involvement in what they study (Harding, 1986; Stanley and Wise, 1983; 1993). They dispute conventional notions about, and the so-called procedures for ensuring, objectivity (Harding, 1991). Feminists are also sceptical of the notion that there is one true *real* reality, which is somehow external to and there for the researcher to discover (Stanley and

Wise, 1983; 1993). They have expressed concern about ways of obtaining knowledge which emphasize rationality, impersonality, predictability, measurement and control, at the expense of emotionality, empathy, rapport and contradictions (Nielsen, 1990). Criticism has also been levied at the emphasis on generating quantifiable and numerical data which, certainly in a social context, produces a falsely concrete body of information and atomistic facts, in both a static and an atemporal fashion (Graham, 1983).

Yet, some feminists, along with other scholars, have also questioned whether the assumptions of positivism really reflect the ways in which natural science itself is practiced and the extent to which claims about value neutrality, rigorous methods and the search for objective facts are legitimate (Haraway, 1989; Keller, 1985). As Hilary Rose points out in Chapter 2, the 1980s and 1990s have been characterized by heated debate as to the extent to which science is or is not a social construct and the implications of this for statements about truth. Thus, given the increasing ambivalence with which many have written about the philosophical underpinnings of a scientific methodology, it is hardly surprising that there has been a tendency for feminists to shy away from engaging with the more substantive issues which science addresses. For reasons such as this, then, feminists have tended, as Birke puts it 'to leave science to the boys' (1994, 192).

Where there *has* been a concern about the sciences in relation to women, however, it has largely taken one of the following forms, as Jordanova has demonstrated (1995). The first has been to recover the lost women of science, those whose contributions have been marginalized or rendered invisible, often because it has been misattributed or thought to be the work of men (Bleier, 1984; 1986). The second involves charting the progress of women's access to science education and their success in becoming science professionals, in both historical and more contemporary contexts (Rossiter, 1982). A third approach has been to analyse how scientists have theorized womanhood, femininity and sexual difference. This is important since scientific knowledge has been used to prove that women are inherently incapable of certain kinds of activity or modes of thinking. Indeed, such arguments have been employed to show that they are less well equipped to do science than men (Tuana, 1989). Fourth, an alliance of the sociology of science with feminist epistemology has produced critiques of scientific knowledge as itself a gendered construct (Haraway, 1989; Keller, 1985; 1993). This has focused on the gendering of scientific inquiry and knowledge production. Finally, there has been work on the impact of science, technology and medicine on women's lives, with an emphasis on how the practices of science enter into the fabric of everyday life. For women, particularly, this affects their experiences in the household, through, for example, domestic technology, and their relationship with their bodies, as with contraception or abortion (Cowan, 1983; Stanworth, 1987).

As Jordanova discusses, these five approaches are not mutually exclusive (1995). Most of the focus, however, is on the nineteenth and twentieth centuries, with very little interest being shown in earlier historical periods. Overall, three main goals appear in the literature. One is to use the topic of women and science as a vehicle for critiquing modern western science, with a view to changing its very nature. Another is to discover the mechanisms whereby women are excluded from the practice of science, with the aim of getting more of them involved in it. The last is to understand the nature of science in relation to certain themes (colonialism or class, for example), of which gender is just one. Unlike the other two, no direct pay-off may be intended or sought with such an approach (Jordanova, 1995).

With the extension of work such as this, there are signs that feminism and women's studies might be becoming more open to engaging with issues of a scientific and technological nature. This would appear to be for several reasons, both intellectual and pragmatic, as contributors to this book demonstrate. For instance, the rapid development of information technology and the internet is making it increasingly impossible to avoid critical engagement with such practices. Similarly, advances in so-called fertility treatment, genetic engineering and other medical interventions have made it difficult simply to consider them under the category *health* (This issue is addressed in Chapters 8 and 9). The proliferation of feminists' interest in science fiction has encouraged speculation as to how far science might act as handmaiden to women's liberation and the search for utopian solutions associated with this. We are also, as Rose notes in Chapter 2, currently in the middle of two oppositional forces in the public representation of science. One, the realist position, exemplified by the old scientific élite, asserts that science is the purveyor of truth. The other, that of relativism, offers a range of contradictory expert views on issues such as BSE, radiation and global warming, indicating a clear lack of consensus as to what might even approximate the truth in each case. Media exposure of such contradictions is fuelling public uncertainties about the nature and role of science. Although it appears to work in particular circumstances, a mood of scepticism is developing as to what science actually *is*. For all these reasons, then, science is increasingly becoming an area for feminist concern and attention. The next section considers some of the related issues raised within this book.

Science, Technology and Power

Western feminists' critiques of science and technology span a range of areas, from the workplace to the household and from the military to medicine and the pharmaceutical industry. Commentators have suggested that such discussions about technology are, in general, less developed than those concerning science (Fitzsimons, 1994; Wajcman, 1991). Not only have they tended to borrow unproblematically from the sciences the idea that technology is used by men to subordinate and control women and nature, they have also frequently conflated the notions of science and technology. For instance, Margaret Low Benson has written that:

power is the most important message that male use of technology communicates. Power over technology and the physical world is just one aspect of men's domination of this society . . . Male power over technology is both a product of and a reenforcement for their other power in society. Even at the household level, every time a man repairs the plumbing or a sewing machine while a woman watches, a communication about her helplessness and inferiority is made (1992: 37).

The idea that science and technology are deeply implicated in the domination of women has two corollaries. The first is to position women as the passive victims of both men and the science and technology employed over them. The second is to suggest that science and technology are detrimental to the welfare of women and should, therefore, be opposed. Now, there is certainly much in the literature concerned with women, science and technology to support these views. In the household, for example, Ruth Schwartz Cowan's pioneering work demonstrated how the possession of labour saving devices only raised expectations about higher standards of cleanliness and the production of gourmet meals (1983). Anne Gray's research on domestic video and computing technology found that decisions as to its purchase, the buying itself and the routine operation of this equipment is largely the prerogative of the male of the household, who from his position of knowledge comes to command control over its use (1992). Similarly, it is well-known that the introduction of technology into the workplace has done little to challenge either the sexual division of labour or the ascription of women's work as being low skilled (Webster, 1995). In fact, feminist research points to the continuing exclusion of women from the processes of scientific research and design, production and decision-taking in technology, as well as to a plethora of long-established patterns of work organization in women's jobs which seem to have been affected little by scientific and technological change (Cockburn and Fürst Dilić, 1994; Cockburn and Ormrod, 1993; Webster, 1995). Further, despite the fact that women pioneered the occupation of computer programming, they were forced out of this by men, once the occupation was seen to be creative and important, only to be allowed to return once the work had been reduced to something like ordinary clerical labour (Dain, 1991; Fitzsimons, 1994). This is important since, first, it hints at the gendered process of deskilling which has taken place within the history of the computing profession. It also indicates that women can, and indeed have, taken the lead in technological developments (Wajcman, 1991).

So, it would appear that feminists have identified much which is negative for women concerning science and technology. Yet, the latter should not be dismissed out of hand. In fact, three major reasons for not doing so are advanced by the contributors to this collection, each addressing, in different ways, the question of power. These are: the ability of science and technology to make a difference; the need for engagement with them in order to redefine their parameters and content; and their future potential. Each will be briefly discussed in turn.

The work of Annette Fitzsimons on women and computing provides a useful context for the argument about the potential of science and technology to make a difference for women, that is, their power to intervene to bring about change in certain circumstances. Fitzsimons argues that: 'there is no *necessary* antagonism between women and technology' and 'women's relationship to technology is not necessarily that of passive victim' (1994: 128). Drawing on Foucault's notion of the productivity of power and the idea that it is never entirely repressive, she distinguishes between micro- and macro-practices of power. While power at a macro-level focuses on institutional relationships relating to phenomena such as patriarchy, the economy and the state, at a micro-level it is concerned with practices that occur in everyday life. Fitzsimons argues that, whereas the former may operate to women's overall disadvantage, the latter can provide openings and spaces for women at a local and personal level. In fact, technology has the potential to bring autonomy to individual women.

Similar sentiments appear in a number of the chapters featuring in this book, but a particularly powerful argument is presented by Cecilia Ng Choon Sim and Rohini Hensman in Chapter 6 on Third World women. Like Fitzsimons, they also make two important conceptual distinctions. One is between technological developments *per se* and how these are used by those who have control over them. The other is between the potential inherent in scientific and technological innovations and how these may be applied to support the economic and political purposes of those in power. While feminists in the West may bemoan the ways in which technology has affected women there, Ng Choon Sim and Hensman indicate how very little influence it has had on most women and children in the world, who are still plagued by problems of poverty, malnutrition, sickness and natural disasters. Yet, many of these issues could be ameliorated by the application of technological and scientific developments which are widely available in the West. Although not denying the detrimental uses to which technology has been put, they argue strongly that this depends on who has the power of control and whose interests are being served. From a whole world perspective, science and technology have enormous positive potential to transform the lives of women, providing that the purpose is 'to nurture and conserve' (this volume, p. 103). Ng Choon Sim and Hensman thus warn against the uncritical adoption of western ethnocentric assumptions that science and technology are *inherently* inimical to the welfare of women and ought, therefore, to be opposed. One reason for this, they argue, is that it cannot be assumed that science and technology affect all sections of women in the same, or even similar, ways. In this, they reflect Rose's admonition in Chapter 2 that feminists avoid unhelpful either/or dichotomies when addressing issues concerning science and technology.

A number of contributors to this book also point to the need for a second way of thinking about science and technology, in terms of a critical engagement with its content and practices in order to offer reworked meanings and new definitions. This is, in part, because science is regarded as a masculinized form of knowledge, both in terms of its content, what is researched and how this is conceived, and the practices adopted for researching and generating knowledge. These activities, it is claimed, are undertaken by men concentrating on their own agendas and interests. Spallone, for instance, demonstrates in Chapter 8 the difference between gender-blind and gender-sensitive analyses of reproductive technologies. She points out, along with Sourbut, that some of the techniques currently associated with the term have little to do with technology *per se*, since they do not require scientific knowledge and expertise, and neither are they new. Spallone argues that the term *technology* is doing a lot of hidden work in these kinds of discourses and her chapter explores the extent to which this involves projecting social meaning on to certain kinds of technological methods. Arguing that the technical and the social are not entirely separable, she raises questions about why certain issues are raised or not, how decisions are made about them and the implications for science and technology when reproductive technologies are examined using the lens of gender.

In Chapter 7 Scott aims at challenging conventional notions as to the content and practice of science. Disatisfied with both biologically essentialist and social constructionist analyses of the body, she seeks to establish it as an agent in its own right, rather than as unintelligent, static and passive. Scott draws on the quantum model of the body to argue that the latter has its own energy field which controls the growth and healing processes. By using the perspectives of alternative sciences, it is possible to undermine the mind/body distinction which lies at the foundation of modern science, thereby leading to new understandings and enhanced healing practices. Scott argues that these are at the cutting edge of knowledge and in advance of, rather than in opposition to, mainstream scientific research. Further, reconceptualizing the body as dynamic and aware has epistemological implications. This is because of the implication that bodily experience will overflow the bounds of social discourse, thereby offering the potential for new kinds of meanings and knowledge. She, thus, critically deconstructs conventional understandings of science, offering, instead, an alternative, feminist, theoretical strategy.

The third issue concerning science, technology and power addressed in this book concerns their future possibilities. In this, for instance, both Sorbut (Chapter 9) and Wolmark (Chapter 10) draw on feminist science fiction, Wolmark particularly on cyberpunk, which offers alternative visions of women's social roles and relationships in the future. Science fiction elides the distinction between the social and the natural, creating both utopian and dystopian imagery. It has been of interest to feminists because, although it offers fictional opposition to the status quo, this fiction is based on the social transformations unleashed by scientific and technological developments. Ideas about what is natural or unnatural are challenged, as are the perceived boundaries between human, animal and machine.

Sourbut, for example, discusses the possibilities of gynogenesis, the fusing of two ova with two biological mothers and no father, to challenge preconceptions about who can benefit from reproductive technologies and who has power and control. Pointing out that lesbians are marginalized in current debates about assisted reproduction, she demonstrates some of the heterosexist assumptions which prevail. Sourbut argues that: 'procreation is a culturally constructed activity, but that part of the construction is to view it as a "natural" process' (Chapter 9, p. 142). She draws on science fiction to offer a range of images of childbearing which do not oppress women.

In Chapter 10 on the uses and abuses of cyberspace, Wolmark is concerned with new ways of conceptualizing the relations between space and place and of thinking about embodiment and gendered identity. Sensitively steering clear of arguments that new forms of information technology are either all good or all bad, she argues, instead, that any liberatory potential for women to be found in electronic communication is not being fulfilled. Despite the efforts made in cyberpunk, for example, to transcend binary oppositions, these tend to be reinscribed. This is because cyberpunk narratives envision cyberspace as a place with determinate and known boundaries, which are circumscribed in the interests of a hegemonic masculinity. Wolmark writes: 'only within cyberpunk narratives written by women are cyberpunk and cyberspace explored from a differently gendered perspective in which spatial boundaries are disrupted and gender identity can be detached from fixed definitions of "masculinity" and "femininity"' (Chapter 10, p. 162). As with Ng Choon Sim and Hensman, she sees technology as being used only to empower women when existing structures of power have been disrupted, a move she describes as being in 'everyone's interests' (p. 178).

Feminist critiques of western sciences, therefore, challenge the assumption that they are, or have been, entirely progressive forces. However, this does not mean that feminists are (or should be) inherently against science and technology. Instead, the latter contain both regressive and progressive tendencies, which only become apparent by examining the social and gendered nature of their construction, production and use (Harding, 1993).

Science, Racism and the Development Process

There are two other important and linked issues relating to the western sciences and power, which need to be given greater prominence and attention within these debates than they are usually afforded. These are to do with the interconnections between racism and science and the role of science and technology in the development process.

While feminists are increasingly able to document the gendered nature of science and technology and the sexism of the knowledge which is often constructed, less attention has been paid to the question of race. Yet, modern scientific discourse, which emerged in nineteenth-century Europe, was demonstrably racist. The historical development of European colonialism, with its practices of expansion and domination, was linked to the typological construction of race. The white, European male was taken as representing the most civilized of the human species, having superior intellect and morals as well as physical form. Any difference perceived from the white male was understood as a sign of inferiority and evolutionary immaturity (Stepan and Gilman, 1993). Thus, through the construction of racial classification, white male European scientists naturalized social hierarchies and also helped to justify exploitative colonial practices. Colonialism was dependent upon a fundamental belief in Eurocentrism, that is a world-view which placed Europe at the centre of civilization. Science and empire combined to produce both ideology and behaviour designed to bring progress, through technological and spiritual development, to peoples perceived to be less culturally and biologically evolved.

In her landmark volume, *The 'Racial' Economy of Science*, Sandra Harding shows how such Eurocentric (to include people of European descent in the Americas and elsewhere, as well as Europe itself) and racist views still exist (1993). She points out how western sciences and technology are still transported to other parts of the world, with little attention paid either to their appropriateness or to the harm they might cause. People constructed as racially or ethnically different or *other* from dominant groups in the West have been exploited and the sciences are heavily implicated in the processes of underdevelopment. This is what Harding means by the racial economy of science. She writes: 'I mean those institutions, assumptions and practices that are responsible for disproportionately distributing along "racial" lines the benefits of Western sciences to the haves and the bad consequences to the have-nots, thereby enlarging the gap between them' (1993: 2).

Harding's analysis is extremely fruitful because it highlights both the historical and the contemporary continuities between science, racism and development processes. Increasingly, feminists are at the forefront of attempts to challenge the idea that development should be concerned primarily with the goal of modernization/westernization – some kind of inexorable linear move towards catching up with the West in terms of growth and progress (Marchand and Parpart, 1995). It has become clear that development has not brought the promised improvement in living conditions to those in the Third World. Instead, it has contributed to increased poverty and degradation of the environment, to the particular detriment of women (Braidotti, Charkiewicz, Häusler and Wieringa, 1994; Mies and Shiva, 1993; Shiva, 1989). Soil and water contamination, depletion of natural resources, deforestation are only some of the consequences brought about by the use of science and technology in development strategies which threaten the environment and the ecosystem. As one set of writers has put it: 'the belief in the limitless manageability of nature with the help of science and technology has by now rendered entire landscapes uninhabitable and beyond repair for the next centuries' (Braidotti *et al.*, 1994: 1). Thus, in addition to those previously advanced, another clear reason why science is a women's studies issue is because of the way in which it is linked to concerns about the situation of women world-wide. Feminist concern for the position of women in the current environmental and developmental crisis necessarily involves foregrounding matters relating to race, power, domination and science.

Note

1 Although acknowledging that the terms *feminism* and *women's studies* are not necessarily coterminous, I am using them interchangeably here since I am concerned with feminist forms of women's studies.

References

ARDITTI, R., DUELLI KLEIN, R. and MINDEN, S. (Eds) (1984) *Test Tube Women: What Future for Motherhood?*, London, Pandora.

BECK, U. (1992) *Risk Society*, London, Sage.

BENSON, M. L. (1992) 'Women's voices, men's voices: Technology as language', in KIRKUP, G. and KELLER, L. S. (Eds) *Inventing Women: Science, Technology and Gender*, Oxford, Polity Press with Open University Press.

BIRKE, L. (1994) 'Interventions in hostile territory', in GRIFFIN, G., HESTER, M., RAI, S. and ROSENEIL, S. (Eds) *Stirring It: Challenges for Feminism*, London, Taylor & Francis.

BLEIER, R. (1984) *Science and Gender: A Critique of Biology and its Theories on Women*, Oxford, Pergamon.

BLEIER, R. (Ed) (1986) *Feminist Approaches to Science*, Oxford, Pergamon.

BRAIDOTTI, R., CHARKIEWICZ, E., HÄUSLER, S. and WIERINGA, S. (Eds) (1994) *Women, the Environment and Sustainable Development*, London, Zed.

BRYMAN, A. (1988) *Quantity and Quality in Social Research*, London, Unwin Hyman.

COCKBURN, C. (1983) *Brothers: Male Dominance and Technological Change*, London, Pluto.

COCKBURN, C. (1985) *Machinery of Male Dominance: Men, Women and Technological Change*, London, Pluto.

COCKBURN, C. and FÜRST-DILIĆ, R. (Eds) (1994) *Bringing Technology Home: Gender and Technology in a Changing Europe*, Buckingham, Open University Press.

COCKBURN, C. and ORMROD, S. (1993) *Gender and Technology in the Making*, London, Sage.

COWAN, R. S. (1983) *More Work for Mother*, New York, Basic Books.

CROOK, S., PAKULSKI, J. and WATERS, M. (1992) *Postmodernization*, London, Sage.

DAIN, J. (1991) 'Women and computing', *Women's Studies International Forum*, **14**, 3, pp. 217–25.

ENLOE, C. (1989) *Bananas, Beaches and Bases: Making Feminist Sense of International Politics*, London, Pandora.

FITZSIMONS, A. (1994) 'Women, power and technology', in LENNON, K. and WHITFORD, M. (Eds) *Knowing the Difference: Feminist Perspectives in Epistemology*, London, Routledge.

GRAHAM, H. (1983) 'Do her answers fit his questions?', in GAMARNIKOW, E., MORGAN, D., PURVIS, J. and TAYLORSON, D. (Eds) *The Public and the Private*, London, Heinemann.

GRAY, A. (1992) *Video Playtime*, London, Routledge.

HARAWAY, D. (1989) *Primate Visions: Gender, Race and Nature in the World of Modern Science*, New York, Routledge.

HARAWAY, D. (1991) *Simians, Cyborgs and Women*, London, Free Association Books.

HARDING, S. (1986) *The Science Question in Feminism*, Milton Keynes, Open University Press.

HARDING, S. (1991) *Whose Science? Whose Knowledge?*, Milton Keynes, Open University Press.

HARDING, S. (Ed) (1993) *The 'Racial' Economy of Science*, Bloomington and Indianapolis, IN, Indiana University Press.

JORDANOVA, L. (1995) 'Women and science – what does history have to offer?', public lecture in the series, *Women and Science*, University of York, 26 January.

KELLER, E. F. (1985) *Reflections on Gender and Science*, New Haven, CT, Yale University Press.

KELLER, E. F. (1993) *Secrets of Life, Secrets of Death*, London, Routledge.

LYKKE, N. and BRAIDOTTI, R. (Eds) (1996) *Betwen Monsters, Goddesses and Cyborgs*, London, Zed Books.

LYKKE, N., BRYLD, M. and MARKUSSEN, R. (1992) 'Groundpaper', *Gender–Nature–Culture Newsletter*, **1**, 1, Autumn, pp. 4–10.

MACKINNON, C. (1982) 'Feminism, marxism, method and the state', in KEOHANE, N., ROSALDO, M. and GELPI, B. (Eds) *Feminist Theory*, Brighton, Harvester Press.

MARCHAND, M. H. and PARPART, J. L. (Eds) *Feminism/Postmodernism/Development*, London, Routledge.

MIES, M. and SHIVA, V. (1993) *Ecofeminism*, London, Zed.

NIELSEN, J. M. (Ed) (1990) *Feminist Research Methods*, Boulder, CO, Westview Press.

ROSE, H. (1994) *Love, Power and Knowledge*, Cambridge, Polity Press.

ROSSITER, M. (1982) *Women Scientists in America*, Baltimore, MD, Johns Hopkins University.

SHIVA, V. (1989) *Staying Alive*, London, Zed.

SMITH, D. (1974) 'Women's perspective as a radical critique of sociology', *Sociological Inquiry*, **44**, 1, pp. 7–13.

SPALLONE, P. (1988) *Beyond Conception: The New Politics of Reproduction*, London, Macmillan.

SPALLONE, P. (1992) *Generalizing Games: Genetic Engineering and the Future for Our Lives*, London, Women's Press.

STANLEY, L. and WISE, S. (Eds) (1983) *Breaking Out*, London, Routledge.

STANLEY, L. and WISE, S. (Eds) (1993) *Breaking Out Again*, London, Routledge.

STANWORTH, M. (Ed) (1987) *Reproductive Technologies, Gender, Motherhood and Medicine*, Cambridge, Polity Press.

STEPAN, N. L. and GILMAN, S. L. (1993) 'Appropriating the idioms: The rejection of scientific racism', in HARDING, S. (Ed) *The 'Racial' Economy of Science*, Bloomington, IN, Indiana University Press.

TUANA, N. (Ed) (1989) *Feminism and Science*, Bloomington, IN, Indiana University Press.

WAJCMAN, J. (1991) *Feminism Confronts Technology*, Oxford, Polity Press.

WEBSTER, J. (1995) 'What do we know about gender and IT at work?', *The European Journal of Women's Studies*, **2**, 3, pp. 315–34.

Chapter 2

Good-bye Truth, Hello Trust: Prospects for Feminist Science and Technology Studies at the Millennium?

Hilary Rose

Changing the Subject?

Feminist science and technology studies (STS),[1] like every other field within feminist scholarship are normatively driven. Even though there are complicated debates and divisions between those of us engaged in this expanding field, these are characterized by intense moral and political preoccupations. As feminists we are concerned with women, though we have learnt (not without struggle) that such a category only makes sense in relation to that of men, and that both gender and the social processes of gendering must be situated in time, space and culture. Whether we speak of social divisions or of difference, the feminisms today are intensely aware of social and cultural complexity. Nor is that complexity just 'out there', for most of us have accepted with a mixture of relief and pleasure that conceptual gift from postmodernism – the multiple hyphenated self.[2] But throughout the turmoils of feminist theorizing of the last two, almost three decades, this particular group of feminists carry an acute consciousness that science and technology, in today's increasingly globalized context, matter and matter in specific ways to women in all our diversity. For this *us*, the task of changing the subject is experienced with both urgency and intensity.

However, it is as well to recognize that many scientists and engineers who are quite friendly to the social justice claim to change the gender of the subjects who produce science and technology, are often distinctly uncomfortable about the idea of changing its content. Further, that sense of discomfort is not exclusively felt by men. As I explore in this chapter, changing the subject in terms of the content can make these partial allies wish to change the subject in yet another sense, in their embarrassment and even irritation at the feminist presumption that actually existing science and technology is not immutable, but has been socially shaped and thus could potentially be reshaped. In the less friendly milieu of élite scientists who feel threatened by the outrageous suggestion that scientific knowledge is socially constructed, a backlash has been launched against any and all critics of science. This backlash has to be read against the achievements of feminists' critique of science and technology a rich and extraordinarily diverse corpus of engaged scholarship. Of course, one short chapter cannot do more than trace the outlines of this now huge corpus of feminist scholarship from one location and celebrate the depth and the multi-disciplinarity of feminist science criticism.

Let me begin with what feminists engaged in feminist science and technology studies have in common with scientists and engineers, namely the shared recognition that in today's world natural science and technology are hugely powerful. Like them we see science and technology as both shaping culture in the sense of constructing our ideas about nature and ourselves as part of nature, and also in the sense of creating new physical artefacts which impact on culture and nature alike. But where scientists and engineers recognize the importance of science and technology, they mostly attribute neutrality to it, so that for them, it can be used or abused; many feminists see the problem as deeper. For feminists in STS it is not simply that we are aware that science has a long and increasingly well studied history of representing natural difference so as to legitimize existing social hierarchies[3] notoriously of constructing scientific racism as the crucial cultural support to imperialism,[4] and scientific sexism as the cultural support to the political project of keeping women in our place.[5] A large body of feminist research on biomedical innovation has sceptically evaluated its loud claims to being 'in our best interests'.[6] Feminists in STS argue that science and technology are socially shaped and that gender is crucial within that process. Thus the trouble for many of the diverse feminisms is not just use or abuse, it is the nature of modern science and technology itself.

In Anglophone culture the concept of *science* works to prioritize knowledge of the physical world relegating the social sciences and the humanities culturally and politically to a less important space. In this hierarchy of the knowledges, mathematics as the guarantor of disembodied abstraction has been recruited as natural science's close ally. This narrow Anglophone focus has to be set against the broader approach of most of continental Europe, where science is understood as *Wissenschaft* and thus as including the whole of systematic enquiry and knowledge. My focus here on the natural sciences stems not from my enthusiasm for Anglophone constructions, but from my recognition of the immense power of the natural sciences and technologies in contemporary society. In extending what was a specifically western approach to the study of nature over the world, modern science was a pioneer of globalization. But the other part of that immense power comes from the natural sciences' capacity to denigrate other knowledges by insisting on their historically unique claim to speak truth to power.

This claim to speak truth descends from the mythic birth of science in seventeenth-century England. Here modern natural science was given a distinctive character, which set it apart from other historically located forms of knowledge production. Bacon crucially proposed that providing methodological procedures were followed scrupulously, any man might create the new knowledge. This new masculine knowledge would represent nature faithfully, it would hold up nothing less than a glassy mirror to reality. Thus scientists do not make science up as the storyteller makes up stories, instead they discover, find, uncover, reveal, show, what is in nature. Whatever the social history of truth, one of the organizing beliefs which held the practitioners of the new knowledge together was that the production system was in this way both truth claiming and profoundly democratic. The truthfulness of the reflection in the glassy mirror was all that mattered. While the glassy mirror with its lack of concern about the relationship between the word and the thing has received rather extensive consideration in the philosophy of science, for natural scientists there is an everyday sense that they must believe both that there is a thingness out there, and that in some sense they can faithfully represent it.

Bacon's new mode of production of knowledge about nature separated the observer from the observed, and through forceful intervention, produced an abstract disembodied knowledge (ideally expressed in mathematical form) which claimed objectivity and thereby truth.[7] This modern, as against premodern science, was never content simply to represent nature, but always to intervene, to change, to dominate the natural world. Thus modern science has from the beginning carried within it the generative connection of science with technology. This marriage of science and technology has long held ideologically, even though the historical record points to the rather frequently different social origins of technology (for example, a number of important technological innovations in nineteenth-century England had rather little to do with scientists or science). Nonetheless, at the ideological core of modern science (displayed vividly in the entire post-1945 discussion of science policy), science and technology are locked together, each seen as nourishing the other's growth.

Shifting Boundaries

Even though I speak of science and technology, as if these are self evident, neither are fixed entities. What is and is not science or technology is subject to historical context, above all to the political question of which groups have the power to define the boundaries. Thus to give a not insignificant example, the feminist historian of technology Ruth Schwartz Cowan (1983) includes the development of the baby's bottle as a technology of tremendous social significance, whereas the dominant androcentric history of technology had excluded the baby's bottle as too trivial to be of historical note. The new histories of science and technology have not only been subject to such feminist moves to redraw the boundaries, but have more generally been reconceptualized to understand science and technology as no longer the products of the isolated genius outside culture and society. Thus today the history of both is rather rarely told as the story of great men with great ideas. Instead science and technology are increasingly seen by all the disciplines engaged in the STS (chiefly history, philosophy and sociology) as both shaped by, and shaping culture and society.

Among ourselves we may argue about our theoretical preferences for SCOT (the social construction of technology) or ANT (actor network theory) or SSK (the sociology of scientific knowledge) or the case for holding on to some variant of externalism (the political economy of science), but the language accepted by all, a sort of lowest common denominator in the field, is social shaping. However this shaping is not a world of stasis, of mirrors in which society and science mutually and statically reflect one another, so that the question of their separateness comes under question, but also of relentless change.

Change, Risk and the Technosciences

Whatever scientific and technological change does for economic growth within a market economy, through the continuous provision of new sophisticated artefacts, there is rather little doubt that relentless change over the course of the twentieth century has left nature in rather a bad shape.

Today global warming, the risk of nuclear or biological warfare, pollution, the hazards of biotechnology and the new genetics, together with the relentless use of finite natural resources, have moved onto the political agenda. There is intense debate between experts as to how serious specific risks are, and if they are real, how should we respond to them? Is it a question of moral panic – or is the climate really warming up and what might this mean for millions of people and the possibility of life in huge regions of the world? Society increasingly feels that although no one knows exactly which is the greatest risk, there is something wrong, and that it is science and technology which is somehow causing the trouble. This concern with the risks to nature, both those which have historically happened or nearly happened and those which threaten, has in its turn both given rise to positive attempts to theorize living in a risk society[8] and also, in a culturally defeatist vein, to nostalgic appeals for the return of a never existing golden age when things were *natural*.[9] These nostalgic longings, not least within ecofeminism, for nature as some fixed eternal entity, ignore both her own dynamic history, and her relationship with culture. By contrast I want to conceptualize both culture and nature as interacting together through time and in space constituting both local and global ecosystems.

In recent years this generative relationship between science and technology has dramatically speeded up. Increasingly the new powerful fields coming into existence are fusions of science and technology. Here the old distinction between science and technology falls away, and to grasp this transformation the hybrid concept of the technosciences comes into play. Chief among these new technosciences are information technology and the new genetics, including both human genetics and biotechnology. Many of us feel about these new hybrid forms pretty much as Virginia Woolf did, when she reflected on the electrically powered lifts in Selfridges. She explained that she knew so little about electricity, that so far as she was concerned, the lifts might as well have moved by magic. Sixty years later as I gossip by e-mail with a friend in India I have a distinctly similar feeling. The possibility of my knowing what goes on inside the grey plastic box that performs this marvel, well, dream on. But it is not just the writer or the sociologist who 'black box', and who necessarily have to trust the capacity because we do not understand the innards; today natural scientists, not least when they are working in their laboratories, must also black box. The scientists using their computer controlled equipment, like Woolf in her lift and me with this computer, have to advance their specialist field with the aid of sophisticated equipment without understanding what goes on inside.

Goodbye Truth, Hello Trust?

Today we have everywhere, but most dramatically in the laboratory, an extraordinary combination of specialist expertise and technological illiteracy, the gap between them can only be crossed by trust. This mix of tremendous expertise and illiteracy is historically relatively new: even 50 years ago, natural scientists – if nobody else – could have a reasonable grasp across the whole of the sciences. The fragmentation/specialization of knowledge so evident at the end of the twentieth century means both that it is hard for scientists to talk to one another and even harder for them to talk with those outside science. When the sciences look at nature from so many different approaches, the old cultural authority of the scientist to speak for science as some unified entity is eroded. Indeed, insofar as this chapter speaks of science and technology in the singular it tends to reproduce this longing for unification. Yet what is so conspicuous today is, first, the plurality of the sciences and technologies and, second, the development of the new hybrid forms. These diverse approaches are not easily translatable from one to another, as it were from the biochemistry to the physiology of an organism, but instead often offer conflictual accounts. In the life sciences, those discourses of nature most strongly under criticism from feminism, the crucial difference lies between the *lumpers* (whole organism explanations) and the *splitters* (reductionist explanations). Thus although the story of the development of science as an institution is the story of how one gendered and raced group of people won the cultural authority to exclusively name – to represent – nature to us, the new fragmentation and the intensified conflict erodes the old monovoiced authority.

Within the institutions of science there are evident moves to restore this dream of the unity of science. In the life sciences this longing is very much associated with the intense reductionist programme associated with the new genetics. The splitters (the genetic reductionists) are dominant and despite widespread opposition the geneticization of the culture proceeds apace. In the cultural and political project of sociobiology there are strong moves to reduce both nature and culture to our selfish genes.[10] Physicists continue to long for the possibility of realizing either GUTs or TOEs[11] as a means of restoring their diminishing cultural authority. While I have not the space to explore these changes within the sciences and the attempts to return to some dream of a unified past in any detail, this turbulence is part of the reason for the social standing of science coming under question. Instead of the old status of Science as Truth with unique capacities and duties to speak to Power, we have the emergence of the expert who perhaps has rather little to say about universal laws but who can contribute reliable knowledge to feed into specific local problems.

Such a transition is not taking place without contest. Today, as society faces unprecedented risks stemming from science and technology, we are in the middle of two contradictory pulls, one by the old scientific élite trying to hold onto the past where they were the unique purveyors of truth, and the other from our experience of listening to a plurality of experts. Such experts, as we all know from problems of science and technology in everyday life, no longer have the unique claim to speak the truth, whether about BSE (mad cow disease), how to clean up oil spills, safe contraception, radiation leaks, etc. Experts today often make conflictual claims and leave the rest of us to make sense of what they are saying. The old asocial concept of the rationality of science is seen as manifestly inadequate to help us cope with risk and feminist and other social theorists increasingly argue for a new normative concept of rationality.[12]

This cultural turbulence around the social standing of science and its authority to represent nature, is the current foreground.[13] Although the empirical surveys suggest that science is still well regarded by the public, the scientific élite feels that science is not understood, and is no longer trusted in quite the same old way. The Royal Society's Committee on the Public Understanding of Science is symbolic of élite science's feeling nervous about the weakening cultural deference truth commands. Behind this present unease with the shifting of scientists from being the purveyors of truth to becoming the purveyors of expertise, there is a background of a troubled relationship between science and society. It is not just feminists who are influenced by the memory of Nagasaki and Hiroshima or who are angered by the latest contraception scare, or who are concerned least the new genetics are inexorably eugenicist.[14] In general society no longer quite trusts science in the big cultural sense, even though in everyday life we must and do trust all sorts of scientific knowledges and technologies to work for us. So I am sitting here more or less trusting my computer and this morning I took my drugs to control my genetic disorder, but I remain fairly sceptical about screening and suspect that I only take part when my conscientious GP catches me. Many of us share these societal mixed feelings about science: fascination, amazement, gratitude, revulsion, distrust, anger even boredom, even while we accept or reject particular bits; nonetheless over the past two decades, science and technology have unquestionably come onto the cultural and political agenda – and feminists have had a good deal to say.

Moving in from the Periphery?

First into Feminism

Although feminists surveying the field of feminist STS tend to put the various different strands together (and I have myself, Rose, 1994) here I want to look at them as addressing rather different audiences. Then the question of whether feminist STS has or has not moved in from the periphery and changed the subject becomes not one question but a whole series of questions. But the first is surely the question of science and technology or the technosciences in feminism itself.

In the first phase of feminist science studies, and certainly to the end of the 1980s, the field was widely spoken of as the feminist critique of science. In similar vein, Judy Wacjman's widely read book was called *Feminism Confronts Technology* (1991). FINNRAGE was the Feminist International Network Against the New Reproductive Technology and Genetic Engineering. Such a confrontational relationship was scarcely surprising when we recall that the first time that the equal rights amendment was proposed in the USA was the same year, 1975, that Steven Goldberg published *The Inevitability of Patriarchy* and E. O. Wilson published *Sociobiology*. Though the former placed his claim for essential difference on hormone theory which was just moving past its cultural zenith, while the latter, with a sharper sense of where the power centre of science was moving, placed his claims on genes, they were as one in their desire to show that nature was sexist.

For that matter the cultural attempt to renaturalize women was preceded by a corresponding attempt to show nature as inexorably racist. This attempt was initially made with the rather weak tools of psychometry, as it were from Arthur Jensen and Hans Eysenck with their obsession with IQ measures to Richard Herrnstein and Charles Murray's recent *The Bell Curve*.[15] Today the power charged discourse of molecular biology takes over and race is currently being resuffused with tremendous energy from the life sciences. The need for feminist rebuttal and confrontation so evident in the early days of second wave feminism, has intensified, not decreased.

To take the example of the highly culturally problematic development within the life sciences of the reappearance of a biologically defined concept of race. For many social theorists of race who have by and large taken the UNESCO 1946 statement on race as a definitive ruling that the concept of race has no biological meaning, this development is immensely serious. This new genetically defined concept is no longer part of a project of the demonstration of racial superiority, but instead has been constructed under the banner of good intentions of identifying the gene implicated in breast cancer.

It seems churlish to question this well-intentioned gift from technoscience, for women are indeed dying at an appalling rate from breast cancer. Nonetheless it must be questioned. First there is a problem around the identification of a gene for breast cancer, which, in the context of the US marketized medical care, has led to the medical advice being given (and sadly increasingly taken) for radical double mastectomy as a prophylactic measure where no cancer exists. To resist such monstrous biomedical advice, we need the steady reminding from feminist and left-wing biologists that genes are not determinant. Alone, genes can determine nothing. Genes can only be expressed within context, which is itself immensely varied. (Hubbard and Wald, 1993; Rose, Lewontin, Kamin, 1984). Second, one of the genes for breast cancer is claimed to be particularly present among Jews of Eastern European origins. This racial identifier, whatever the intentions, occurs in a historically negative context, including the widespread rise of neo-Nazi formations in Europe and the US together with genocide and ethnic cleansing in the former Yugoslavia and Rwanda. It is this identifier which threatens to take those carefully constructed brackets off 'race'.

This recent example of feminism's continuing need to watch, question and where need be, confront the power of the technosciences is expressive of our political and cultural experience of science and technology over the past three decades. We have seen both an acceleration of the biomedical invasion of human, especially women's, lives and bodies and a recognition that there is a deep impulse in the life sciences which constantly seeks to determine our nature. The period has also seen a massive expansion and industrialization of the life sciences so that this impulse has tremendous technological capacity brought into existence by vast state and venture capital investment.

That early indifference of second wave feminism to science and puzzlement towards those feminists who were either interested in science or, even more disturbingly, actually were scientists, is today more or less a historical memory. *The Science Question in Feminism* as Harding (1986) so memorably proposed it in the mid-eighties is unquestionably central to the agenda today. The primary audience to which this feminist science criticism is directed is other feminists in and out of the academy, and indeed anyone, anywhere who cares for social justice.

Partly, that sense of indifference and puzzlement on the part of the feminist movement changed with the advent of the new sociobiology which sought to return woman to 'a woman's place' precisely at the moment when women were demanding to enter history as subjects and not as objects. Partly it changed with the speed up of research within the life sciences, and the proliferation of biomedical technologies. In this situation feminist biologists suddenly became precious knowers with the skill to rebut and hold back the avalanche of sexist science. Among the names conspicuous in this struggle have been those of Ethel Tobach, Betty Rossoff, Ruth Bleier, Ruth Hubbard, Marion Lowe, Lynda Birke, Gail Vines but also many, many more. Some have also played an important role in helping construct a new knowledge of women's health, which sought to bring together subjective feeling and traditional objective knowledge. Biomedical feminists were active in the women's health movement which sought to empower women to take charge of *Our Bodies:*

Our Selves (Boston women's Health Book Collective, 1973) – to cite the feminist seventies classic – which in its various editions and languages has sold more than 4 000 000 copies.

Those strong politics of empowerment in the women's health movement meant that, while the feminist biomedical experts were a thread, they did not, as in other male dominated social movements, ever constitute the whole cloth. It has been easier within the context of feminism to locate scientific and technological knowhow within a responsible rationality, as against examples, such as that of Greenpeace and Brent Spar, where the experts single handedly appropriated the task of defining the objectives – and quite disastrously got them technically wrong. Instead feminist biomedical expertise has been a continuing resource, from contributing to understanding both the increasingly technologized issues around reproduction in the seventies and eighties, to the challenge of the Human Genome Project,[16] and the dangerous proliferation of diagnostic genetic tests in the nineties. The struggle for women's reproductive freedom has constantly to shift its ground as the technological challenges change, but the old political struggle remains – who is to decide which women shall mother and if, and when. Maria Meiss's (1992) bitter analysis that while biomedicine seeks to push (white) women in the North into motherhood, women in the South are to be denied, reminds us that the historic alliance between old and new forms of imperialism, racism eugenics and biomedicine are by no means played out.

For that matter the massive growth of the brain sciences over the past two decades has witnessed the development of an entire subgenre devoted to demonstrating the causal links between brain structures or genes and sexuality. Thus while there are rich cultural debates around sexuality, and the gay and lesbian movement has proclaimed a politics of identity, a small industry of biomedical researchers has explained that it is the shape of particular brain regions, the current rivals are the hypothalamus (Levay, 1993) and the corpus collusum (Allen, 1994) which are determinant. But where brain structure is part of a discourse extending back into the earliest days of science the new hot claims are made by molecular biology, with the proclamation of the gay gene (Hamer *et al.*, 1993). While such reductionist claims about sexuality have long been part and parcel of the life sciences, they are for much of the time relegated to a minor cultural space, but today, when sexuality is under intense cultural scrutiny and new groups are seeking to come into public existence, such determining claims are powercharged. Today the claims are being made by biological researchers working in élite institutions, using some of the most sophisticated techniques available and are published in the world's leading scientific journals. Exposing such claims to rigorous scrutiny from within the canon of science becomes of increasing cultural importance and is recognized as such by the feminist movement.

The introduction to Anne Fausto Sterling's second edition of *Myths of Gender* (1992) gives us something of the sense of this tedious task of rebuttal as necessary political labour. Locating and critically reading the scientific papers on which the wilder claims of masculine, heterosexual, racial and class superiority are based is not in itself an attractive task. Evaluating sample size, the presence or absence of controls, the legitimacy of inference are the routine business of the construction of good science. These then have to be harnessed to the critical exposure of bad science with, in this case, its association with reactionary politics.

Not only have feminist biologists moved into a new relationship with the feminist movement both because of their skilled resistance to the determining patriarchy of the biomedical sciences, and also in constructing better accounts of our bodies, they have also made strategic moves to change fundamental evolutionary accounts – our origin myths (Zilman, 1978). In human cultures origin myths are of enormous cultural significance; the stories of who we are, where we come from, who we might become, give meaning to our lives. From the perspective of the historian or the anthropologist it does not matter very much whether these origin myths are framed in magical, religious or scientific terms, although as inhabitants of a deeply scientific culture we want the most reliable scientific account. Here feminist evolutionary theorists have wrought a small cultural revolution which has been so successful that it has entered popular culture. Thus today popular culture pretty much takes for granted the evolutionary account summed up as 'man the hunter and woman the gatherer', and we suspect that the men were busy prancing about occasionally getting meaty treats while the women quietly supplied the basic necessities of life. But this evolutionary story was constructed by feminists and had to replace – as better science – the old story of man the hunter in which women were cast as mere dependants, waiting for man the meat winner to come triumphally home. To speak of such a cultural shift in our popular origin stories as 'coming in from the periphery' is surely an understatement.

There are numbers of examples of changing the subject in the life sciences, particularly in ethology, where feminists have pretty much decentred the male primate in the construction of primatology, and from human epidemiological studies which are equally beginning to decentre the human male from the scientific construction of heart (and other) diseases. These changes, although far from complete, are an integral part of feminism's long struggle to reconstruct the life sciences. Although I write *complete*, cultural struggles concerning nature's body have an inherently unfinished and contested character. However, what we can see (despite the renewed onslaught from genetic determinism) is that there are significant and positive changes made over the past two decades. Perhaps the most precious gain has been a wide spread understanding that having feminists in biomedicine makes a difference.

And Equality Feminism?

Equality feminism's demands (typically with a judicious wrapping of labour market efficiency arguments) for access to occupations and promotion in the research system are increasingly acknowledged as morally just and economically rational (see Nancy Lane's Chapter 3 in this book). These claims are made and heard both at the level of the nation state and at the level of international organizations, most recently the EU[17] and UNESCO.[18] This new equality feminism is a substantial improvement on from that peculiarly victim-blaming analysis so widely promulgated in Britain during the eighties. This mixed a litany of complaint against dire statistics together with a psychologistic view that there is something lacking in women and girls, which renders them unable to compete in the academy, and above all, in the laboratory (Kelly, 1978; Whyte, 1986). The new approach no longer asks women to overcome their deficiencies, instead it asks what the institutions of science and technology are doing for women? *The Rising Tide* report (Cabinet Office, 1994) even suggests that children are part of women's lives, and that to enable women scientists to contribute to their full, issues of child care must be addressed. However such a suggestion in an official document is radical only in a UK context, which under an extreme right-wing government, has resisted recognizing the need to reconcile labour market participation with child care. In such a hostile context the report cannot quite bring itself to say that many men scientists are also the partners of women scientists and the fathers of children and need to do more, much more, about parenting. In this backward British environment the report fails to insist that scientific institutions support new and responsible constructions of fatherhood. (Thus where responsible fatherhood has been the subject of a leader in *Science* – the US counterpart to *Nature* – it is difficult to imagine the British journal urging men scientists to share parenting.)

Nonetheless, an international rising tide of the women in white coats has decisively broken away from the eighties victim-blaming analysis and is demanding that institutions change to match women's lives. This demand is supported strongly by those feminists in STS who are convinced that the strategic goal of changing the content of science and technology is, in the context of a global feminist movement, most likely to be achieved by diversifying the human subjects producing science and technology (cf. Harding, 1991; Rose, 1994; Scheibinger, 1993).

However, although second-wave academic feminism has successfully pointed to the massive over-representation of men in the research system, and specific countries and specific institutions have taken steps to modify this, the issue of over-representation, particularly in the research centres of excellence, is still a huge problem. For science it still more or less remains that power is where women are not. Thus in Britain, while a minority of research centres of excellence such as University College and King's in London have worked hard to secure an increased percentage of women particularly at the senior levels – so they now have 10 per cent of the professoriate – other institutions such as Cambridge remain bastions of male employment but seek to produce a cultural smoke screen by appointing a handful of brilliant feminists. The Royal Society similarly offered itself as the launch place for the government's report on *The Rising Tide* (Cabinet Office, 1994), but when challenged by the SET Policy Forum's proposal that as a condition of its grant it should be required to improve its miserable performance on the election of women fellows (currently slightly worse than 40 years ago), the retiring president showed, in his irritated rejection, that wherever reforms were going to begin, it was not to be at the top.

Of course, these are not the completely unreconstructed days as in the 1930s when the physicist Otto Hahn thought that his research director was quite enlightened to permit his co-researcher Liese Meitner[19] to work in the wood store (the director felt that her presence among the men researchers would be too disturbing), or when Svante Arrhenius, as chair of the Nobel Prize felt that he could ask Marie Curie not to come to Stockholm to take her second prize in 1911, because of the scandal of her sexual relationship with fellow physicist Pierre Langevin. Instead we see small auguries of progress. The venerable Royal Institution in 1994 decided that its annual Christmas lectures for children should at last be given by a woman scientist, and set about locating their ideal. Susan Greenfield's successful lectures and thence entry into becoming one of the few women media scientists and her subsequent appointment as the first woman Gresham professor,[20] speaks both of her talents and also of the continuing power of men as gatekeepers who can recognize or refuse to recognize the contribution of women. What about those other gifted women they decided against? Was 1994 a tokenistic one off or an augury of change?

Recognition is surely overdue not least because the historical record shows that when women have been admitted they have been at the frontiers of science. Thus they have been at the forefront of new disciplines, for example, in crystallography: Dorothy Hodgkin and Kathleen Lonsdale and many others, or Marjory Stephenson and Dorothy Needham in biochemistry, and countless unnamed women in the prehistory of computing in the Manhattan Project which built the first nuclear bomb. The point is that in innovatory moments in the production of scientific knowledge when danger and uncertainty are abundant and the career structure non-existent, only fools and angels enter. For fools and angels in the history of British science read the Braggs and Hopkins and the women of incredible talent they let into science. The intelligent generosity of these men only underlines the power of men scientists as gatekeepers.[21] Then and now such gatekeepers can either let women in or deny them access and recognition.

Despite the continuing power of men, the questions of women's access to science and the recognition of women's scientific contributions are recognized as being on the agenda, even if implementation is uneven and scarcely rapid. Unquestionably since the question was sharply posed in *Science* by the feminist sociologist Alice Rossi: 'Women in science: Why so few?' in 1965, feminism has successfully called into question the mono-gendered production of science. But since those uncomplicated days of the sixties the feminisms have proposed that feminism is about much more than gender. Nonetheless monodimensional politics are conspicuous at the level of official discussion, so that in Britain, Europe and even UNESCO the questioning of the maleness of the scientific labour force has typically been made separately from that of its paleness. When it comes to discussing access to the scientific and technological labour market, it more or less remains that 'all the women are white while some of the men are black'.

In the US these questions of gender, racism and multi-culturalism have been even more intensely debated and fought, as the persistent disadvantage of African Americans and Native Americans are rooted in the evil histories of slavery and genocide, are contrasted with the fast rise of Asian Americans, not least in scientific research. While many US feminists fight to keep hold of both postcolonial and feminist projects, unquestionably a persistent strand of white supremacism sees the increased recruitment and promotion of women as a means of excluding people of colour, even if that lets a few women of colour slip through. Thus even when gender becomes politically prioritized in changing the subject, feminism has learnt to insist on the multiplicity of our identities and to argue for the diversity of our – racialized, differently abled, sexualized and aged – hyphenated selves. For feminism at the end of the twentieth century changing the gendered subject is not enough. Thus, it is slightly ironic that at the very moment that the political demands of early second-wave feminism are beginning to be taken on board, the feminist movement stays partially on the periphery, making more complex demands. The sigh from some of our allies, as we extend the definition of the subject, is almost audible.

From Erasure to Cautious Welcome, and Now to Backlash!

While ANT, SCOT and SSK have commanded considerable academic interest, they have been marked by an inability to see either gender in the laboratories they study so meticulously or to cite feminist researchers who do. This has long been a weakness of British mainstream sociology of scientific knowledge (SSK) and would include the work of Ashmore, Barnes, Bloor, Collins, Mulkay and Woolgar. Nor did Bruno Latour as the most authoritative voice advocating actor network theory (ANT) across the Channel do any better, until his enthusiastic appreciation of Donna Haraway (Latour, 1993). In his work on reproductive technology Mulkay begins to cite a (very) small number of feminist texts (Mulkay, 1995); Woolgar together with Grint is beginning to acknowledge feminism in relationship to constructivism (Grint and Woolgar, 1995). Shapin[22] now working in the US, has clearly been made much more aware of the feminist literature, even if he feels unable to integrate it into his otherwise extensive review of the field. Indeed he still demonizes unnamed feminists in science studies for 'essentializing' gender.

Until these hints of conversion, this highly professionalized grouping has been singularly hostile to normative critics of science, dealing with them by erasure and silence. During the eighties natural science journals were more open to feminists than science studies journals. Thus *Science*, the powerful voice of US science, has for some years had an annual issue devoted to feminist debates in science, and even *Nature*, its UK counterpart, reviewed Evelyn Fox Keller's brilliant biography of Barbara McClintock, while the lead STS journal *Social Studies of Science* did not. Instead mainstream sociology, despite their claim to be interested in the political role of science, has chosen to mirror science's claim of being a gender–race-free culture. Thus Collins and Pinch's (1993) construction of the political is pretty much synonymous with Sandra Harding's concept of 'weak reflexivity' as they persistently restrict their analyses to the 'micro processes of the laboratory explicitly excluding race, gender and class relations' (Harding, 1991: 162).

The unquestioned success of this highly professionalized approach to SSK is running out[23] and there are hints that more normative approaches, such as those of feminism and environmentalism, look to be more fruitful. Democracy in science and technology is on the agenda again.

Today mainstream journals and the national and international meetings increasingly make cultural space for feminists. But while mainstream STS extends a cautious welcome to feminism, the mainstream has itself come under sharp cultural attack. The old élite of science, those whom I characterized earlier as wanting to hold onto a conception of science as truth, have launched a backlash against the whole of STS (including mainstream, feminist and postcolonial variants) as well as a whole other group of critics (new agers, environmentalists, etc.) as the collective destabilizers of science's hegemony as the purveyors of truth.

Numbers of the élite within science are turning their rage on these outsiders, who dare to criticize what they unquestionably see as 'their science'. Now, while I do not think that all natural scientists regard all the outsiders who are interested in science as the monolithic and monstrous enemy of science, unquestionably some powerfully located scientists do. In Britain the most visible of these defenders is the biologist Lewis Wolpert (1992) and in the US the biologist Paul Gross and the mathematician Norman Leavitt (1994). These are not isolated voices, they are well supported by other élite scientists and élite institutions. These conflicts – the science wars – are not identical in the two countries (and they are shaping up in others) but there are considerable parallels. Those who are part of British feminist science studies may perhaps be forgiven a mild relief that this round excluded us. However, it would be a mistake to see ourselves as safely outside the battle zone, as US feminist science critics are massively under attack. It may not be comfortable to be on the receiving end of such splenetic rage, but the pages devoted by Gross and Leavitt (1994) to attacking Harding are a perverse indicator of her achievement in precipitating questions about the pale and androcentric character of modern science.

By contrast, the UK canvass covered by the public and acrimonious debate between the embryologist and chair of the Royal Society Committee for the Public Understanding of Science, Lewis Wolpert, and the sociologist of science, Harry Collins, has been much narrower. The issue which occupied the 1994 meeting of the British Association for the Advancement of Science, pages of the *Times Higher Educational Supplement* and a special meeting in Durham, was that SSK claimed that science was a 'social construct'. Yet for sociology the claim is tautologous, as to observe that knowledge is socially constructed says in itself rather little about the truth status or otherwise. The testerical insistence by a number of élite natural scientists (Atkins, Dawkins and Wolpert) that science is 'not a social construct' left many social scientists, and a few less anxious natural scientists, quite puzzled. What then was this knowledge untouched by human effort – divine revelation? To be fair within this blunderbuss charge the precise target was a relativism which put the claims of scientific knowledge on the same epistemological level as that of any other narrative.

While sharing this basic questioning of relativism, Gross and Leavitt took on the entire gamut of science critics, including feminists, multiculturalists, poststructuralists, sociologists of scientific knowledge, new age thinkers, deep ecologists, etc. Smart enough to recognize that this grouping is not exactly homogenous, Gross and Leavitt ingeniously argue that these disparate social criticisms work by refraining from attacking one another, and that this unacknowledged combination serves to damage the cultural status of science. They name their grouping the *academic left* and denounce its alleged project as the Higher Superstition.

Thus the backlash works by homogenizing plural positions. Nonetheless at the core of these ill-tempered science wars is the argument between relativists and realists. This earlier erupted in the seventies as a debate within the radical science movement. In that conflict, while both agreed that science was shaped by the social relations of its context, the realists defended the truth claims of good science, both because they believed in its possibility, and because they saw truth claims as crucial for the movement's struggles – the so called 'good science, bad science' debate. By contrast the relativists questioned the possibility of truth claims, seeing science as not simply shaped by social relations but as synonymous with them. During the same period a professionalized version of relativism was developed by the strong programme elaborated by the Edinburgh School (notably the sociologist Barry Barnes and the philosopher David Bloor).[24] This was followed by a variety of theoretical modifications (SCOT, SSK, ANT, etc.) and became during the eighties the dominant stance in the social studies of science and technology.

Initially feminists active in the critique of science and technology were opposed to such relativism (Harding, 1986; Rose, 1978). With an epistemologically level playing field how could *we*, not least the feminist biologists to whom this chapter pays tribute, argue against sexist or racist science as bad science? And, given that criticism is a much weaker cultural move than the rival offer of a better theory, relativism also denies the possibility of feminist scientists constructing better accounts. Up to the early eighties there was some considerable agreement in feminist STS that the task was to rebuild the life sciences, as these were the ones so drastically impinging on women's lives and bodies.

This provisional agreement ceased with the advent of post structuralism and that entire cultural shift loosely called postmodernism, when the relativism/realism debate was taken up with new energy, not least among feminists engaged in science and cultural studies. This time the debate has not been restricted to that small group of feminists, left and mainstream academics interested in science and technology studies, but has been given much wider circulation as the question of the social standing of science and technology has come into the foreground of cultural debate. Behind this debate around ideas lie all the issues of the changing and diversifying structures of the sciences, the growth of risk, the emergence of the technosciences, the loss of Truth (with a capital T) as the big cultural claim, the problem of trust and expertise, and the weakening of the status of the old cultural élite of science.

With so much at cultural stake, especially for the old élite, the public debate has been unusually vitriolic, but the issue itself is important enough, and it has certainly occupied feminists. Within feminism the matching debate has been between standpoint theory (approximately equalling realism) and feminist postmodernism (approximately equalling relativism). What began in the early to mid-eighties with an evident strain appearing between the standpoint theorists and the more postmodernist in the science debate has changed to arguments of tremendous tension and complexity.[25] The central example has to be drawn from the US debate as they have been so dominant in feminist science theory. This shifted over the eighties from being confronted by the choice, either to follow influential theorists such as Donna Haraway's move towards postmodernism, or equally influential others such as Sandra Harding's defence of standpoint theory. But it was the exchanges between these feminist science theorists themselves which led to the choice itself being transformed. This transformation occurred partly because of feminism's widespread philosophical distaste for either/or dichotomies, and partly because of a deep commitment to the democratic construction of knowledge which has characterized feminist science theory building.

Over the nineties science theory feminists have developed an increasingly complex theorization, refusing the either/or choice. Instead concepts from both potentially antagonistic discourses of standpoint and postmodernism: situated knowledge, standpoints, revisioned rationality, feminist objectivity essentialism, social constructionism, etc., take their places.[26] Today very few feminists engaged in these strategic debates occupy either a purely relativist or a purely realist position in the manner that has been so denounced by the backlash.

This deep commitment to democracy means that feminists in STS show a strong sense of both the difficulty and necessity of building alliances between feminists in and outside the sciences. Of course, this does not always mean that we are successful but is has meant that the exchanges within feminism have been, thankfully, unlike those of the science wars. This is not to gloss over what I suspect is a basic conversational problem between an epistemological critic of science and a natural scientist – even between feminists. There is an underlying suspicion that the critic is not only explaining, but explaining away, the cultural constructions of the scientist.

What has enabled the multiple epistemological approaches of feminism to the sciences and the technologies relatively able to talk together is the normative commitment of late twentieth-century feminism to both diversity and to democracy. There is an evident longing to construct new democratic knowledges of both nature and culture with no excluded others denied their voices. This concept of citizenship without boundaries is a historically new political and cultural project. My hunch is that such a project can be read in two ways and that the choice may tell us as much about biography and generation as deep theoretical difference. Thus I suspect that this unboundaried citizenship can be claimed quite comfortably either as the project of postmodernity or, for those of us who suspect that modernity never quite arrived, as a radical revisioning of the Enlightenment project.

Here I want to make the connections with modernity and with the Enlightenment, for this richer concept of democracy, of citizenship with no group systematically excluded, has historical links with science's own self understanding of its knowledge production as democratic. That historically constituted scientists, along with Athenians, liberal democratic theorists, or even the theorists of the twentieth-century welfare state had rather restricted constructions of both citizenship and democracy is not denied. Nonetheless it is worth developing and building alliances with the very idea of democracy in scientific production.

As we approach the millennium we see feminist approaches to science and technology in a tremendous diversity of places, by no means agreeing with one another, but with a cultural achievement of having developed a shared language and practice of intellectual and political respect. Building this democratic and mutually respectful culture offers the best possibility of finding the trustworthy knowledges our world so needs. Mediating between these knowledges and holding them together is a historical view which sees that, as science and technology ever more pervade the culture, explanation inexorably becomes more local and more complex, and tailor-made expertise replaces universalism. Currently global and local scientific discourse jostle one another, but while we suspect we know who still shapes those old master narratives, the question of whose voices are to shape new global and local discourses remains on the political table.

What feminist science and technology studies offer at their most utopian is a project of profound democratic renewal, to reshape both science and society. At its heart lies the belief that, in the context of a world historical feminist movement with its celebration of both difference and commonality, if those who produce scientific knowledge become more like the diverse publics for whom they produce science, then through this new inclusiveness, the knowledges can be transformed, becoming more responsible to the diversity of people and nature alike.

Notes

1 Although here I speak of STS as an interconnected field my own work has lain primarily in science and the new genetics as a technoscience.
2 This includes the otherwise staunchly realist philosopher Kate Soper (1991).
3 The founding mother of feminist resistance to men's claims to know women's nature is Christine de Pisan and her fifteenth-century defence of women, *The Book of the City of the Ladies*, translated by E. J. Richards, 1982.
4 The potential references are immense key names would include: Gould, 1981; Haraway, 1989; Muller Hill, 1988; Procter, 1988; Rose *et al.*, 1984; Stepan, 1982; 1991.
5 Fausto-Sterling, 1992; Hubbard, 1990; Lowe and Hubbard, 1979; 1983; Sayers, 1982; Sunday and Tobach, 1985; Tobach and Rossoff 1978; 1980.
6 Technologies both to assist and to prevent conception have been subject to fierce criticism throughout second-wave feminism: Arditti, Duelli Klein and Minden, 1984; Petchesky, 1984; Pfeffer and Woolet, 1983; Rothman, 1988; Stanworth, 1987.
7 Carolyn Merchant's (1980) pioneering analysis revealed both the sexual violence at the metaphorical core of Bacon's conception of modern science and the extension of that violence against the whole of Nature.
8 There is a vast literature on risk following Ulrich Beck's pioneering text *Risk Society* (1992).
9 The novelist Fay Weldon and the journalist Brian Appleyard are conspicuous figures amongst the romantic anti-science current.
10 A story which has run from E. O. Wilson, *Sociobiology*, 1975 to Richard Dawkins' endless recycling of his thesis of *The Selfish Gene*, 1976 to *River out of Eden*, 1995.
11 GUTs are Grand Unifying Theory and TOEs: Theories of Everything. For an example of the physicists' longing, see Weinberg 1993.
12 See 'Thinking from caring' for a discussion of the feminist attempt to construct a responsible rationality (Rose, 1994), and Irvin and Wynne's (1996) attempt to construct a social rationality.
13 The turbulence is mapped by the response to the Science Wars in the special issue of *Social Text* (Sokal, 1996), the insertion of a spoof article by Alan Sokal a physicist, in the issue, and the ensuing US journal and huge international net debates.
14 Many of the sharpest critics of the Human Genome Project are drawn from the US the centre of the Genome production system and from a Germany acutely conscious of its past.

15 *The Bell Curve* by Herrnstein and Murray is the latest high publicity text drawing on psychometry, a technique which has a long history in locating the subordination of oppressed groups in nature. The book defends and justifies the racialized and gendered social hierarchy of the USA.

16 The international project of molecular biology which aims to map and sequence the entire Human Genome.

17 All three co-decision makers, the Council of Ministers, the Commission and the Parliament, in the post-Maastricht Europe, are on public record as supporting the claims of women to be fairly represented within science.

18 The *1996 UNESCO World Science Report* includes a whole section prepared for Beijing on gender and science.

19 Meitner was one of the greatest physicists of the early mid-century. As a Jew she had to flee Nazi Germany, and in 1944 her close collaborator Hahn was given a Nobel Prize. Many regard this as one of the most outrageous erasures of brilliant women scientists.

20 Gresham College was the precursor to the Royal Society of London.

21 The possibly most brilliant woman scientist of that generation, Dorothy Wrinch, was, when she went to the States, systematically excluded by the Nobel Laureate chemist Linus Pauling. (Kay 1993).

22 Steve Shapin seminar paper Science Theory Department, Göteborg May 1996.

23 At a recent international meeting discussing 'Has SSK a Future?' (University of East London, 1996) a substantial group took the view that the paradigm was played out.

24 Barnes at this meeting rebutted the charge that he and Bloor were ever relativists. How far this is seen as a judicious reconstruction of positioning, or they convince their critics, that they were mistaken remains to be seen. For a definitive statement of the position see David Bloor (1976) *Knowledge and Social Imagery*, Chicago, IL, University Press.

25 See Chapter 4 in Rose (1994) for a detailed discussion of this debate.

26 The theoretical accommodations in recent feminism are evident not least around essentialism. Demonized by influential Marxist feminist currents in the eighties, and only preserved theoretically by standpoint theorists and feminist biologists, essentialism, qualified, refined but *still* essentialism, is now making a comeback in both cultural studies and sociology (cf. 'Essential Differences' a special issue of *Differences*, 1996, and Benton, 1991.)

References

ALLEN, L. (1994) 'Anatomical and physiological correlates of sexual orientation', paper given to National Organization of Gay and Lesbian Scientists and Technical Professionals, Annual Meeting of the American Association for the Advancement of Science, San Francisco, CA.

ARDITTI, R., DUELLI KLEIN, R. and MINDEN, S. (Eds) (1984) *Test-Tube Women: What Future for Motherhood?*, London, Virago.

BECK, U. (1992) *Risk Society: Towards a New Modernity*, London, Sage.

BENTON, T. (1991) 'A cautious welcome to the return of the repressed', *Sociology*, **25**, (1), pp. 1–29.

BLOOR, D. (1976) *Knowledge and Social Imagery*, Chicago, IL, University Press.

BOSTON WOMEN'S HEALTH BOOK COLLECTIVE (1973) *Our Bodies, Ourselves*, New York, Simon & Schuster.

CABINET OFFICE (1994) *The Rising Tide: A Report on Women in Science, Engineering and Technology*, London, HMSO.

COLLINS, H. and PINCH, T. (1993) *The Golem: What Everyone should Know about Science*, Cambridge, Cambridge University Press.

COWAN, R. S. (1983) *More Work for Mother: The Ironies of Household Technology from the Open Hearth to the Microwave*, London, Macmillan.

DAWKINS, R. (1976) *The Selfish Gene*, Oxford, Oxford University Press.

DAWKINS, R. (1995) *River Out of Eden*, London, Weidefeld and Nicholson.

DE PISAN, C. (1982) *The Book of the City of Ladies*, translated by Richards, E. J., New York, Persea Books.

Differences: A Journal of Feminist Cultural Studies, special issue-'Essential Differences' March 1996.

FAUSTO STERLING, A. (1992) *Myths of Gender: Biological Theories of Women and Men*, New York, Basic Books.

GOLDBERG, S. J. (1975) *The Inevitability of Patriarchy*, New York, Morrow.

GOULD, S. J. (1981) *The Mismeasure of Man*, New York, Morton.

GRINT, K. and WOOLGAR, S. (1995) 'On some failures of nerve in constructivist and feminist analyses of technology', in *The Gender Technology Relation* (Eds) GRINT, K. and GILL, R., London, Taylor & Francis.

GROSS, P. and LEAVITT, N. (1994) *Higher Superstition: The Academic Left and Its Quarrrels with Science*, Baltimore, Johns Hopkins.

HAMER, D., HU, S., MAGNUSON, V. L., HU, N. and PATTATUCI, A. (1993) 'A linkage between DNA markers on the X Chromosone and male sexual orientation', *Science*, **261**, pp. 421–7.

HARAWAY, D. (1989) *Primate Visions: Gender, Race and Nature in the World of Modern Science*, New York, Routledge.

HARDING, S. (1986) *The Science Question in Feminism*, Milton Keynes, Open University Press.

HARDING, S. (1991) *Whose Science? Whose Knowledge?*, Milton Keynes, Open University Press.

HERRNSTEIN, R. and MURRAY, C. (1994) *The Bell Curve: Intelligence and Class Structure in American Life*, New York, Free Press.

HUBBARD, R. (1990) *The Politics of Women's Biology*, New Brunswick, NJ, Rutgers.

HUBBARD, R. and WALD, E. (1993) *Exploding the Gene Myth*, Boston, MA, Beacon.

IRWIN, A. and WYNNE, B. (Eds) (1996) *Misunderstanding Science: Science in Everyday Life*, Cambridge, Cambridge University Press.

KAY, L. (1993) *The Molecular Vision of Life*, Oxford, Oxford University Press.

KELLY, A. (1978) *Girls and Science: International Study of Sex Differences in School Science*, Stockholm, Almquist and Wiksell.

LATOUR, B. (1993) *We have Never been Modern*, Cambridge, MA, Harvard University Press.

LEVAY, S. (1993) *The Gay Brain*, Cambridge, MA, MIT Press.

LOWE, M. and HUBBARD, R. (Eds) (1979) *Pitfalls in Genes and Gender Research*, New York, Gordian Press.

LOWE, M. and HUBBARD, R. (Eds) (1983) *Women's Nature: Rationalisations of Women's Inequality*, Oxford, Pergamon.

MEISS, M. (1992) 'What unites, what divides women from the South and from the North in the field of reproductive technologies?' in AHKTER, F., VAN BERKEL, W. and AHMADDHAKA, N. (Eds) *The Declaration of Commilla*, Finrrage and Ubinig.

MERCHANT, C. (1980) *The Death of Nature: Women, Ecology and the Scientific Revolution*, London, Wildwood.

MULKAY, M. (1995) 'Parliamentary ambivalence in relation to embryo research', *Social Studies of Science* **25**, pp. 149–63.

MULLER HILL, B. (1988) *Murderous Providence: Elimination by Scientific Selection of Jews, Gypsies and Others: Germany 1933–45* Oxford, Oxford University Press.

PETCHESKY, R. (1984) *Abortion and Women's Choice: The State, Sexuality and Women's Reproductive Freedom*, New York, Longman.

PFEFFER, N. and WOOLET, A. (1983) *The Experience of Infertility*, London, Virago.

PROCTER, R. (1988) *Racial Hygiene: Science Under the Nazis*, Cambridge, MA, Harvard University Press.

ROSE, H. (1978) 'Hyper-reflexivity: A new danger for the counter movements', in NOWOTNY, H. and ROSE, H. (Eds) *Countermovements and the Sciences: Alternatives to Big Science*, Dordrecht, Reidel.

ROSE, H. (1994) *Love Power and Knowledge: Towards a Feminist Transformation of the Sciences*, Cambridge, Polity.

ROSE, S., LEWONTIN, R. and KAMIN, L. (1984) *Not in Our Genes*, Harmondsworth, Penguin.

ROSSI, A. (1965) 'Women in science: Why so few?', *Science*, **148**, pp. 1196–1202.

ROTHMAN, B. K. (1988) *The Tentative Pregnancy: Prenatal Diagnosis and the future of Motherhood*, London, Pandora.

SAYERS, J. (1982) *Biological Politics: Feminist and Anti-Feminist Perspectives*, London, Tavistock.

SCHIEBINGER, L. (1993) *Nature's Body: Sexual Politics in the Making of Modern Science*, London, Pandora-HarperCollins.

SOKAL, A. D. (1996) 'Transgressing the boundaries: Towards a transformative hermeutics of quantum gravity', *Social Text*, 46–7, pp. 217–48.

SOPER, K. (1991) *Troubled Pleasures*, Brighton, Harvester Wheatsheaf.

STANWORTH, M. (Ed) (1987) *Reproductive Technologies: Gender, Motherhood and Medicine*, Cambridge, Polity.

STEPAN, N. (1982) *The Idea of Race in Science: Great Britain 1800–1960*, London, Macmillan.

STEPAN, N. (1991) *The Hour of Eugenics: Race Gender and Nation in Latin America*, Ithaca, NY, Cornell University Press.

SUNDAY, S. and TOBACH, E. (Eds) (1985) *Violence Against Women: A Critique of the Sociobiology of Rape*, New York, Gordian Press.

TOBACH, E. and ROSSOFF B. (Eds) (1978) *Genes and Gender: On Hereditarianism and Women*, New York, Gordian Press.

TOBACH, E. and ROSSOFF, B. (Eds) (1980) *Genetic Determinism and Children*, New York, Gordian Press.

UNESCO (1996) *World Science Report*, Paris, UNESCO.

WACJMAN, J. (1991) *Feminism Confronts Technology*, Cambridge, Polity.

WEINBERG, S. (1993) *Dreams of a Final Theory*, London, Huthinson Radius.

WHYTE, J. (1986) *Girls into Science and Technology*, London, Routledge.

WILSON, E. O. (1975) *Sociobiology: The New Synthesis*, Cambridge, MA, Harvard University Press.

WOLPERT, L. (1992) *The Unnatural Nature of Science: Why Science Does Not make Common Sense*, London, Faber and Faber.

ZILMAN, A. (1978) 'Women and evolution, part 11: Subsistence and social Organisation among Early Hominids', *Signs: Journal of Women in Culture and Society*, **4**, 1, pp. 4–20.

Chapter 3

Women in Science, Engineering and Technology: *The Rising Tide* Report and Beyond

Nancy J. Lane

The Context

On 24 February 1994 a booklet, entitled *The Rising Tide*, was published by the Cabinet Office through Her Majesty's Stationery Office. It was concerned with the current position of women employed in scientific pursuits within the UK and I was chair of the working party which wrote the document. In this chapter I will draw on my experience of working on the report, together with some of the findings which it included, in order to explore the difficulties still encountered by women wishing to follow scientific careers. The fact that the British government initially supported the working party, but subsequently felt unable to endorse some of its more important proposals, is indicative of the kinds of public and political obstacles which women still face.

The British government's current concern with the issue of women in science arose originally with William Waldegrave, who was the Secretary of State for Public Service and Science when the working party began its labours in April 1993, a position he held until the 1995 summer cabinet reshuffle when David Hunt took over this particular portfolio. Waldegrave had been given the go-ahead by the Cabinet to produce a new White Paper on Science and Technology, through which it was intended he should establish new structures for running the scientific community in Britain. In the event, however, the White Paper heralded the advent of a focus on wealth creation by scientists, rather than on basic research activities, to the deep regret of many in the country's research community.

My personal involvement in all of this was due to the fact that I was at that time serving on the Cabinet Office Advisory Panel for the Citizen's Charter, a group of six individuals who advise the Prime Minister on how to raise the public image of the various public services that government has in place. These services include education, the national health service, social security benefits, prisons and all manner of other activities. I was the advisor on the educational side. When I asked the Prime Minister whether William Waldegrave was being encouraged to include a consideration of the position of women in his White Paper on science, the Prime Minister suggested that I go and talk to Mr Waldegrave himself, which I then did.

Mr Waldegrave was very preoccupied at that time because he had found himself the chief protagonist in an amusing Christmas card issued by the organization, Save British Science, in the winter of 1992. As the Christmas card intimated, he was meant to be putting forward a paper on his long-term policy on science and technology, yet the 'batteries were missing', because Waldegrave was not himself a scientist. Since Mr Waldegrave lacked an understanding of the position of UK scientists, he went around the country talking to them and taking advice on what to include in his White Paper. Many scientifically trained women hoped that he would seek the opinions of women scientists as well as those of men, about their particular career problems and difficulties. In the event, when the White Paper, *Realizing Our Potential* (Cabinet Office, 1993) was published in May 1993, it contained only one paragraph dealing with women. This stated that the UK was not realizing the full potential of women as a resource in general and in the field of science and technology in particular. The single, most undervalued and, therefore, underused human resource in the country, it said, are women.

However, Waldegrave clearly ultimately did put his mind to the problem for women, in that he spoke to the then Chief Scientific Adviser to the Cabinet, a plant scientist called Professor Sir William Stewart. In March 1993, Stewart and Waldegrave called upon me to chair a working party, to investigate, first, if there were any problems with respect to scientific activities and careers for women in the UK and, second, if it emerged that there were such problems, what should be done about them to improve the current situation for women. So, some 11 women from various parts of the country and from various scientific disciplines were identified to form the working party and we gathered together at regular intervals at the Office of Science and Technology (OST) to prepare a report on this topic. In the autumn of 1993 we finished the writing of it in collaboration with another, more senior committee of women, set up and chaired by Sir William in the late spring. The document was not made public until February 1994, however, owing to the Cabinet Office's publications' section having a backlog of documents to publish.

We entitled our report *The Rising Tide* in an allusion to lines by Shakespeare, hoping that we would stimulate debate among Ministers about the problems for women in science. At one point in the text of the play, *Julius Caesar*, it is said, 'There is a tide in the affairs of men, which taken at the flood leads on to fortune . . .' Many women would like to think, of course, that this is what *The Rising Tide* was all about, since it noted the benefit or good fortune available to the UK, by making greater use of the potential of its women scientists.

The government did not respond to our report until July 1994. When it did so there were some recommendations it agreed to accept or consider, but there were also a number of suggestions, particularly that on tax relief for child care, which it felt unable to implement. The government did, however, agree to one of our major requests, which was that there should be a Development

Unit, set up in the Office of Science and Technology, dedicated to look into the issues raised by the report.

The Problems for Women in Science, Engineering and Technology

What problems did we discover when we made our investigations for *The Rising Tide* (Cabinet Office, 1994)? An initial problem was that it was quite difficult in some cases to obtain relevant data because, although we could get figures from certain branches of government, notably the Department for Education and the Employment Department, it was almost impossible to get material from industrial sources. Industry didn't seem to want to impart information about those women they employed in science and technology. It soon became apparent that one reason that this was the case was that, in general, women employees were not being treated particularly favourably. Companies were obviously very embarrassed to have to admit what an exceedingly tiny percentage of their senior management were women. Basically, the business community appeared to recognize that the dearth of women in senior positions was not very palatable news, and so they were not eager to make it public.

Most of the data available comes from the Labour Force Survey and, in *The Rising Tide*, is based on 1991 figures (Office of Population, Censuses and Surveys, 1992).

Figure 3.1 illustrates the numbers of men and women employed in science and engineering and other related occupations in Britain in 1991. The numbers of women are astonishingly low. There are only a few women working successfully on a technical level, and a few women in town planning. Very few women are employed in engineering and electronic work, and but a small number in chemistry. Only tiny numbers of women are working in fields other than the biological sciences, and there they are mainly laboratory technicians. The lab technician's job is, however, by far the most menial of positions in the lab. So women are not only underemployed in science and technology for the most part, but when they are employed, they are positioned, not in the exciting and interesting aspects of lab work, but rather the opposite. Projected figures show that by the time we reach the year 2006, four-fifths of the increase in the civilian labour force will be women (Department of Employment, 1993). So, if something is not done about training women in science and technology, there will be a shortage of trained scientists in the workforce by then. Hence, the UK needs to train more women in science and technology, and having trained them, women need to have access to jobs with decent career development, to ensure that they can have a reasonable lifestyle, enabling them to cope with their domestic responsibilities, while they carry on doing scientific work. Unfortunately, it seems that unless companies or the institutions can see some sort of economic advantage to be gained by employing and promoting women, then they fail to do so. If there is no economic advantage, no improvement in the bottom line, then employers are not usually enthusiastic about instigating

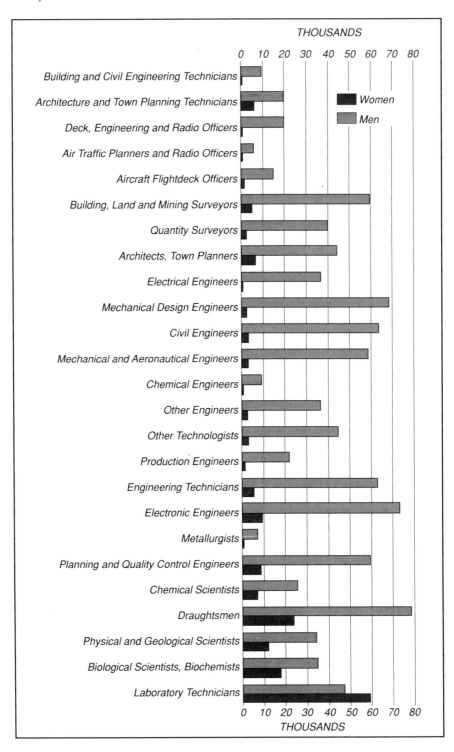

policies that are 'female friendly' (Cabinet Office, 1994). However, one can hope to show a benefit to the employer if women stay on after child-bearing, since employers often put a great deal of money into training their women employees, and this is money wasted if they do not retain these members of staff, quite apart from the fact that they are losing experienced, and hence, valuable, personnel.

If we turn to universities as employers, there were roughly 24 000 academic staff in full-time higher education work during the academic year 1991–92 and, from the data available, it emerges that women account for only 15–16 per cent of that workforce (Universities' Funding Council, 1993). As one progresses up the academic ladder, moving into senior positions such as readers and professorships, fewer and fewer women are to be found, and the women all tend to be in 'other' grades, that is grades other than readers, professors or even lecturers. Other grades usually means short-term contracts, jobs that are the lowliest of the low, very junior positions. In all the sciences, there are only tiny numbers of women who are professors. In 1995 only two women professors of physics and one woman professor of chemistry existed in the UK.[1] The biological and medical sciences do rather better but, even so, the percentage of women in professorships is not very large; within the biological sciences, only 30 per cent of university posts are held by women; one would have expected rather more than that, given that there are a large number of women, almost 50 per cent, reading the biological sciences as undergraduates, as well as a good number at graduate level (Universities' Funding Council, 1993).

With regard to the professional institutions, and the numbers of women in the various classes of membership, the 'higher the fewer' is again the case. Fellows, the top-most senior position, are followed by members, associates, graduates and students, descending down the levels of seniority. Women are in their largest numbers in the student category. At the level of fellowships, there are very few women in the engineering professional institutes, physics, chemistry or even biology (Cabinet Office, 1994). In biology, of those who have achieved fellowship level, only 5 to 6 per cent of these are women, even though 50 per cent of the student members are female. This is both surprising and distressing.

Engineering is particularly significant, because it is a subject where women are currently catastrophically underrepresented. Has there been an improvement over the last decade? Statistics reveal the difference between the position in 1980 and that in 1990 (Engineering Industry Training Board, 1981;

Figure 3.1: Numbers of men and women in employment in science, engineering and related occupations, Great Britain, 1991
Source: Labour Force Survey

1992). There has been some improvement in the numbers of women in administrative and professional staff jobs over the last decade, but very little change in the numbers of actual engineers. This is not the substantial improvement that one might have expected. In fact, women scientists, in general, show no real improvement in their position over the last 10 years. What is unnerving is that the largest numbers of women in engineering, between 70 and 80 per cent, are to be found in the clerical staff (Engineering Industry Training Board, 1992). So it is clear that they are not practising engineering or science in the true sense of the word.

A similar picture emerges if we consider the research councils, in this case as they were before the White Paper on Science, Engineering and Technology, *Realizing Our Potential*, which changed their names (Cabinet Office, 1993). In 1992 there was a huge discrepancy in the numbers of women versus those of men on the government boards or councils, such as the Medical Research Council (MRC), which ran science in the UK (Cabinet Office, 1994). The women were primarily noticeable by their absence, although there was one lone woman on the Natural Environmental Research Council (NERC), and small numbers in a few of the others. There were none, however, on the Advisory Board to the Research Councils (the ABRC) and this was the place where science policy was made in the UK. When the 1993 White Paper changed the names and activities of these Councils, a new Council for Science and Technology was established to replace the ABRC, and one woman was appointed to serve on it! In fact, rather more would have been desirable to more closely approximate gender parity. Another powerful new committee, the Foresight Technology Committee, was also set up to assess the future directions of UK technology and that initially had no women serving on it at all. Given that these committees were being established in 1994, this struck many women scientists as being really rather extraordinary. After all, government had let it be known that attempts would be made to improve the numbers of women on public committees to ensure, it had been said, that women were well represented, in decisionmaking and in all manner of other ways within Britain.

If one analyses the élite research societies to which the crème de la crème of our scientists and our engineers would wish to be elected, very few women are encountered.[2] To be elected as a Fellow of the Royal Society, or a Fellow of the Engineering Academy is extremely unlikely for a woman, because of the total fellowship of the Royal Society, which in 1995 numbered over 1000, only 3 per cent were women. In the Royal Academy of Engineering, out of a total fellowship of 901, only three fellows were women. So no woman should hold her breath if she is hoping to be elected to a fellowship in one of these eminent Societies! The odds are very much against it happening. Moreover, there has been no improvement over the last few years since, of the new fellows elected to the Royal Society between 1989 and 1993, only 3.5 per cent were women and, in 1994, only one woman was elected to a fellowship. Each year sees about 40 fellows elected, so one is not an encouraging figure.

It is sometimes suggested that the situation regarding women's position in science, engineering and technology is much better in North America, where progress for women has been underway for quite some time. It is, therefore, surprising to discover from data presented in the journal, *Scientific American*, that women scientists are faring no better in the United States than in Britain (Holloway, 1993) and that the situation in Canada is also very similar. This suggests that women are either being excluded, possibly by the theoretical glass ceiling, or are not putting themselves forward for posts in science, engineering and technology (SET). One reason often suggested is that the educational system fails to direct or encourage girls into science (Acker, 1994; Berryman, 1983; Byrne, 1993). It is claimed that there are relatively few women science teachers, especially in primary schools, and, in the latter, those who are there tend to be inexperienced in science subjects.

What is needed, it is argued, are enthusiastic and able scientists who are capable of demonstrating to young people, and particularly to girls, the excitement and significance of subjects such as physics or chemistry. Mentors, in short, are very important. The lack of female role models or mentors in SET is quite deleterious from the point of view of girls continuing in science. It is also clear from recent evidence that girls receive less attention from teachers, even though teachers fail to realize they are neglecting them in favour of the boys (Alper, 1993). It appears that, if you actually add up the time spent, more minutes per hour of teaching attention are given to boys than to the girls; this is not just the case in science, it is so in every subject (Acker, 1994; Byrne, 1993). Thus, the main message from all this research is that teachers' attention at school is terribly important in terms of encouraging girls into science (Cabinet Office, 1994). If girls are not encouraged in school, they may not take up science or study it at university, so, of course, they will not, as a result, have a career in science. The same situation is greatly exacerbated in engineering.

It is also reported that, in the US, women claim to have less general encouragement, less mentoring, and less help with their professional advancement than men (Holloway, 1993). Further, as adults, women are less likely than men to be asked to serve as members of editorial boards, direct group research projects, or speak at meetings (Holloway, 1993). They also have the problem of harassment. It appears, however, that very few women will actually admit to being sexually harassed. When one asks for figures of how many people are complaining of sexual harassment, the answer is essentially none; but when one interviews university students, it emerges that a huge percentage of young women on any university campus will admit to having experienced some form of sexual harassment (Holloway, 1993). But they rarely actually publicly admit it or complain to the authorities. This may be a question of how one defines sexual harassment, but what the reasons are for the reluctance of girls to come forward have not been entirely satisfactorily established. At Oxbridge, the suggestion has been made that the harassers may, in some cases, be the supervisors or Directors of Studies to the students, which places the young woman who complains in an unenviable position as regards advancement.

Another problem that women have to endure, although there is little data currently available on the situation in the UK, is that when their husbands or partners are relocated owing to a job change, they must move with them if their family unit is to survive. It is claimed that, in 1993, 43 per cent of women in the US were relocated and, if you are a scientist, relocation leads to difficulties because the chances of getting a post in your particular specialist subject elsewhere are often very remote (Holloway, 1993). Such women are often demoted to a more junior position in their new lab. In contrast to the women, only 7 per cent of men in the US were relocated (Holloway, 1993). If a partner refuses to relocate, then couples are likely to be separated and often have to travel very long distances to maintain their relationship.

A further major problem for women scientists is that of child bearing/ rearing. Data on the ages when women and men are being employed in science, engineering or technology, indicate that men who join this work force between the ages of 25 to 29 continue to be employed until their early fifties, after which their numbers only gradually begin to drop off as some take early retirement (Office of Population, Censuses and Surveys, 1992). If one considers all the women working in science in the UK, although there are fewer than the men, at least there are women employed in science between the ages of 25 and 30. However, after that, there is a significant decline in their numbers. One way to interpret this decline would be that if women want to have children and have not done so by the age of 30, they tend to think that they really ought to proceed immediately to have a family, since their biological time clock is inexorably continuing to tick away (Cabinet Office, 1994). The problem appears to be that after they have their children, women often take time off from work, but then seem not to be able to get back into scientific employment. They may be on a short-term contract that will have come to an end by the time their child is born, for example. If the maternity leave being given is not only limitless, but also unpaid, then women scientists have a serious problem. In short, there is often no maternity leave policy in science labs, which might encourage women scientists to take time off from work and then to come back to the lab (Cabinet Office, 1994). While off work there should be maternity benefits and a percentage of pay available, so that the woman is able to return to employment with her position waiting for her. Sadly, this is frequently not the case in science labs, often owing to short term contracts. This is another of the problems for women in science, which needs to be addressed by persuading employers to put good maternity benefits and policies into place, so that the money spent on woman's training is not wasted.

Overall, the data collected for *The Rising Tide* report suggested there were three major areas of concern about women in science, engineering and technology – education, employers and the media (Cabinet Office, 1994). The report, therefore, first addressed education, considering what was happening in schools, in further education colleges and in universities. Why are more girls not encouraged to go into science? The UK needs more science teachers who are women, both because they act as role models and mentors and because they positively encourage girls to go on with science. Employers of women scientists, the second category to be addressed, included universities, industry and the civil service, and they all need to ensure that equal opportunities are in place. Proper maternity leave should be available and other family friendly policies should be in existence. The monitoring of progress also needs to be maintained. Finally, the report considered that the public image of women scientists should be heightened; they should be given more coverage by the media, particularly by TV and radio, and when individuals are being considered for public appointments, women should not be excluded from the process.

Women and Science Education

Although *The Rising Tide* considered, and acknowledged the significance of, a range of issues, it is clear that education, providing part of the basis from which young people go on to make choices about their future, is particularly important. It is, therefore, worthwhile considering some of the current educational factors in relation to young women and the science subjects a little further. For instance, it is clear from comparing the results of 1970 with those of 1992 that there has been a gradual improvement in girls' performance in passing at grades A to C at GCSE, with an increasing number of them doing well; in 1992 girls did not merely equal the performance of the boys, they actually surpassed them (Department for Education and Science, 1971; 1993). In 1994/95 the girls were also seen to be surpassing the boys in science subjects at A level, although fewer of them were doing physics or chemistry (Department for Education, 1995). So it cannot be that girls are intellectually inadequate to cope with science subjects, because these results show that they are entirely capable of doing so. Yet, if we consider the new entrants to higher education in 1991, there were very few women in subjects such as engineering, maths and physics (Cabinet Office, 1994).

Only with regard to the biological sciences and subjects allied to medicine did the numbers of women equal those of men. However, a slight improvement has taken place since 1991. The latest available figures, those from 1994, indicate that women are now outnumbering the men reading biological sciences in the UK, with 59 per cent of undergraduates currently women (Department for Education, 1995). In the veterinary subjects and agriculture, there are 51 per cent women to 49 per cent men. In physics, nearly a third of the physicists are women. But there are rather smaller numbers in maths, information technology and engineering. Comparing the situation between 1992 and 1994, though, it can be seen that there has, in fact, been very little change. Although women comprised 59 per cent of the total number of students studying the biological sciences in 1994, the percentages for 1992 and

1993 were 57 and 58 per cent respectively. If we consider maths, engineering, technology and physics, there is essentially no change, with women still numbering 30, 25, 14 and 12 per cent respectively of the overall student numbers.

If we turn to 1992 postgraduate numbers, evidence suggests that women were present in rather small numbers in engineering, maths and physics, but in biology they were almost up to equal numbers with the men, and they were actually more numerous than men in medicine (Cabinet Office, 1994). In 1994–95, there were very few girls doing PhDs in science subjects and they represented around 16 per cent of the total numbers in physics, maths and engineering (Higher Education Statistics Agency, 1996). Without PhDs girls cannot hope to go on into university positions, so there can be little improvement in the dreary situation in UK universities until more girls are persuaded to stay on and become PhD students in physics, chemistry, engineering, etc. Although there are a reasonable number of women doing their PhDs in subjects like biochemistry, which is, of course, a biological subject, they mostly end up in jobs with short-term contracts, and relatively few become lecturers, senior lecturers, readers or professors.

The question as to why fewer girls continue with science subjects and why their numbers decrease the further one moves up the educational hierarchy has been addressed in a study, which focuses on Oxford and Cambridge, by Dr McCrum at Hertford College, Oxford (McCrum, 1994). McCrum looked into what happens to girls after they come into university at Oxbridge. He claims that there is a *gender deficit*, because men and women at Oxford and Cambridge enter with three A grades at A level, and yet, by the end of their 3rd year course, fewer girls get first class marks than the boys; they may achieve good second class degrees, but they rarely obtain firsts. Dr McCrum has put forward four possibilities to explain this gender deficit. The first, that women have smaller brains, and so cannot cope, can, I think, be safely disregarded. The second reason, Dr McCrum suggests, is that the Oxbridge male admissions tutors are so swayed by the pulchritude of certain women candidates that they select the beautiful rather than the able ones. There are two issues here: one is that it is very irritating for women to be told that girls cannot be both clever and beautiful; the other is that it is outrageous that beauty should be what admission's tutors are allegedly seeking in students, rather than ability. This phenomenon may, of course, if true, be peculiar to Oxbridge. The third explanation McCrum offers is more interesting, since it relates to the issue of gendered variability in performance. Women, it is alleged, obtain more second class degrees and men more firsts and thirds. Men, it is thought, will 'chance their arm', by writing something quite provocative in an examination, and for that they may be either extolled by the examiners and given a first, or deemed to be totally on the wrong tack and given a third. On the other hand, women, it is suggested, play safe, and present cogent and well-argued cases, putting forward much organized data and well-structured supporting evidence. Yet this is likely to be deemed a second-class answer and one which is inferior to the lateral thinking and flamboyancy presented by men. Unfortunately, some institutions are now refusing to fund for a science doctorate individuals who fail to obtain a first class degree. So, if a student is awarded a 2.1, as many girls are, then they have no chance to do a PhD. Hence, fewer women are studying for higher degrees in spite of their obvious ability.

A further, and contentious, issue raised by McCrum is that of premenstrual syndrome (PMS). There is the question of whether girls, who happen to be having a period with concomitant headaches and discomfort, do less well, if suffering from PMS during a single event assessment, i.e., an exam, than they would do if being judged on a long-term project. There is very little data on this, although there are anecdotal reports which suggest that girls do equally well whether being assessed short term, or doing a long-term project (McCrum, 1994) at Cambridge University. Interestingly, a small preliminary study indicates that this does not seem to be the case.[3] This study suggests that girls do better on long-term projects than they do in exams; whether that evidence can be pinned down to PMS or not is unclear. However, if candidates for Oxbridge degrees continue to be assessed by examination alone, PMS, if truly a problem, could work against the success of girls.

Yet, more positively, even if McCrum's data shows Oxford and Cambridge women to be suffering from a gender deficit, men and women in other universities in the UK can be seen to do equally well (McCrum, 1994). Although men tend to beat women in terms of degree classification in certain subjects, such as maths, physics, languages (interestingly) and history, women beat the men in biology, biochemistry, geography, law and economics. And they perform equally well, (amazingly enough), in chemistry and engineering. Even though there may be fewer women doing engineering, those who do choose to study it are able to perform as well as the men. This means that it cannot be argued that there is any problem with women's brains or that they are intellectually incapable of becoming engineers or chemists. It is still, however, a question of enquiry as to what we have to do to improve the position for women in these fields.

Recommendations and Good Practice

The Rising Tide report made recommendations on many different levels. With regard to education, the report recommended that there should be a broadening of the A-level syllabus. If individuals did not have to restrict themselves to three subjects at A level, it suggested, then more young people might be prepared to include science among their options and, perhaps, more girls would actually study science (Cabinet Office, 1994). The moment one has to make a choice at an early age, many girls opt out of science because, it is alleged, they are frightened they will not do as well in it as they would in history, languages or English. They are aware that one needs very good A levels to be accepted at university to study and so they opt for the subjects in which they think they will do best. If there was a broad spectrum of subjects to study, as is available in Scotland, where they have the Highers, or in France, where they have the Baccalaureate, then students would be able to take on a wider range of subjects, and perhaps maintain their science studies until they reached an age of greater maturity and self-confidence. If, then, students realize that they are good at science, they may opt to continue with it. The UK is presently losing many potential scientists by having this possibility cut off (Cabinet Office, 1994).

The government's response to this recommendation was negative, possibly because the A-level system has been in existence for a long time and it would take a great deal of effort to change it. Yet, it was surprising that the government also vetoed the suggestion that the interest of both girls and boys be maintained in science, when it came to the training of teachers. Government claimed that it could not interfere with the training of teachers in any way. Instead, it was suggested that some move could be made through the Office for Standards in Education (OFSTED) to enhance the effectiveness of equal opportunities policies in schools.

With regard to employment, the report recommended that equal opportunities policies for staff recruitment, retention and promotion should be part of any organization's policy and strategy; this should be implemented and then monitored (Cabinet Office, 1994). A report at the end of each year is ideally required to see if progress has been made and improvements noted. It is also very important, it was thought, for line managers to know that they have to have these requirements in place and, moreover, that they themselves are going to be appraised on their implementation. As a line manager, if part of your job description is making sure that equal opportunities policies are in place and recruitment is unbiased, and if it is also clear that your job is on the line, as well as your incremental salary, then you are more likely to ensure that such policies are well established.

Also important for women are maternity benefits, together with the childcare facilities required for them to return to work after having had a child. Women need to be able to work part-time, or to job share, and to have access to other comparable kinds of flexible policies. Amazingly, many employers have no such policies, operate terribly strict 9.00am to 5.00pm daily hours arrangements and do not permit job sharing or working flexible hours (Cabinet Office, 1994). These policies regarding flexibility, often called family friendly policies, reflect how crucial it is that the attitudes of men change in recognizing that women, including their own wives, may be as important for their earning power as they are themselves. As a result, job sharing should be seen to occur, not just in the workplace, but also in the home environment. In addition, monitoring of the success of these policies, and hence of their progress, is essential, yet is often not in place.

The Rising Tide report also acknowledged that Britain should be doing better with regard to childcare for pre-school children. In 1988/89, only 2 per cent of children under three years in Britain had access to publicly funded childcare services, compared to 20 per cent in France and 48 per cent in

Denmark (Women of Europe, 1990). Similarly, only 35–40 per cent of children from three years to school age, (i.e. five or six years) are catered for in Britain, compared to 95 per cent in France and 85 per cent in Denmark (Women of Europe, 1990). Hence, compared to the rest of Europe, Britain is doing poorly in terms of providing childcare facilities for mothers who wish to work and who need someone to look after their children while they return to the workforce. Yet, one of the report's suggestions that the govenment considered it could not implement was to allow tax relief on childcare costs for working women; this, it was claimed, would not be cost effective. Those of us who have spent the bulk of our salary on paying for the costs of our offsprings' childcare consider, of course, that this would be very cost effective indeed from the mothers' point of view. So, it is to be hoped that the Chancellor of the Exchequer will keep the suggestion in mind and reconsider it again at some point in the future. It could be deemed a vote winner, at least as far as women are concerned.

Another issue to be addressed is how to establish more flexible arrangements for research funding. If a woman scientist does have a baby she should be able to take time off for maternity leave and subsequently, when back at the lab, obtain help in childcare in order to go to scientific meetings. Women who take extensive time off to have children should be able to come back into science and have an opportunity to be retrained. As a scientist, it is not possible to go straight back into the lab after a lengthy absence because one needs to be retrained to cope with new techniques and equipment. There needs to be some sort of scheme to pay for that retraining, and returner schemes should be in place to facilitate such activities. Returner schemes have been set up at the Open University although, sadly, those schemes are currently not being adequately funded. The Wellcome Trust and the Royal Society also have recently established some returner schemes, but the numbers of scientists these can support is obviously very small.

One of the deficits noted in *The Rising Tide* report was the lack of a central focus for actively making more use of the currently undervalued and, hence, underused, potential of women in science, engineering and technology (Cabinet Office, 1994). It was, therefore, recommended that a Development Unit, for women involved in SET, be set up in the Office of Science and Technology, for at least three years, to take forward the recommendations of *The Rising Tide*. It is gratifying to report that such a Development Unit has been set up, as from December 1994, under the Directorship of Lynda Sharp, although for two years only. One problem here may be financial, as the extent of the budget is not clear. However, the Unit has already established a central catalogue of databases and it plans, ultimately, to give careers advice in the provinces. An initiative from the Science Museum will circulate in the provinces to help women use the information superhighway and become more aware of IT in general. The Unit will also monitor events in government and research councils, to check current policies, establishing those which are successful and then disseminating details of these. An attempt will be made to monitor the impact of the Development Unit itself, by surveys gathering responses from various establishments and measuring the numbers of groups contacting the Unit, to try to make an assessment of its success from such sources.

The Rising Tide report also considered it desirable that the Development Unit for women in SET should interact with Opportunity 2000 and, possibly, with the Investors in People (IIP) scheme. Opportunity 2000 was set up in 1991 by the organization, Business in the Community. This initiative tries to persuade all the different businesses, companies and universities in the UK to promote more women to senior positions within their organizations and to do so by the year 2000. It puts the case that it is of economic advantage to utilize the resources of the women in the workforce to their full potential. Each member organization decides how it wants to approach such goals, by instigating more training or other initiatives for women or instigating a target for the percentage of women to be in senior management by a certain predetermined time. Progress towards the attainment of their targets or benchmarks are normally monitored year on year and the Development Unit will use the targets of Opportunity 2000 in order that its own progress might be assessed. The IIP scheme is non-gender based and aspires to persuade employers to take more care with their policies concerning the fair treatment and career development of staff; assessment of success in this regard is rewarded with an IIP stamp of approval.

Examples of companies operating in the UK with good policies, in relation to the above kinds of schemes, include Lucas, the car manufacturing firm, which is setting up placements in schools, trying to show the students there that women engineers actually exist; they are working on this in collaboration with the University of Warwick. Nuclear Electric has also put forward various initiatives to encourage more women graduates to apply to them and has established workshops for the personal development of their female staff, since one of the problems women often confront is a lack of self-confidence. Smith and Nephew, the international health care company, has objective assessment centres judging all their staff with a view to increasing the percentage of women in senior positions in their workforce. Northern Electric has a special liaison with schools and Midlands Electricity is sponsoring some splendid schemes with WISE (Women into Science and Engineering), under the auspices of the Engineering Council. Unilever, the chemical company, has schemes in place for a flexible working environment and Texaco, the industrial firm, has implemented awareness training and dignity at work policies. These relate as much to the male employees as to the female. The National Health Service has some wonderful development programmes for women; SmithKline Beecham, self-awareness programmes and maternity packages; Glaxo, childcare initiatives; British Gas and British Telecom, workplace nurseries or childcare vouchers, all of which are very good value for the companies because it means they retain their valuable, highly trained, workforce. Much of this information about employers has been published in a brochure compiled by the Office of Science and Technology, together with Opportunity 2000, called *Making the Most* (Office of Science and Technology/Department of Trade, 1995).

The Wellcome Trust, like the Royal Society, is setting up a number of flexible fellowships, with schemes for returners. The fellowship initiative that the Royal Society has put in place is to ensure that women have access to a career development scheme. These flexible fellowships will also provide an example to persuade universities and other funding bodies to change their previously inflexible approach. Their policies include maternity leave and additional help in attending conferences if childcare is required. The Royal Society is also making efforts to include more women on decision-making bodies, and to monitor the success of such ventures. They hope to use *academic age* rather than chronological age in judging success. So, if an individual has five years out of science for child-rearing, the academic age is the chronological age minus those five years. Moreover, rather than judging publications by sheer numbers, the quality of the publications is to be taken into account. The Royal Society is also setting up a Daphne Jackson Memorial Fellowship scheme, in memory of Professor Daphne Jackson, a physicist, who during her lifetime made great efforts to help women to carry on with a career in science.

The data collected for *The Rising Tide* also suggests that it would be helpful if national targets could be set up in relation to women and SET. Accordingly, it was recommended that at least 25 per cent of qualified women should be raised to senior positions in SET by no later than the year 2000. Unfortunately, the government felt unable to respond positively to this recommendation. As has been seen, in industry, unlike universities, data is not readily available and so the current percentage of women in senior SET positions is not accurately known. Although, 25 per cent is not a very high figure in itself, the government argued that, since it was not entirely clear what the current position actually was, it was being asked to agree a percentage increase from an invisible baseline.

The Rising Tide also argued that it is important to try to raise public awareness by more interaction with the media, in order to explain to the general public that women scientists have an important contribution to make and that they are not eccentric 'blue stockings', but ordinary women (Cabinet Office, 1994). The media could very much help with this by presenting, on TV and radio, women scientists as interesting people undertaking significant and exciting work. In this way, they could provide valuable role models for girls contemplating a scientific career. Thus, efforts are being made to encourage the media to raise the profile of women scientists, as well as science in general. To this end a joint media–scientist evening was held at the Science Museum in London in 1995. The Royal Institution (RI) Christmas TV lectures for 1996 are being given by a woman, for the first time in 165 years! Some of us, together with colleagues who are expert TV writers, are producing TV scripts on the lives of fictional women scientists in an attempt to demonstrate that women who do science have existences outside of work, and can have an interesting social life linked to their laboratory activities. Such soap operas, set in labs, will hope to show that science is fun and that any young woman may aspire to be a scientist.

A number of further developments have also recently taken place. Early in 1995 the House of Lords set up a Select Committee to look into academic courses for graduate scientists in SET and they are taking a particular interest in career development for women. Opportunity 2000, the Business in the Community scheme, has a number of admirable initiatives, to encourage more school girls to go into science; they are publishing a brochure of best practice. Springboard programmes, involving lectures and workshops are being devised for undergraduate women scientists at universities such as Cambridge, in an attempt to improve their self-confidence. There is a development called AWISE–Forum, which has sprung up at regional centres all over the country, to encourage networking among women scientists. Databanks have been set up by the Committee on the Public Understanding of Science (COPUS), Women into Information Technology in the European Community (WITEC) and the Office of Science and Technology (OST), to facilitate finding women working in science, engineering and technology to serve on national or international committees or councils.

Concluding Remarks

A year after *The Rising Tide* was published, the Foundation of Science and Technology, a body which supports science by arranging discussions on topical issues, held an anniversary gathering at the Royal Society in London, to celebrate the success of the Development Unit for Women at OST. David Hunt, then Secretary of State for Public Service and Science, spoke, as did Lynda Sharp, the mathematician who runs the Development Unit. Dr Bridget Ogilvie, Director of the Wellcome Trust, which has put a number of admirable initiatives in place, also gave an address. It was one of those occasions when one felt a buzz of excitement from the people attending. The audience was roughly fifty–fifty men to women, which was splendid, for if key men are not persuaded of the importance of the venture to improve the lot of women in science, then success is unlikely to follow. It is, therefore, imperative that men should be persuaded of the economic benefits to be gained for the UK from having a good number of women in science and engineering.

The wastage, as regards human resources, if one ignores 50 per cent of the population, as well as the loss of potential diversity and balance in the work force, with the concomitant loss of customer satisfaction, should be apparent to all. Women's particular strengths lie in areas such as team working and cooperative ventures. Perhaps, then, given that women often actually operate rather differently than men, what really needs to be done is to change the current system which historically was designed by men. It is alleged that women prefer work that has a relevance or is of benefit to society, that they like to collaborate rather than to compete, that they prefer non-confrontational situations and that they often possess a rather different, less hierarchial, managerial style to that of men (Holloway, 1993). It may be, therefore, that these are the reasons why it is often difficult for women to fit into the schemes that have long been established by men. Should certain aspects of our scientific organizations be changed? Perhaps they are already beginning to be modified, as hardened attitudes are eroded with the advent of increasing numbers of able women into the scientific work place, and the concomitant policy changes being set up by enlightened employers. It is to be hoped that the economic benefits of these policies will soon be apparent to all employers so that ultimately we will have a gender balance not only in the workforce of science, engineering and technology, but also in all positions of seniority and authority in the UK. It is to this end that the content of *The Rising Tide* report can be seen to lead the way.

Notes

1 Office of Science and Technology, personal communication.
2 Office of Science and Technology, personal communication.
3 G. Horn, unpublished observations, 1994.

References

ACKER, S. (1994) *Gendered Education*, Toronto, Canada, OISE Press.

ALPER, J. (1993) 'Is there a female style in science?', *Science*, **260**, pp. 384–429.

BERRYMAN, S. E. (1983) *Who Will Do Science? Minority and Female Attainment of Science and Mathematic Degrees*, New York, Rockefeller Foundation.

BYRNE, E. (1993) *Women and Science: The Snark Syndrome*, London, Falmer Press.

CABINET OFFICE (1993) *Realizing Our Potential – A Strategy for Science, Engineering and Technology*, London, HMSO.

CABINET OFFICE (1994) *The Rising Tide: A Report on Women in Science, Engineering and Technology*, London, HMSO.

DEPARTMENT FOR EDUCATION (1995) *Statistics of Education: School Examinations, 1994*, London, HMSO.

DEPARTMENT FOR EDUCATION AND SCIENCE (1971) *Statistics of Education: School Examinations, 1970*, London, HMSO.

DEPARTMENT FOR EDUCATION AND SCIENCE (1993) *Statistics of Education: School Examinations, 1992*, London, HMSO.

DEPARTMENT OF EMPLOYMENT (1993) *Employment Gazette*, **101**, pts. 1 and 2, London, HMSO.

Nancy J. Lane

ENGINEERING INDUSTRY TRAINING BORAD (1981) *Annual Report and Accounts 1979–80*, London, HMSO.

ENGINEERING INDUSTRY TRAINING BORAD (1992) *Annual Report and Accounts 1990–91*, London, HMSO.

HIGHER EDUCATION STATISTICS AGENCY (1986) *Qualifications Obtained by and Examination Results of Higher Education Students in England and in the United Kingdom for the Academic Year 1994/95*, Cheltenham, Universities Statistical Record.

HOLLOWAY, M. (1993) 'A lab of her own: Trends in the sociology of science', *Scientific American*, **269**, 5, pp. 68–77.

McCRUM, N. G. (1994) 'The academic gender deficit at Oxford and Cambridge', *Oxford Review of Education*, **20**.

OFFICE OF POPULATION, CENSUSES AND SURVEYS (1992) *Labour Force Surveys*, London, HMSO.

OFFICE OF SCIENCE AND TECHNOLOGY/DEPARTMENT OF TRADE (1995) *Making the Most*, London, HMSO/Opportunity 2000.

UNIVERSITIES' FUNDING COUNCIL (1993) *University Statistics 1991–2*, **1**, Cheltenham, Universities' Statistical Record.

WOMEN OF EUROPE (1990) *Childcare in the European Community, 1985–1990*, Supplement 31, Brussels, Women's Information Service, Commission of the European Communities.

Chapter 4

Against the Odds: Women Developing a Commitment to Technology

Ailsa Swarbrick

Introduction

Women are still under-represented in science, engineering and technology (SET). After ten years of reports, campaigns and schemes, the proportion of women in these professions had risen by 1990 from 2 per cent to 5 per cent (Devine, 1992). This chapter is based on research data on 275 women technologist returners who studied on the Open University's Women in Technology (WIT) scheme between 1981 and 1988. In a larger project which also includes a comparative group of 90 women new to technology, I have questioned employers' and trainers' perceptions of the *career-break*; explored aspects of the WIT women's discontinuous work-histories and argued that their experience exposes existing concepts of *career* as gendered constructs (Swarbrick, 1993). An ideology based on the separation of the public and private spheres enables the breadth and variety of the unpaid half of the WIT women's experience to be devalued, and their commitment to the public sphere of technology to be dismissed.

In terms of a traditional career, the WIT women's withdrawal to the private sphere, though temporary, makes problematic their commitment to the public world of technology. On the one hand, they have qualifications in an area of knowledge constructed as male; their experience has been in an occupation noted for its gender segregation; and their earlier employment patterns assumed a career of unbroken progression. To have overcome the gender-based barriers to technology, the women had needed a strong commitment to the public sphere. But their present status as returners shows that they had also made a second family commitment. The public/private dichotomy polarizes these commitments, reducing them to simple alternatives. The women's experience suggested a more complex interpretation.

The Research Approach

My enquiry is based on a feminist approach. I began by recognizing the women technologists' demonstrable commitment to both public and private spheres, and aimed to explore what that meant for the women themselves. A full discussion of current debates on feminist research processes is beyond the scope of this chapter. The features relevant here are first, that knowledge itself is held to be a gendered construct (Harding, 1991; Smith, 1987). The concepts so produced cannot accommodate women whose experience is rendered invisible or deviant (Ramazanoglu, 1989; Thiele, 1987). Second, a project to reconstruct knowledge must adopt a feminist standpoint position (Lather, 1988). This is not an additional variable, but 'raises questions about . . . a relationship between gender and power' (Ramazanoglu, 1992: 209). Third, women's experience, examined from their perspective, is seen as a valuable empirical resource. Placed within a theoretical framework concerned with gender divisions, such research cannot be politically neutral (Maynard, 1994).

These are the issues which distinguish my feminist research. My priorities were to listen to the women's own presentation of their experience, but also to use the large-scale characteristics of the WIT project. This resulted in a combination of methods. Quantitative data on the full sample of 275 women provided a framework for analysis. The insights gained from this were explored through interviews with 17 women.

The period examined here extends from their education up to the time when the women first came out of full-time technological employment. I explore the beginning of the women's commitment to a profession in technology: how long it took to develop, at what stage it became clearly formulated, and the extent to which they felt hindered or supported in their choice. Different patterns are identified at three key stages. The first is that of establishing an interest in science or engineering during education and training. The second is when consolidating that interest in employment. The third occurs with the approach of the family commitment, and the beginning of the period of discontinuities known as the career-break. Their entry and progress in professional technology is analysed in terms of gendered power relations and based on a feminist critique of the public/private dichotomy.

Establishing Commitment: Education and Training Choices

The WIT women include both graduates and technicians who had been in education and training mainly during the 1970s. They were part of a tiny minority on two counts. As Table 4.1 shows, the majority had either a university degree or technician qualifications in mathematics, science or engineering. To be part of this tiny minority suggests at least unusual determination – a necessary ingredient for future commitment.

A working definition of technology is the application of scientific knowledge to the solving of practical problems, and is perceived as directly vocational. The 41 per cent of WIT women who chose to study for technological qualifications, therefore, appear to have made an early commitment to technological employment. Table 4.1 further suggests that academic, as distinct from vocational, courses may have been seen as more suitable for girls. This is

Table 4.1: Women technologists: First educational qualifications

	WIT Population		Interviews
Technological qualifications (ONC/HND)	55	20 per cent	2
BSc English	56	21 per cent	3
BSc (Maths; Physics; Chemistry)	96	35 per cent	8
BSc (Life Sciences; Biology; Geography)	23	8.50 per cent	3
Other Qualifications	42	15.50 per cent	1
Not Recorded	3		
TOTAL	272		17

Table 4.2: Further Qualifications

	WIT Population	Interviews
PhD/MSc	11	4
Professional Engineering Institutes	11	3
Chartered Engineering	6	2
TOTAL	28	9

supported by an examination of the *kinds* of degrees studied. More than twice as many women had degrees in pure sciences (subjects perceived as more academic) than degrees in engineering or technology. The questions are *why* any women chose technology (as distinct from pure science) at 16–18 years old, and how those who did choose science came to move into technology later?

In the 1970s, when the WIT women were making course choices, there would have been little encouragement to have opted for engineering. By 1979 only 0.5 per cent of UK engineers were women (Finniston, 1980). The 21 per cent of the total WIT sample who made such a choice show some level of commitment. Pure science would have been both more familiar and more accessible for the 43.5 per cent who chose it at the age of 18. That they later used their scientific knowledge for a move into its practical application suggests an awakening commitment. This may also be the case for the 15.5 per cent with other qualifications. For example, a number of arts or modern language graduates went straight into Information Technology jobs. A further indication of developing commitment maybe seen in Table 4.2, which shows qualifications gained later. But whenever the WIT women found their way into technology, they would invariably have been in a tiny minority.

What were the influences which led this minority to make a non-traditional choice of post-school qualifications? The interview accounts in my research suggest that for many, the choice was a process over time, sometimes extending into their first job. That choice could be haphazard, depending on factors like school or family background, as other research on women engineers has noted (Carter and Kirkup, 1990; Walshok, 1981). Three broad and sometimes overlapping categories could be identified: the women engineers; the scientific technologists; and the latent technologists.

Early Commitment

Five of the 17 women who were interviewed had made an early commitment to technology – three graduates, in civil, chemical and aeronautical engineering and two technicians in electrical and mechanical engineering. How had they come to make their choices, and how clearly did they regard their courses as vocational? Were there any common features which might have encouraged an earlier commitment to technology than that made by the other 12 women?

The Women Engineers

These five women moved immediately into post-school technological higher education or training. None had spontaneously considered engineering as their first option. They had all enjoyed maths at school, and science where it was available, but their original plans for further study had been either more conventional or less focused. For all five, the influence of family or mentor appeared to have been a crucial factor. Active encouragement helped three women to widen their horizons. For example, a friend of the family arranged for Margaret to visit aerospace firms in the school holidays, while Chris's year at technical college opened options lacking at school.

> I had no idea what I wanted. I hadn't a clue. Then I was offered a technical drawing job in the local factory. The head of the department was a female, a fully qualified engineer, and within a month she was saying, 'would I like to go on, take an apprenticeship?' (Chris).

Two further women were influenced by direct parental intervention. Anna, with excellent A levels in maths, had been turned down by 15 teacher training colleges because she had no art or craft subjects.

> Nobody would have me. Would you believe it? I couldn't get in anywhere. They were looking for junior school teachers and I suppose they weren't interested so much in a higher level of maths. I had fallen between two stools really. Perhaps I should have tried to get into university (Anna).

Instead, on her engineer father's advice she went to work for a local firm and studied for technician qualifications in electrical engineering. Mira's family intervened in the absence of any firm plans on her part.

> I did what they said really. My brother who's an electrical engineer, *he* said 'Why don't you go into chemical engineering?' So I thought 'Oh, why not?' Very immature, just left to chance really (Mira).

Catherine changed from the more conventional choice of maths, her favourite school subject.

> I was eased in through the maths. One of the maths teachers was an ex-civil engineer. He told . . . us that there was almost as much maths in the engineering course. But there were so many branches of engineering, you might have a choice to go into something else (Catherine).

For all five, the interest of people close to them influenced the choice to which they became committed, but which was not an obvious one for girls of 16–18. I referred above to the haphazard nature of decisionmaking. Here the influences and circumstances vary, but all five had either parents, family friends, or elder brothers who were in engineering themselves. They may well have contributed to the familiarity of engineering as a field of study and as an occupation.

Other research has reflected the significance of encouragement from male relatives or friends who were themselves from an engineering background on women technologists (Carter and Kirkup, 1990; Newton, 1987; Swarbrick, 1978; Warren, 1986). Given the effectiveness of exclusionary practices by employers and unions in industry (Cockburn, 1986; 1988; Drake, 1987; Walby, 1986; 1988), support from insiders would appear to be important.

Later Commitment

Twelve of the women interviewed had moved to technology after completing their studies in mathematics or science. Two broad and sometimes overlapping categories could be identified: the scientific and the latent technologists.

Scientific Technologists

These were six women who developed an early enthusiasm for the study of science which became more specifically focused into technology at university. Two dated their interest in science from a crystallizing experience. For example, a particular incident had sparked off a curiosity in physics for Louisa.

> I remember once, my father was asking somebody to repair a bank of
> light switches, and the man said 'No, one switch isn't working, you
> will have to replace the whole bank'. I said, 'I'll have a go at it', and
> I was only about 12. So I switched off the mains and I fiddled about
> with the spring. It was one of those old tumblers you know . . . I got
> it working and he was very impressed (Louisa).

Doing post-graduate study to build on a central scientific interest offered
another route into technology. Three women had moved into specialized
applications which gave them an extra advantage for later employment. Val
stayed on after graduating in chemistry.

> It was a bad year for employment and the research department had
> a good reputation. It was almost a trivial step from the MSc to my
> PhD in nuclear magnetic resonance spectroscopy (Val).

Hannah followed her geography degree with an MSc in hydrology, and Louisa
began a part-time MSc in microwave engineering during her first teaching job.
The experience of a work-placement could also provide inspiration. Mavis, a
physicist, had no definite employment plans until well into her degree, when a
vacation studentship at Harwell focused her interest into nuclear physics.
Lorna, a microbiologist, became interested in a medical research career after
a sandwich year in the pharmaceutical industry.

A fourth route from science to technology was that taken to escape from
a course which was dauntingly academic.

> Well I went to do pure maths, but I actually changed. I went to a girls'
> grammar school, I had a father who was an engineer, I could do
> maths without working on it, to be honest, at school anyway, so you
> were channelled, you did the degree in the subject you had done at A
> level. There were only six of us, and to some extent you were consid-
> ered the élite of the school (Alice).

That confidence soon disappeared at university. Other research (Thomas,
1990) also shows how girls who did well at school in physics, felt their confidence being destroyed by the dominant male ethos at university. At the end of
Alice's first year she switched to the general degree with more practical work,
which later led her into technological employment.

The experience of both the women engineers and the scientific technologists shows that there was no readily recognizable or uniform route into
technology for young women at the time they were making crucial choices
for their future employment, though the pure academic route was the most
accessible.

The Latent Technologists

The third group of women came to technology much later than either the women engineers or the scientific technologists. Unlike the engineers, they did not have the influence of mentor or family. Nor did they, except for one, have a clearly focused interest like the scientific technologists. These latent technologists did not develop a commitment to technology until after they graduated. They appeared less aware of their own potential in this field until external or random factors stimulated it into growth. In two cases, commitment to technology did not emerge until the end of the first stage of employment, when priorities were starting to shift towards the private commitment. It then lay dormant until reactivated by the effects of WIT. The end of their degree studies left them all in a state of uncertainty. Decisions were taken by default, different options were sampled and choices were taken for pragmatic reasons.

Commitment developed *after* the choice had been made. In Rachel's case, the discovery of technology came through an advertisement for a government-funded PhD in hypersonics in the aerospace industry. This random chance finally gave shape to a hitherto rather aimless drift through mathematics and a first job in teaching. She had not been aware of areas of employment where a mathematical background could be applicable. One factor influencing most of the women was the perceived need to fit in with a new husband's career plans. For example, Deborah newly graduated, married a PhD student. Recognizing the dual commitments opening up before her, she chose post-graduate training in information science for its flexible and widely available job opportunities.

Latent commitment can take as long as six years to emerge. Two women eventually developed an earlier brief or passing interest. Deidre recognized with greater maturity, how to use her mathematical ability to her own satisfaction.

> I was nowhere near as good then as I am now. And that's because I hadn't judgment. Particularly in software and control systems, you need judgment (Deidre).

Jenny, a geography graduate, took five years to find intellectual stimulation in training for a new career in computing.

Finally, a commitment can remain latent through force of external pressures. A web of cultural and gendered family constraints delayed the sixth woman developing her commitment to technology until much later.

> I wanted, I *especially* wanted to do a pharmacy course of some kind . . . My parents were both retired teachers, and in our country, teaching is a good professional job, a respected job especially for a

lady. It was only a two-year course, and my husband wanted me to finish the course very soon so I could come over here. I did science because I'd always been interested in it, all the time . . . actually I shouldn't have done the teacher training, because I was educated in my medium and not in English, but everyone preferred it, so I chose it . . . I had no other choice (Sylvie).

School played little part in opening access to technology as an employment option for the WIT women. Academic higher education was seen as the main route for acquiring qualifications, and many simply continued to study their favourite subject at university. But once they had started on technological employment, their commitment grew. As Rachel said, 'I've got more determined and channelled as I've got older.'

For none of the women interviewed had technology been the first choice. Their experience confirms that at the time they were making decisions about higher education or training, it was conventionally outside the range of options for young women. To enter further or higher technological education was to enter a gendered domain, where all of the women had been aware of their conspicuous minority status. The WIT women had survived by finding ways to protect their vulnerability. These early lessons in the development of coping strategies were essential not only for survival in this first stage of establishing commitment to the public world of technology. They were necessary for the will to sustain that commitment through the period known as the career-break. The women's experience would also be the basis for combating the variety of exclusionary practices encountered when they were reclaiming their full technological commitment in the post-WIT period. Meanwhile, having acquired the necessary foundation for a commitment to technology, the women moved on to develop that commitment.

Consolidating Commitment: Employment

The first period of employment was a time when the WIT women consolidated their interest in technology and also began to diversify. Evidence suggests that once their choice was made, the majority stayed in technology. Of those with technological qualifications, 64 per cent had worked solely in that field until they first left paid work. But by then 27 per cent had already had some experience of teaching, with either a professional qualification, or employment, or both. A further 9 per cent had acquired other qualifications in subjects such as management, accountancy, catering, youth and community work, agriculture and tourism, while still maintaining links with technology. So a significant minority of 36 per cent, while not abandoning their commitment, had begun to widen their options. Was this a dilution of their technological commitment or a pragmatic response to other circumstances? It is not only the actual jobs that are of interest, but also the context in which job-seeking decisions were made. The full WIT sample of 275 women technologists had on average 6.9 years experience in the first stage of employment. Without this solid professional base, it is more difficult to retrieve the public commitment later. The rich variety of employment patterns illustrated in the interviews cannot be contained within one monolithic model of career. Instead, five broad pathways can be identified: the engineering career; the tenacious career; the tryout career; the pragmatic career; and the aborted career. From the strategies the women developed to overcome constraints, all of these demonstrate commitment to technology. The first path was that adopted by the five women with engineering qualifications, who had also slightly longer employment experience.

The Engineering Career

Engineering is still largely organized on the basis of male experience (Devine 1992; McRae, Devine and Lakey, 1991). Women are not formally excluded, but remain a very small minority in terms of involvement. To establish themselves in the inflexible structures of engineering, in effect they are required to behave like young male engineers (Compton and Sanderson, 1990). The WIT engineers were able to demonstrate the gendered form of commitment up to the end of the first stage of employment. This was only possible because of their compromises and ingenuity in coping with the demands of a gendered profession – an extra, though unrecognized dimension of commitment. But once this gendered pattern of professional behaviour becomes untenable, there is no acceptable alternative model for an engineering career. Sooner or later the women found it difficult to comply with many of the characteristics which are taken to demonstrate professional commitment. Two examples are mobility and the acquisition of varied experience.

The first 5–10 years in engineering, as in any profession, is a critical period when mobility is seen as essential for acquiring a wide practical experience. This assumes that the engineer is free from other constraints so as to give priority to professional development. All five WIT engineers had been mobile in this period and had thoroughly enjoyed the travel and variety. As long as they felt free to go wherever the contracts were placed, their careers continued to develop on conventional, gendered, lines. But while they were developing their professional skills, they also got married – four to engineers whose careers were similar to their own. At first, this made little apparent difference because of the joint strategies they devised to cope with the situation, for example living half-way between two workplaces, or moving only when both had found jobs. But eventually a husband's career took priority, as did that of Catherine's husband when he was posted abroad, or Mira's who was moved on promotion. Both these women responded with initiative and determination that in itself constitutes unrecognized professional commitment. Without the career structure provided for her husband, Catherine wrote to all the consultant civil engineers in the phone book. Without the benefit of in-service training, she tracked down and got to grips with a foreign code of practice. Without colleagues, with whom to share ideas, she learned how to work independently.

Catherine's efforts to continue to exercise her professional skills in these circumstances demonstrate the extra dimension of commitment referred to above. Mira demonstrated a similar commitment. Finding no jobs locally in her field of chemical engineering, she got a job installing a computer system, where she met all the targets against opposition from older members of the company.

Margaret showed commitment to remaining in technology by extending her base of experience beyond the technical side of aeronautical engineering. Over eight years she became more involved in administration and finance.

> I moved from aerodynamics to the sales department because they were reducing numbers even then. There were fairly frequent redundancies, 4000 while I was there and you had to leave yourself with another way out ... Then I moved on to contract administration because Sales had a big upheaval. I took over bringing in some computer systems for Contracts throughout the factory ... I suppose it helps to know what the parts of an aeroplane are that you're talking about (Margaret).

The pathways of the two technicians were similar. Anna completed her HND and technician apprenticeship in electrical engineering the same year she got married. She consolidated her career with 10 years' varied experience in industry, finishing as a design engineer making aircraft simulators. With her second commitment now looming she tried to ensure her future employment credibility by achieving Chartered Engineer status just before the birth of her first child.

> After I became a graduate engineer of the Institute of Electrical Engineers, you just need experience and age on your side, so you can't in fact apply for full membership until you are 27, and you have to have a certain degree of responsibility. By the time I was 27 I was about five months pregnant, so I filled in all my forms – hastily! I was eight months pregnant when I finally staggered out of work (Anna).

Chris's commitment was strong enough to survive the industrial recessions of the 1970s. She struggled to improve her qualifications while unemployed, and used her initiative after a change in company policy to enable her to move into research and design.

> Working things out, and the design work and getting into problems that need thought, I enjoyed that. That's when I started to find the

disadvantage of having only a Full Technology Certificate. I found it limiting because I didn't know enough (Chris).

This first employment period was crucial for the five engineers. They were using their education and training, acquiring experience of different work-place environments, and learning that other skills like communicating effectively, cooperating with colleagues, and negotiating with management were also important. Their experience would be applicable to all young people starting out in the engineering industry. There are, however, other socially constructed factors relating to gender which they were already learning to cope with and plan for, in order to sustain their commitment. Factors from the private sphere such as partner's career aspirations and family formation were unlikely to affect their male contemporaries. The extra dimension of commitment found in the women's career strategies is unrecognized. The point is that once the gendered pattern of professional behaviour becomes untenable, there is no acceptable alternative model for a career in technological industry. How far did this apply to the 12 women who made a later commitment as scientific and latent technologists? The diversity of their experience suggests four further pathways.

The Tenacious Career

The tenacious career typifies those women who determinedly pursued a technological interest developed during their studies, from a purely theoretical interest in sciences. They had all made a later start in technology than the women engineers and from a range of different routes. But once they had made the move, they consistently demonstrated their commitment. Like the women engineers, constraints arose from the beginnings of their family commitment, and did not appear to affect their partner's careers. Tenacity could take different forms. For a physicist who wanted to get married, but also did not want to waste her start on a career, it meant a year of weekend cross-country travelling. She made it quite clear that while she was prepared to move, she would not have considered taking a chance on the job market.

> The first job was definitely the sort I was looking for. The second came about because I got married. We met when we were both working in the same area, for different employers. Then he got moved away . . . I had invested so much into getting to where I'd got. It was such a huge investment in terms of time that it wasn't something to be discarded lightly (Mavis).

Mavis's tenacity finally enabled her to widen her experience, and consolidate her commitment to technology in this first stage of employment.

I'd never contemplated working on a power station before. If you were in the labs, you didn't. Power stations were something else. It actually turned out to be a very good move, in fact, I ended up enjoying that job even more than the one I'd had before (Mavis).

Determination was a consistent characteristic. Two women pursued post-graduate qualifications, though not yet for a clearly focused technological commitment. But having committed themselves thus far, they stayed in their chosen specialisms until their first pregnancies. The hydrologist worked with two water authorities after her MSc, and was then sponsored by the Manpower Services Commission to do a PhD with another. Like the technician who achieved her CEng when seven months pregnant, she 'went to the graduation ceremony . . . and Mark was born two months later. Youngest child with a PhD!' (Hannah). While Deborah's husband completed his PhD, she worked in jobs of increasing interest, setting up a local authority information service for planners and engineers and finally taking responsibility for a technical library with a major power industry. This last especially satisfied her abilities, using information science to link the chemical abstract database. In spite of dependent mobility, these women did their best to build up experience for an effective return to work later.

Two more graduates, in applied physics and maths, who had moved to engineering after teaching, also displayed tenacity. Louisa recognized early the need to develop a dual strategy to fulfil her professional and family ambitions. Her aim was to gain experience in both education and engineering. In contrast to the sexist and racist attitudes she met in unsuccessful interviews for industry, she was pleasantly surprised when she turned to the education sector.

I thought if I was going to have a family, teaching would be a handy thing to have. So anyway I tried three schools and within a week I got three offers. Fantastic. Even then they were short of physics teachers . . . usually you didn't get a grade 1 post until you were experienced, but one of the heads rang me up at home and offered me a graded post. 'You are the answer to our dreams' . . . I mean to have a woman (Louisa).

Later, with a part-time MSc in Microwave Engineering to strengthen her professional credibility, she started the first of the three engineering jobs she had before her son was born. Her commitment to technology is evident in her planning for the future. Rachel's tenacious pattern is different. After a few months teaching maths, she worked almost entirely in the aerospace industry.

I'm one of these people that has lots of changes . . . I wanted something that was exciting and interesting . . . At least all the moves gave me experience before breaking off. I really enjoyed it in the last year, working on the simulator. They were very keen for me to stay. I said I'd go back, and I did for a while part-time, before it got too much (Rachel).

These are women whose education had been confined to science or maths rather than engineering, but they had developed an interest in technology early enough for them to have made a significant commitment by the end of the first stage of employment.

The Tryout Career

In contrast to the tenacious model, the tryout is one where women with much the same kind of background did not develop an interest in technology until the very end of the first stage, that of employment. With no clear employment aims, two spent much of this time trying out a variety of jobs. After five years of sampling different jobs in the service industry, Jenny discovered the field to which she became committed. 'I did an Adult Training course in programming. The programming was the first job that I'd really enjoyed, but after two years there I got pregnant' (Jenny). Deidre, a maths graduate, summed up her early career briskly. 'When I left university, oh, I was a different person then. I did a year's programming, I didn't like it. I did four years' teaching, I did six months as a statistician, then I finished work, I was pregnant' (Deidre). Her commitment to technology only developed with her part-time work at a training centre in her career-break. Both Jenny and Deidre were eventually able to build on one of the jobs sampled in this first period of work. Their tryout approach had enabled them eventually to make an informed decision for their post-WIT employment.

The Pragmatic Career

The pragmatic career pattern results more directly from the constraints of being restricted to a particular geographical area than from preference. Job choice is determined solely by what is available. Five of the women with science qualifications had been in this situation. Their work histories show that this does not necessarily prevent the development of commitment. For some, the pragmatic career opened up a new interest. One example was the experience of Pam, who began work as a computer programmer in aerospace. 'I must say that the one thing I wasn't willing to do was computing and I ended up taking that job because I couldn't find another one at the time – related hardly at all to my maths degree' (Pam).

After a year she moved into university research, where she stayed for five years until her first baby. For Val, the pragmatic career signalled the beginning of commitment to a different area of technology. She had used her highly specialized knowledge in industrial research for just one year. Then marriage to a colleague led to her resignation, since her husband's promotion meant a transfer. After a fallow year in a clerical job, Val showed her adaptability by moving into another field, where she spent two enjoyable years building up a new career before leaving to have her first child.

> Eventually I got a job working with the Poly here in computers, which was a complete change of area. It was starting from scratch, but I got promoted to Senior Programmer Analyst, and if I'd stayed on, I would have taken some kind of diploma, looked for some qualifications. I was very sorry to have given up the job because I enjoyed it (Val).

Alice's pressures came from her parents who urged her to look around locally.

> So I did, just to see what there was. I was offered a job in the research labs at this chemical plant for more money than the London job, so I took it. I'm not sure that it was the right thing to do, but I stayed there until I had Matthew (Alice).

These experiences illustrate that the random outcomes seen earlier in education continue into employment. The above developed their commitment within the pragmatic career. The next two could not. In similarity of background, they fit the pragmatic model, but found difficulty in fulfilling their commitment, despite long-standing ambition or careful preparation. Their experience suggests a model of aborted career.

The Aborted Career

Women who have very clear aspirations from an early age can be prevented from achieving them and are unable to find an alternative commensurate with their abilities. In the case of the two women here, the constraints are clearly gendered.

> When I graduated the wedding date was already set and my husband had got a job near here ... So it was a matter of just writing to anyone who would employ a microbiologist saying are you interested? Most of them were not (Lorna).

In the only job available locally, commitment remained underused.

The consultant wanted an assistant who would help him in his research . . . but the job never actually materialized and I got drawn into working on the bench. I ended up sticking numbers on specimens or inoculating plates. No responsibility at all. I hated it. I was doing pregnancy tests most of the day. So I thought maybe the time had come to have my own family (Lorna).

Sylvie actually worked only one year as a science teacher, before finding her reluctantly acquired qualifications were not recognized in the UK. She joined a local electronics firm as an unskilled operator – 'the worst time in my life'. Then her abilities were recognized and she trained as an electronics technician. 'My favourite job, very interesting, time flies, you know you never notice the time. I liked it'. For women technologists, having ability and motivation are not in themselves enough. Individual qualities have always to be used within social and economic structures, which are more likely to constrict than enable women.

Reviewing Commitment to Technology

The period when the women technologists were establishing their commitment to an occupational career in the public domain is not what it seems. To assess it simply in terms of professional career development is to judge it on the gendered model of employment. The superficial similarity of improving qualifications, exercising professional knowledge and skills and gaining wider experience actually conceals profound differences. The male technologist can assume single-minded progress. This is not to say that he may not encounter obstacles or diversions. The point is that these are likely to arise from personal individual circumstances, whereas women are always operating in structures based on gendered power relations. Even when a couple openly addressed the issue of combining profession and family, the result was invariably the same. The male technologist could ultimately assume both freedom of mobility and delegation of day-to-day family responsibilities.

There is a further difference. The emphasis in this first stage is on acquiring the skills and knowledge which form the basis of a commitment to technology. For the WIT women it was also marked by a growing awareness of the second major life commitment, that of children and family. Their attempts to grapple with strategies which might enable them to combine those commitments as discussed above, should not be seen as a diffusion of their technological interests. Their efforts should be seen as a determination to challenge exclusive structures based on a recognition that both public and private spheres are important. The situation is, therefore, far more complex for women technologists as they begin to take these issues into account. The process of the women's stock-taking covered both their occupational career and their decisions on future family organization.

The Public Commitment: Employment

The WIT women's assessment of their progress in a technological career depended on such factors as their level of expectations, recognition of their own worth and acceptance or assimilation of constraints. Most were reasonably satisfied with their achievements so far, though all expressed some reservations. The hydrologist, while critical of training on her first job, considered that most of the time she had been doing work that was fulfilling and used her knowledge, 'I wasn't being paid properly for it, but the recognition was that they sponsored me to do the PhD' (Hannah).

Though Deborah had adapted her commitment to fit around her husband, she had begun to think about her own career development in information science.

> It was all right, it wasn't very dramatic. There wasn't a terrific career path, there were some promotion jobs, you could be the Senior Information Scientist but there wasn't a dramatic future within that organization (Deborah).

Mira assessed her achievements completely in terms of the gendered career model, and inevitably found them wanting.

> I suppose I was doing averagely well. I wasn't doing extremely well, but I wasn't doing badly either. I was handling projects that had quite a high value on them. You need a lot of ambition. If you have ambition you look further than you do today, and I didn't have that ambition because all along I looked upon it as a job I would do until I had children. So, to me it was a matter of just getting the job done well, reasonably well but not so well as to go round saying, 'Well what are you going to promote me to?', which is what I think people who go up the ladder do. Not at all single-minded (Mira).

A career model which gives recognition to achievements in both private and public spheres would enable Mira to see that in her twin ambitions she was indeed 'looking further than you do today'. Single-mindedness is not usually available to women. Two women ended this period in frustration. The microbiologist cut short her employment career at the age of 25, because the family option offered an escape from a monotonous job. She was one of the few who had specifically chosen her degree course as a preparation for employment. However, an early marriage and the combined effects of both public and private constraints meant that her occupational career was very restricted. Her experience had fallen far short of her hopes. 'I was totally disillusioned. I realized it wasn't for me and I wasn't going back into the Health Service again' (Lorna). Chris had been discontented for much of the time through the lack of opportunities to use fully her energy and abilities. It was only at the end of this first stage that she began to realize the limitations of her qualifications. 'I needed to be better qualified to get anywhere.'

The Private Commitment: the Family

The second commitment, family, was now coming to the fore, with a priority on child-rearing. For some women it was to be their single-minded occupation for several years. 'I thought I'd spend the rest of my time bringing up children . . . but it didn't work out as I expected' (Deidre). Only when the demands of infancy lessened did boredom set in.

> The first three or four years were just so busy I had no vision of anything. There was just two years between the girls. Then when they went to school it was just mundane things to fill the day. I felt I was wasted (Val).

Others had always intended to stay at home with their children, at least until primary school. This was a positive decision and seen as one which still kept open a future occupational career.

> I thought of returning, but not when they were tiny. . . I didn't have any family round about to help me with the children. I wasn't keen to put them with the childminders as babies, so even though I did have an idea I would want to go back in the future. I resigned, and just accepted it (Deborah).

Child-rearing was an important function they wanted to fulfil themselves, but was not expected to last forever. The employment/family strategy was perceived as a joint partnership decision, democratically arrived at.

> We felt if we had to move for my husband's career we would con- centrate on him for four or five years until the boys went to school, and then I would consider going back to work. We decided to give them the time, and I was quite happy giving them the time (Catherine).

In practical terms such outcomes were then almost inevitable. It is very difficult to organize differently. If both partners work part-time, there are immediate and long-term financial losses in terms of current pay, tax allow- ances, and future benefits or pensions. The unreliability and short-term aspect of part-time work also makes mortgage payments precarious. The effect on the women technologists with young children who attempted to continue with their professional employment, without the security of comprehensive local childcare facilities, was one of continuing stress.

So far the women had experienced only the occupational and public half of their life careers. Most accepted being at home with varying degrees of resignation. In effect, they were presented with a rigid set of alternatives, structured by the public/private divide, each of which assumed a total commitment. Women do not all have the same priorities. In the case of the women technologists, different – sometimes unexpected – choices were made. Two examples follow which illustrate the situation of women with two commitments which are structured to conflict rather than combine. For both, the arrival of their babies led to a complete reversal of their original plans. Mavis, who had had a very strong employment career motivation, had taken maternity leave, only deciding afterwards that she would want to stay at home. The appeal of her family career became equally strong. 'It's a difficult thing. Once it's your baby, you are at home with it. I wanted to be the one to look after it. So I decided that I wouldn't go back to work' (Mavis).

Mira's reversal of plan went the other way. She felt she had done well in employment so far, but was now ready to commit herself exclusively to the family commitment.

> I was 30 and the next stage was to stay at home and look after my children. It was only when I started doing that, that I realized that I didn't quite fit into the mother-at-home-with-children thing ... I then felt it was in the best interests of everyone – particularly me! – to go back to work (Mira).

The ideal solution suggested by Alice would have been 'to have kept something going' while her children were young.

> I suppose because I had him when I was older, I was 30, I actually enjoyed it. Some people seem to want to get back to work straight away; I never wanted to do that. It's not all question of organization, it's a question of what you like doing as well (Alice).

The evidence from the women technologists is that a combination of the public and the private is what they would have liked.

Planning for the Future

None of the women had clearly formulated plans for a return to professional work. Most had spent the first stage of their employment in working towards a satisfactory occupational career. Just as they were reaching some understanding of their preferences and strengths, and an awareness of the structural constraints on their progress, they were faced with the other completely new half of their life career. A future return to work could seem remote, and so plans were vague.

I thought I'd want to do something (Hannah).

I had no intention of spending the rest of my life in the house (Chris).

I thought I might go back, but it seemed a long time away (Pam).

I thought well, I'd be able to start again later. But you don't have one baby, you have two, time goes on (Lorna).

The lack of firm plans could be seen as no bad thing since it could allow them to be open-minded about options. 'I was one of those people who didn't really plan things out. I don't know, things just happened really. In a way it's been fortunate to have been like that, looking back' (Rachel).

But although few of the women interviewed had specific plans for their future return to work, they had all established themselves, by the end of this first period of employment, with a solid body of experience for a technological career. Eight had improved their vocational qualifications, two engineers had been admitted to Chartered Engineer status and a technician had gained her Full Certificate. One of the scientific technologists had gained the MSc which enabled her to enter industry, two more had been sponsored by their employers for doctorates while working in industry, another had a diploma with which she could enter a field she thought compatible with her family career, and one had been stimulated by a programmer's training course into a late commitment.

Conclusion

My aim has been to explore how the experience of the women technologists related to the public/private dichotomy. There were two main concerns. One was with the process by which they had established a commitment to technology in the public sphere. The second was with the structures of education and employment in which this process took place and how far these constrained or enabled the women. Three possible stages have been identified at which commitment might begin: at the end of school education for the women engineers; during degree studies for the women scientists and mathematicians who had the opportunity of practical experience; and through chance or sampling during the first employment period for others. For none of the 17 women interviewed had technology been formally presented as a employment option. At whatever stage they had come to it, it was as individuals who happened to have personal contacts or random experiences. In largely, if not formally, excluding women, technology operates as a gendered area of knowledge and employment. As such it demands the characteristics of its majority participants which include mobility and widening experience. My argument is that in striving to counter gendered constraints, the women cogently demonstrate commitment to a technological career in the public sphere. At this stage, the public/private dichotomy appears to have little relevance. The gendered nature of the conventional career model becomes apparent as the women near the end of their first period of employment. The approach of their second major commitment, associated with the private sphere, marks the beginning of the career-break, a period marked as problematic in itself and in its potential effects on career. The implications of the public/private dichotomy begin to emerge, even for those women with a demonstrable public commitment, such as Hannah, graduating with her PhD in hydrology and seven-and-a-half months pregnant.

References

CARTER, R. and KIRKUP, G. (1990) *Women in Engineering: A Good Place to Be*, London, Macmillan.

COCKBURN, C. (1986) 'Women and technology: Opportunity is not enough', in PURCELL, K., WOOD, S., WATON, A. and ALLEN, S. (Eds) *The Changing Experience of Employment: Restructuring and Recession*, London, Macmillan and BSA.

COCKBURN, C. (1988) 'The gendering of jobs: Workplace relations and the reproduction of sex segregation', in WALBY, S. (Ed) *Gender Segregation at Work*, Milton Keynes, Open University Press.

COMPTON, R. and SANDERSON, K. (1990) *Gendered Jobs and Social Change*, London, Unwin Hyman.

DEVINE, F. (1992) 'Gender segregation in the engineering and science professions: A case of continuity and change', *Work Employment and Society*, **6**, 4, pp. 557–75.

DRAKE, B. (1987) *Women in Trade Unions*, London, Virago.

FINNISTON, M. (1980) 'Engineering our future', Report of the Finniston Committee Enquiry into the engineering profession, Department of Industry, HMSO.

HARDING, S. G. (1991) 'Whose science? Whose knowledge?', *Thinking from Women's Lives*, Buckingham, Open University Press.

LATHER, P. (1988) 'Feminist perspectives on empowering research methodologies', *Women's Studies International Forum*, **II**, 6, pp. 569–81.

McRAE, S., DEVINE, F. and LAKEY, J. (1991) *Women into Engineering and Science: Employers, Policies and Practices*, London, Policy Studies Institute.

MAYNARD, M. (1994) 'Methods, methodology and epistemology: The debate about feminism and research', in MAYNARD, M. and PURVIS, J. (Eds) *Researching Women's Lives from a Feminist Perspective*, London, Taylor & Francis.

NEWTON, P. (1987) 'Who becomes an engineer? Social psychology antecedents of a non-traditional career', in SPENCER, A. and PODMORE, D. (Eds) *In a Man's World*, London, Tavistock.

RAMAZANOGLU, C. (1989) 'Improving on sociology: Problems in taking a feminist standpoint', *Sociology*, **23**, 3, pp. 427–42.

RAMAZANOGLU, C. (1992) 'On feminist methodology: Male reason versus female empowerment', *Sociology*, **26**, 2, pp. 207–12.

SMITH, D. (1987) *The Everyday World as Problematic: A Feminist Sociology*, Milton Keynes, Open University Press.

SWARBRICK, A. (1978) 'To encourage the others: a survey of women studying the technology foundation course of the Open University', Internal Report, Open University.

SWARBRICK, A. (1993) *'Revaluing women's work: The combination of commitments career'*, unpublished PhD thesis, University of York.

THIELE, B. (1987) 'Vanishing acts in social and political thought: Tricks of the trade', in PATEMAN, C. and GROSS, E. (Eds) *Feminist Challenges: Social and Political Theory*, Sydney, Allen & Unwin.

THOMAS, K. (1990) *Gender and Subject in Higher Education*, Buckingham, SRHE and Open University Press.

WALBY, S. (1986) *Patriarchy at Work*, Cambridge, Polity Press.

WALBY, S. (1988) *Gender Segregation at Work*, Milton Keynes, Open University Press.

WALSHOK, M. (1981) *Blue Collar Women: Pioneers on the Male Frontier*, New York, Anchor Books.

WARREN, C. (1986) 'British women with interrupted technology careers: patterns of childhood socialization', New Delhi, Conference Paper.

Chapter 5

Women, Science and Adult Education: Toward a Feminist Curriculum?

Jean Barr and Lynda Birke

Getting through a day is like a science for some women [MHC].

That quotation represents many layers of women's lives. It was drawn from our research on women's perceptions of science, which forms the basis of this article. The research was based primarily on interviews with women involved in community groups and/or local adult education courses.[1] Our concern was to explore how women standing largely outside of formal educational structures perceive science and scientific knowledge (the attitudes of women in higher education toward particular subjects, such as physics, have been analysed elsewhere, see Thomas, 1990).

This concern was motivated partly by our work in adult education and partly by our interests in feminist critiques of science. Work with adults has traditionally emphasized the importance of building on prior experience: But how can such practice deal with the relationship of adults to the abstract knowledge that we call science? What prior experience could be incorporated? and whose? Women may not only be excluded from science, but – as several feminists have pointed out – their interests may not always be well served within adult education provision in general (Blundell, 1992; Thompson, 1980).

Women's exclusion matters, because of the power of science and technology in our culture: Exclusion from science thus means exclusion from power. And the exclusion of women's experiences from adult education matters because of the potential of education to play a part in women's empowerment (Thompson, 1988). Our research raises many issues, not only about how women see science and its place in our society, but also about how science is taught. Not least, it also raises questions about women's lives.

We explore these themes in this article, focusing less on the well-known theme of women's exclusion, and more on women's *ways of knowing* (Belenky, Clinchy, Goldberger, and Tarule, 1986) in relation to science. The suggestion that there may be a distinctive 'women's voice' or women's ways of knowing is appealing; it has been argued, for instance, that these should be taken into account in women's education (see Susan Warner Weil, 1988, as a main exponent of this in Britain). Feminists are often only too well aware of the ways in which women's knowing or experiences are downplayed or ignored. But to speak of *women's ways* is also problematic.

One of the central problems in referring to women's *ways of knowing* is that it can become essentializing, obscuring differences between women and focusing on the one thing that women seem to have in common, their biological experiences. Such an approach can ignore important differences among people, based on class or ethnicity, as well as gender, which can affect experience. These must be central to any pedagogy which claims to start from that experience in developing a curriculum, for science or otherwise. We used Belenky, *et al.*'s (1986) notion of women's ways of knowing in relation to science as a starting point for our research, but we were also concerned to focus explicitly on the differences that emerged from different women's experiences of their lives.

The Abstraction of Science

The prevailing image of scientific knowledge constructs it as abstract, removed from everyday life, as knowledge that has to be acquired in the form of systematic facts. It is, moreover, a knowledge from which many adults feel excluded. Yet adults can acquire or develop knowledge which, in other contexts, would be labelled scientific. In this kind of learning, any scientific knowledge that people develop might be an example of what Layton, Davey and Jenkins (1986) have called 'science for specific social purposes'; that is, they seek and acquire knowledge according to particular needs, such as finding out about local environmental issues or about a disease that is inherited in their family (Wynne, 1992). Layton and his colleagues document how, historically, different social groups have acquired scientific knowledge as they wanted it, for specific purposes. But this kind of democratic process was restricted by the development, in the late nineteenth century, of a science education that was explicitly abstract and served the needs of an academic élite (Layton *et al.*, 1986).

For women, 'really useful knowledge' (Johnson, 1988) might be acquired in informal groups in the community – mother and toddler groups, for example, or health groups. The kind of knowledge thus developed is both practical and theoretical, developed through use and through working with other people; it is more closely aligned to the science for specific purposes than it is to the science formally taught in our schools and universities. Self-help health groups, in particular, produced a kind of knowledge about medical phenomena different from that provided by medical science and experts – knowledge and skills which drew on women's own experiences and needs (McNeill, 1987: 24) – including the need to exercise some control over the conditions of their lives.

Jean Barr and Lynda Birke

Women's Perceptions of Science?

In these interviews, we as researchers made it clear that we were interested in their views of science/scientists and scientific knowledge. Some of these views, of course, may not be specific to women; indeed, many are likely to be shared with men who are also outside science. But some undoubtedly have been shaped by their experiences as women – in relation to their role in domestic labour or childraising, for instance. So, women's knowledge could include information about nutrition or reproduction – topics that others might label scientific (Birke, 1992).

Any attempt to investigate women's perceptions of science also invokes the notion of science as a social and cultural activity, which produces meanings and interpretations of the world, rather than certain knowledge. We maintain that any attempt to understand the complexity of women's relationship to society and culture must accommodate the notion of contradiction (see Modleski, 1991: 44).

The story the women told is certainly one of contradiction and of exclusion. At the same time, however, it is one of commonality through difference. It serves as a reminder that women do not always slip easily into their role as women, whether they are black or white, middle-class or working-class, young or old. The women's voices quoted here speak some common ground; they also speak differences rooted in different social experiences.

Similarities

In women's talk about science, some linking themes certainly emerge. Perhaps the strongest were the *impressions* that the women gave to us – in their body language, their pauses, their silences. Science seemed to evoke powerful memories for many of school science – experienced as deeply alienating, or at best as irrelevant.[2] Another strong theme was the notion that science was difficult – summed up eloquently in the quotation at the beginning of this article. Primarily, that quote was intended to mean that women's daily existence is often very difficult, a perpetual struggle. Science here means the epitome of something hard. It also symbolizes the need to plan carefully, as well as the sheer drudgery of everyday work: For several women, science means boredom, a plodding approach to solving problems.

Although the women we interviewed see science in many contradictory ways, two particular tensions stand out. One is that, when they label knowledge as scientific, it usually means something they do not understand: What they understand, by contrast, is likely to be labelled common sense. The second tension can be summed up in the aphorism: 'Science is in everything, but it has nothing to do with me.' Taken together, these themes serve as a stark reminder of the extent of women's exclusion from scientific knowledge.

The interviewees bring out an opposition between *common sense* as *things we know* and *science* as *things we do not know*. For example, in an earlier study, one women said of medicine that 'I don't know enough about it . . . so it must be science' (Birke, 1992). It is in the realm of common sense that they identify what they already know as not really science, for example, nutrition. Through this opposition, the location of the self and of personal experience lies outside what is labelled science. Another respondent, for example, speaks of people's 'instinct . . . compared with science', on the grounds that 'with science you have to have the knowledge' [MPLC]. Formal knowledge of science is thus once again contrasted with common sense.

An overlapping issue is how women perceive the relevance of science; they consider those areas of science more obviously linked to the common sense of everyday lives to be the interesting ones. Thus, one respondent recalls doing experiments with reflection in physics at school and speaks of how this seemed more relevant than chemistry, 'because it was there and you could see and chemistry wasn't something you could see . . . It wasn't part of everyday life, it was something set aside that you had to learn about' [MPLC]. Another feels that physics is irrelevant – a reason for her failure to remember much about it; 'unless it was related to our life . . . now I can't remember laws and that I wanted to but my brain wasn't ready for it' [KMTHA].

Making use of science and technology is seen to differ from understanding their basic principles; several women distinguish, for example, between using science or technology, using the products of previous research (such as domestic appliances or medical treatments), and understanding the principles of scientific knowledge. The former is something to which they can relate; the latter, something in relation to which they feel marginalised.

The tension surrounding science as everywhere, yet 'nothing to do with me' came out when we sought to explore the various contexts in which women would describe something as scientific. Most women resist the scientific/ nonscientific distinction on the grounds that science is everywhere. For example, one respondent feels that 'In a strange way science is around us all the time – in how we live, in hormones in vegetables, pollution in water' [SHC]. Another expresses the view that 'We're surrounded by science; everything in ourselves, our way of life, psychology and computers, is related to science . . . everything to me is science' [ADTHA]. A scientific explanation, in other words, can probably be found for just about anything – why the table stands up, or the appearance of colours in a painting, for example. But at the same time, interviewees often express the contradictory view that science has little or nothing to do with their own lives.

One woman living in a rural area labels as scientific many of the things she does herself, such as cooking or looking after her animals; yet at the same time, she feels that 'Science just doesn't interest me. I'd rather leave it to someone else' [GEWH].

Science affects everything in our lives: 'We can't get away from it', asserts another woman, including many daily activities in the category – hoovering, using electricity (except cookery which is 'sheer pleasure'). Yet, for her, scientific knowledge is: 'all the things I don't know the answers to, things that don't seem to have answers – and I don't want to know' [IWC].

Inclusive versus exclusive definitions of science and scientific jostle with one another in the interviewees' accounts. What women do include in the category of science appears to depend on beliefs and values held. Some women who speak of science as bad then exclude from it what they valued – natural history, and nutrition, for example, are seen as outside the realm of science. Relatedly, pleasurable activities cannot be science; thus, '. . . people would argue that [cooking] is scientific, but as far as I am concerned it isn't, because it is a great pleasure' [IWC].

Contrasting images of science as certainty and science as contingency also appear; 'there aren't any right answers to anything' may coexist as a belief alongside a view of science as facts (right vs. wrong). Recognition of the changing, contingent nature of science makes no difference to the sense of exclusion that women feel, because the self is not part of the negotiation of the facts; this is the prerogative of experts.

Research into how different social groups understand science has shown that people are often quite well aware of its contingencies and uncertainties (Wynne, 1992). Collins (1985) makes a plea for science teaching to include the social science of science, observing that the model of science as certain and of scientists as authoritative tends to be reproduced within normal science teaching. Rather, he suggests, in science papers, 'certainty increases because the details of the social process that went into the creation of certainty become invisible' (p. 160). What the science paper leaves out is experiment as 'a piece of ordinary life', as process. Science teaching and scholarly science papers are a fraud, he believes, at odds with actual practice.[3] The model of science put forward allows lay citizens only two responses to science – either awe at its authority, or rejection – 'the incomprehending anti-science reaction' (Collins, 1985: 161).

For women, the latter response may include their feeling of being excluded from science; thus, one interviewee acknowledges that she has some scientific knowledge from her daily life, but comments: 'But I don't home in on it. It's the hidden part of you. I see talking about science as a man's world and you're not taken seriously if you talk about these things' [MBO].

Another woman, 20 years older, claiming, to admire scientists 'more than all others', nevertheless sees experiments as 'using knowledge to prove a point'. Moreover, 'people are overpowered by it, baffled by it, take it on trust and later its theories are disproved'. For her, then, science is both certainty ('proving a point') and contingency [IWC].

The contradictions between the certainties and the contingency of science are brought out by a younger woman, who is concerned about the ethics of using animals in research: 'We look to them [scientists] to give us rock hard answers, if you get a scientific answer you expect it to be the truth'. Yet she goes on to point out that she feels that testing drugs on animals is inappropriate because the answers are not always correct. When asked about the contradiction, she suggests that perhaps she has not

> got my facts right . . . I think maybe I've been brought up to believe a scientific report. Maybe because I've got this idea that there is lots of test tubes and bunsen burners and that's what they're doing and then maybe I can believe that and what they are testing is right. But where I was actually looking at the side where it wasn't bunsen burners and test tubes any more, it's animals, that's when my opinion changes [CHC].

The stereotype of scientists as other, as unlike ordinary people, was also common. This stereotype is used even by women studying a science course on which all the tutors are women. Scientists are seen by one woman on this course as 'different, quaint, really'; in general as removed from reality, separate, even 'mad' and 'very intelligent'. (We should note here that it was not clear from this interview whether she felt that the tutors were 'not like ordinary people' because they were scientists, or because they explicitly dealt with a feminist curriculum!)

Sometimes gender is mentioned (scientists, unsurprisingly, are men); race and class come up less often. We would have expected, given the research focus on *women's* perceptions, that gender would be foregrounded. But few social or sociological notions were used, the tendency being to answer in individualistic, psychological terms.

A perception of science as an individual endeavour, rather than as a social/political process emerges from the interviews. We see this as linking into what Bhaskar (1989: 61) has described as the positivist, 'spontaneous consciousness of science' itself – that is, to its *own* commonsense view of scientific knowledge as the outcome of special individual brains, unracialized, ungendered, unclassed. This notion of scientific knowledge as something passively acquired by the few, very intelligent amongst us could be graphically expressed: 'How can they *hold* all that knowledge in their heads?' [CHHC].

There are two points of contrast here. The first is that, in relation to scientific knowledge itself, women typically portray themselves as (at best) passive consumers/receivers of knowledge, who might perhaps acquire odd bits of scientific information (reminiscent of the 'passive knowing' that Belenky, *et al.*, described, 1986). The second is to contrast the expert and his possession of élite knowledge with knowledge that women (sometimes explicitly) felt they owned, which 'I'd rather have than all that science stuff'. Referring to the 'science is everywhere versus nothing to do with me' polarity, one respondent says:

> I don't feel it personally . . . I know it but don't feel it . . . that science is everywhere. I pigeonhole it and see it as separate and that's how I divide it from common sense and women's intuition [CHHC].

Bearing in mind that the women knew that the focus of the interview was science, we expected that most would attempt to provide a scientific explanation when we asked, at one point, how they would explain certain phenomena. Yet hardly any of them did so when the question was: Why do we have four seasons, how would you explain that? Here, the narrative was almost always a more intuitive account of nature, taking the form of the Persephone myth: The earth must rest, so that she can bring forth life again in the spring. The appeal of this tale is clearly enough to promote resistance to the rather more prosaic scientific account of planetary motion.

In these accounts, what scientists *do* is perceived as boring, tedious, mathematical. Whereas those with some connection with science tend to see what scientists do in terms of the scientific method (testing hypotheses, for example), others tend to see experiments as luck, a matter of trial and error – although this does not appear to affect their trust or lack of trust in scientists.

These various tensions powerfully reproduce and maintain women's exclusion from science. If science is all around you, for example, then where is the self? If science is an individual endeavor, understood only by those eccentric but clever persons known as scientists, where does this leave women's knowledge, or their common sense? Women's exclusion from science is not only in terms of sheer numbers who drop out of science education; it is more profound than that. It is fundamentally about the status and power of some knowledge claims over others.

Voicing Resistance: Finding Difference

Resistance to scientific accounts is evident in other parts of the conversation (particularly when respondents were asked anything about physics, as opposed to more general topics). It was, moreover, in voicing resistance that differences emerged. Emily Martin, in *The Woman in the Body* (1989) notes how working-class women in particular resist medical/scientific accounts of their bodily processes (such as menstruation and childbirth). This was not, she stressed, that such women were ignorant of the scientific model that their middle-class counterparts immediately recounted: The ignorance, rather, is constructed through resistance.

Women in our interviews sometimes refer self-consciously to their ignorance of science, as a means of challenging it. Thus, one student studying literature is clearly presenting a view of herself-in-relation-to-science in saying:

Scientific knowledge? I find this difficult. I'm obviously ignorant but that sounds as if I think I shouldn't be talking about it. But everyone has a natural intuition about what goes on in the world around them. I'm not scientific but that doesn't mean I don't have an intuitive feeling about things [SFLC].

It is not simply not being scientific which distances her from science and scientific knowledge; it is to do with her views on the nature of science itself, which relate to her own sense of self:

> Science promotes fear in me. It's such a strong power. The power to destroy has come through science, not the arts. We're made with a desire to explore and use our minds but unless we supply a spiritual quality in a working sense, we'll eventually destroy ourselves. In art you can experiment and make mistakes but in science mistakes can't always be remedied, and experiments on animals and humans I find offensive [SFLC].

Science, again, is around us; it is a product of the human desire to explore. Yet it clearly has little or nothing to do with their lives. Rather, it is a power out there that evokes fear for this student, who (elsewhere in the interview) contrasts the remote authority of science with her own 'love affair with words' that motivated her study of literature.

There are clearly differences in these interviews that reflect varied life histories: Age, social class, and ethnicity are all factors that seem to relate to variations in tone and content of response. Younger women, for example, are likely to invoke clear images of school science lessons – the image of the bunsen burner and laboratory bench. Resistance, too, is strongest amongst younger women in our interviews, who were more likely than older women to claim that it had nothing to do with them. One asserts, for example, that: 'My brain has shut off from it completely. I've a lot going on in my head but not methodical, technological tedium. It would drive me nutty' [CHHC]. Another, similarly, says 'I think I wasn't comfortable with it at school. And I just blocked it out' [TCHC].

Black women are more likely to point to issues around science and imperialism, noting how it is rarely women in developing countries who benefit from scientific knowledge. While wanting to emphasize the importance of their own cultures and traditions, black women are nonetheless scornful of what they see as a western fashion for alternative health: Here, we see a specific type of resistance linked to an awareness of the part western science has played in imperialism. Thus, one woman who came to Britain from Zimbabwe, feels that,

> That's one thing I think you western people are crazy about. OK it's important to be careful about what you eat but you can go too far. And if you say to yourself 'I'm thinking positive' you may be dissociating yourself from reality because life isn't always positive [BTHAN].

Similarly, another Zimbabwean woman shows her awareness and disgust at the expropriation of traditional kinds of knowledge by western science:

> Science has improved women's health here but not back home. Cancer of the uterus is neglected and the West is doing nothing about Aids. And experiments done on herbs here don't get fed back to the Third World, another form of exploitation [BTHAH].

Such differences are undoubtedly important in the context of adult education; they form the basis of experiences on which further learning is built. One particularly noteworthy difference among women is that among women from different groups or institutions. Some of these women were attending particular courses; others took part in community groups. There is a tendency for women from the same group to answer in similar ways. The belief, for example, that science means lots of studying by clever people comes from three women in the same group, whereas another four from the same institution (one renowned for its woman-centered approach and its emphasis on experiential learning) share a distrust of experts and a refusal of the notion of scientific facts.

What this illustrates is that the frames of reference women use to construct their ideas and to talk about them with us is developed through sharing ideas in their groups. They knew in advance that we were coming to talk to them about science, but they did not know in advance what we would ask. So, what these differences tap into is the sharing of thoughts about the interview process before we arrived, to create some kind of consensus and common discourse.

This is important for two reasons. First, it flies in the face of any simplistic picture of science and scientific knowledge as fact-driven: These women paint a picture of their ideas about science that is, on the contrary, shaped by their social milieu and processes of learning through sharing (consciousness-raising?). Second, it illustrates an aspect of experiential learning that is inadequately addressed in the adult education literature: The group itself is an important part of learning.

What can be Learned from This? Knowing and Power

We have attempted to show the complex and often contradictory quality of women's relationship to science by focusing explicitly on women as knowers. Such a stance recognizes women's active epistemological status, as agents of knowledge, so avoiding the construction of women as deficient (Michael, 1996). The story that emerges is a complex tale of the relations of power between women and science.

Some of the themes we have identified are not surprising: It is widely known, for example, that women feel excluded from science. But what we want to emphasize here is the way that these themes are rooted in oppositions – between science and commonsense, between owned and alienated knowledge, between science as everywhere but nothing to do with me. In their account of women's different 'ways of knowing', Belenky, *et al.* (1986) distinguish several approaches to the acquisition of knowledge, ranging from the silent knower to the knower who actively constructs knowledge. Several of these are identifiable in interviews, sometimes in the same person. We have certainly witnessed the reflective, critical, many-sided quality of some women's thought about science.

The first point to note about how women talk about science is that these contradictions illustrate an alienation from science far deeper than is commonly acknowledged. There have been plenty of studies which expose the dearth of women entering scientific professions. But for most women, science is completely apart from them; it is not simply something that, with a bit more application, they too could get to grips. The knowledge that they have is labelled as not science; they construct themselves as passive knowers by contrast to the clever people who can actively understand science.

We live increasingly, as Jansen and Van der Veen have recently pointed out (1993), in a 'risk society' that presents particular challenges to adult education. The women we interviewed are well aware of the various ecological risks to which they and their children are exposed – through nuclear hazards, genetic engineering, food additives. The social changes of the risk society, Jansen and Van der Veen suggest, help create a form of individualization: It is people's lifestyles that, in part, contribute to particular risks.

Yet the risk society might also be one in which individuals' experiences become marked by a sense of powerlessness. Adult education, Jansen and Van der Veen note, has devoted much attention in recent years to the issue of experiential learning; in women's education, indeed, that is an important theme. But there is a danger that, in focusing on experiential learning, educators ignore the fact that many of the risks to which people are exposed are beyond daily experience; we cannot know through experience, for instance, how the ozone layer has developed a hole. In their ambivalence toward experts and the authority of science, the women we spoke to are articulating just that sense of science as outside our daily lives.

It would be demeaning to women to see these narratives as reflecting only alienation. What is also evident from them is a sense of active resistance: This may or may not be helpful to women, but it does indicate that women are not necessarily passive in their relationship to scientific knowledge. Science, for example, is held by some women to be the antithesis of real knowledge which they can intuit, or arrive at through their own processes of analysis. This is more meaningful to them than the litany of facts that they saw science to be. The point is not that women are somehow lacking, or unable to construct their own knowledge and meaning: The women to whom we spoke know well enough that they can construct knowledge. But they also know that what they might construct is unlikely to be accepted as scientific.

A central theme of our research is that gender, class, race, age are epistemological factors – that is, that these are factors which shape our knowing (as Sandra Harding has argued in her feminist analyses of the philosophy of science: Haraway, 1988; Harding, 1991; Nelson, 1990). It seems essential in developing critical (in the sense of self-reflective, aware of its own assumptions) science education for adults that these factors should be accorded a more active epistemological status than is common in our education system. This would not only make women familiar with 'the very serious game of the production of scientific knowledge' (Larochelles and Desantels, 1991: 387) but would encourage them to see *themselves* as implicated in this, that is, as 'responsible knowers' (Code, 1989; Haraway, 1991: 107) and creators of knowledge. For, as Harding (1992) would have it, we are all inside science.

Perhaps few now believe in theory-free facts (at least since Kuhn, 1970). There is always a slack between theories and the evidence supporting them (that is, scientific theories are underdetermined: see Knorr-Cetina and Mulkay, 1983: 4–5). This being so, the social factors which shape the direction of scientific knowledge deserve further examination. It is central to recent feminist philosophy of science that gender provides a division in experience deep enough to make a difference to the direction of research and the content of scientific theorizing. It is central, too, to feminist arguments, that there exists the possibility of developing science more democratically, as a mass phenomenon – 'not simply as a democratic duty but as a way of making science better' (Nelson, 1990: 170). Such an approach would be highly appropriate to a number of the adult women involved in our research, for whom contingency and uncertainty are not difficult notions to grasp, yet whose experiences and knowledge have been so often disregarded.

Transforming Science Education?

What would it mean in practice to integrate into science education for adults epistemological reflection on what is at stake in the production of scientific knowledge? In this section, we want to bring the discussion back to the wider feminist critiques of science and knowledge. The first point to address is that we need more openness to different ways of knowing as potential resources in the development of new knowledge of the natural world, but, at the same time, emphasizing women's experiences in this way can also be problematic if it serves to reinforce traditional roles. The recent development of nontraditional courses for women (such as plumbing) can be beneficial for some women but confirm others in their domesticity (Blundell, 1992). It is not necessarily empowering for working-class women, Blundell points out, to learn better how to manage the home (taking on the plumbing as well as the cooking). It is similarly double-edged to base science education for women on what they have learnt through their domestic role (also see Butler, 1993).

However, although we might have reservations about *basing* an education on women's 'different ways of knowing', an equal education for women of all social groups (as for the men of relatively unprivileged groups) cannot be the *same* as the education that has developed in a culture based on the exclusion of some of those groups (Minnich, 1989: 109). It may or may not be the case that women learn and come to understanding differently from men, but it is clear that many people think effectively and well in ways which do not fit the dominant culture's narrow notions of rationality and intelligence. 'Knowledge requires many of us', says Minnich.

We need to find the suppressed voices to change and enrich education. If science itself is to reflect more fully the experiences of all of us, then those suppressed voices must become part of the processes of creating scientific knowledge. Feminist critics of science have stressed, for example, how science needs to include the standpoints of excluded others (see Harding, 1992; Rose, 1983).

Such integration must be critical and sensitive to lived experiences: It is not enough simply to tack a bit of history (the history of the Great Men of Science, for instance) into existing curricula. For adult women – who have already become outsiders to science – that approach simply reinforces the perception that science is done by experts and has nothing to do with me. To build in epistemological reflection would, on the contrary, require integrating science into a more discursive, consciousness-raising approach to adult education. Doing so might create resistance in some circles; we are both familiar with the refrain that a curriculum that was built on women's experiences might 'not be real science any more'. Indeed, it might become better science.[4]

This would certainly broaden the meaning(s) of science and science education to encompass a wide range of people's experiences, as feminist critics have urged. But it might also serve to 'reenchant' science, to make it more fun. That doing science might be fun is a theme that has largely been omitted from feminist accounts (not surprisingly, as we have concentrated effort on criticizing it). Moheno (1993) has urged the need to develop forms of science education that counter the modern 'disenchantment of the world' (and science) by contextualizing science. Such science education, he points out, would not only be fun, but would help to empower people positively to change the world.

Having fun with science, empowering people, and building on experience are notions that would certainly transform science education. To build on experience means moving away from the prevailing model of scientific knowledge as facts and certainty. Narrow notions of reason and science deny us rich possibilities, as does labelling as irrational anything to do with the emotions, experience or intuition.[5] Part of the problem posed by science (and the distance of most of us from it) is to do precisely with that separation of feelings and reason.

So, one way of developing a more feminist approach to science that was rooted in women's experiences would be to bring those experiences consciously into teaching and learning. We could share, for instance, what it *feels like* to learn about (say) genetic disease as part of the process of learning/teaching about genetics.

Yet that kind of awareness is still not enough. Another part of the problem is the persistence of the two cultures. How often is science brought into literature courses (say), or into return-to-learn courses designed for women? One way of making science seem less divorced from everyday life is to bring it into other things; in formal education, this could mean integrating philosophical, historical and sociological approaches, as well as an attention to literary and metaphorical devices used in science (see Haraway, 1991, on science as narrative; Harding, 1986, on self-reflective social science as a paradigm for natural science). One concrete example is our own work with local women artists; working with women's groups, the project (Bridge the Gap) seeks to use the arts and science to ask questions about the world around us.[6]

Through such integration, the notion of science as 'boundaryless' (Nelson, 1990: 11), as 'all around us', as, that is, inseparable from common sense, politics, philosophy, history, language and metaphor (although since the nineteenth century giving every appearance of being so) could become less exclusive, more human, and more ownable by women. Feminist biologist Ruth Hubbard observed that it is as political beings that women will change science – that is, as *citizens* (Hubbard, 1990). A critical science education project would, in consequence, involve working with women's groups in the community, drawing on their own agendas, whether to do with health, housing, roads or the environment, in an effort to develop more broadly based 'scientific communities'.

Science education is conceived here as an aspect of citizenship education, social and political education: Central to it is the notion of 'responsible knowing'. Some of these themes are, of course, central to many feminist approaches to education. But feminists, too, tend to stand outside science: If we are to become responsible knowers (or, we might add, responsible educators), then we cannot afford to do so.

If we are all to be effective citizens, it is not good enough to adopt an antiscience stance, pointing to the abuses of science (important though that is). This stance, evident in some feminist writing, effectively leaves the terrain of science uncontested. And not only does it fail to challenge science; it also fails to challenge the ways that science affects us all, as Donna Haraway reminds us:

> To ignore, to fail to engage in the social process of making science, and to attend only to use and abuse of the results of scientific work is irresponsible. I believe it is even less responsible in present historical conditions to pursue anti-scientific tales about nature that idealize women, nurturing, or some other entity argued to be free of male war-tainted pollution. Scientific stories have too much power as public myth to effect meaning in our lives . . . (1991: 107)

The meanings of science now include the apocalyptic tales, the dystopian visions, to which many of the women referred. Quite rightly, these tales evoked fear. But fear need not mean passivity – meanings can be changed and tales rewritten. As feminists, we want nothing less.

Acknowledgement

The authors thank Annette Kuhn, Lorraine Baxter, Kate Scanlon, and Chris Duke for taking the trouble to read and comment on earlier drafts of this article.

Notes

1 In total, we interviewed 40 women, who were a subset of women drawn from a range of adult education courses and self-help groups in the community. The larger group was approached to complete a questionnaire, and the subset was drawn as volunteers from that group. Some of these courses or groups had a scientific theme (Introducing Science, Ecology); others had no obvious relationship to science (Literary and Cultural Studies). We chose not to identify individuals or courses explicitly and have therefore coded each quotation. The coding system is based on the respondent's name, and the group/institution to which she belonged. As women were sometimes talking about quite personal feelings about their education, we felt it was more appropriate to keep the interviews confidential, rather than to identify either interviewees or institutions. Interviews were semistructured.

2 It is, of course, possible that these nonverbal reactions were to the process of being interviewed. They may partly be, although they were much less noticeable when women were talking about 'safer' topics, such as their children or the course they were doing.

3 Bruno Latour makes a similar point, noting that the construction of the language and argument in a scientific paper 'is chasing its readers away . . . Made for attack and defence, it is no more a place for a leisurely stay than a bastion or a bunker. This makes it quite different from the reading of the Bible, Stendhal, or the poems of T. S. Eliot' (*Science in Action* (1987) Open University Press, Milton Keynes, p. 61).

4 Sandra Harding (1992) suggests that a scientific practice and knowledge that was more responsive to, and inclusive of, the standpoints of excluded others (women, non-Europeans, lesbians, people with disabilities, for example) would be more fully representative. It would thus create what she terms *strong objectivity*, rather than the weaker form in which *objectivity* stands for the position of a select minority.

5 The modern scientific way of finding out about the natural world is, after all, a recent cultural phenomenon (see Keller, 1992). Carlo Ginzburg's fascinating work in historical epistemology (see 1980: 5–36) documents an alternative scientific paradigm with ancient roots, part of an unnamed legitimate traditional epistemology, which he dubs 'conjectural'. Rooted in the everyday and the sensual, but not irrational, this paradigm is based on an understanding of the individual, the qualitative, the semiotic (or reading signs)

and is the property of those in a given society who are not in a position of power. For example, low intuition (akin to penetrating shrewdness) which involves the instantaneous running through of the thought process from the unknown to the known, is different from élite knowledge. Rooted in the senses, but going beyond, it has nothing to do with the extrasensory intuitionism of eighteenth–nineteenth-century irrationalism, and is the heritage of hunters, mariners – and women (Ginzburg, 1980: 36).

6 This is run in conjunction with Coventry Arts Exchange. One theme, for instance, is the body: We can ask ourselves how it can be represented artistically, as well as (scientifically) how it works. Working on this project is, inevitably, fun – something science teaching has tended not to be traditionally!

References

BELENKY, M. F., CLINCHY, B. McV., GOLDBERGER, N. R. and TARULE, J. M. (1986) *Women's Ways of Knowing: The Development of Self, Voice and Mind*, New York, Basic Books.

BHASKAR, R. (1989) *Reclaiming Reality*, London, Verso.

BIRKE, L. I. A. (1992) 'Inside science for women: Common sense or science?' *Journal Further and Higher Education*, **18**, pp. 16–30.

BLUNDELL, S. (1992) 'Gender and the curriculum of adult education', *International Journal of Lifelong Education*, **11**, pp. 199–216.

BUTLER, L. (1993) 'Unpaid work in the home and accreditation', in THORPE, M., EDWARDS, R. and HANSON, A. (Eds) *Culture and Processes of Adult Learning*, London, Routledge, pp. 66–83.

CODE, L. (1989) 'Experience, knowledge and responsibility', in GARRY, A. and PEARSALL, M. (Eds) *Women, Knowledge and Reality – Explorations in Feminist Philosophy*, London, Unwin Hyman, pp. 157–172.

COLLINS, H. (1985) *Changing Order: Replication and Induction in Scientific Practice*, London, Sage.

GINZBURG, C. (1980) 'Morelli, Freud and Sherlock Holmes: Clues and scientific method', *History Workshop Journal*, **9**, pp. 5–36.

HARAWAY, D. (1988) 'Situated knowledges: The science question in feminism and the privilege of partial perspective', in HARAWAY, D. (Ed) *Simians, Cyborgs and Women*, London, Free Association Books, pp. 183–201.

HARAWAY, D. (1991) 'The contest for primate nature: Daughters of man-the-hunter in the field, 1960–80, in HARAWAY, D. (Ed) *Simians, Cyborgs, and Women*, London, Free Association Books, pp. 81–108.

HARDING, S. (1986) *The Science Question in Feminism*, Milton Keynes, Open University Press.

HARDING, S. (1991) *Whose Science? Whose Knowledge?*, Milton Keynes, Open University Press.

HARDING, S. (1992) 'The instability of the analytical categories of feminist theory', in CROWLEY, H. and HIMMELWEIT, S. (Eds) *Knowing Women*, Buckingham, Open University/Polity.

HUBBARD, R. (1990) *The Politics of Women's Biology*, New Brunswick, NJ, Rutgers University Press.

JANSEN, T. and VAN DER VEEN, R. (1993) 'Reflexive modernity, self-reflective biographies: Adult education in the light of the risk society', *International Journal of Lifelong Education*, **11**, pp. 275–286.

JOHNSON, R. (1988) 'Really useful knowledge, 1790–1850', in LOVETT, T. (Ed) *Radical Approaches to Adult Education*, London, Routledge, pp. 3–34.

KELLER, E. F. (1992) 'How gender matters, or, why its so hard for us to count past two', in KIRKUP, G. and KELLER, L. S. (Eds) *Inventing Women: Science, Technology and Gender*, London, Polity/Open University, pp. 42–56.

KNORR-CETINA, K. and MULKAY, M. (1983) 'Introduction: Emerging principles in social studies of science', in KNORR-CETINA, K. D. and MULKAY, M. (Eds) *Science Observed: Perspectives on the Social Studies of Science*, London, Sage, pp. 1–19.

KUHN, T. (1970) *The Structure of Scientific Revolutions*, Chicago, IL, University of Chicago Press.

LAROCHELLES, M. and DESANTELS, J. (1991) 'Of course, it's just obvious: Adolescents' ideas of scientific knowledge', *International Journal of Science Education*, **13**, 4, pp. 373–89.

LATOUR, B. (1987) *Science in Action*, Buckingham, Open University Press.

LAYTON, D., DAVEY, A. and JENKINS, E. (1986) 'Science for specific social purposes (SSSP): Perspectives on adult scientific literary', *Studies in Science Education*, **13**, pp. 27–52.

MCNEIL, M. (Ed) (1987) *Gender and Expertise*, London, Free Association Books.

MARTIN, E. (1989) *The Woman in the Body*, Milton Keynes, Open University Press.

MICHAEL, M. (1996) 'Knowing ignorance and ignoring knowledge: Discourses of ignorance in the public understanding of science and technology', in URWIN, A. and WYNNE, B. (Eds) *Misunderstanding Science*, London, Cambridge University Press.

MINNICH, E. (1989) *Transforming Knowledge*, Philadelphia, PA, Temple University Press.

MODLESKI, T. (1991) *Feminism without Women*, London, Routledge.

MOHENO, P. B. B. (1993) 'Toward a fully human science education: An exploratory study of prospective teachers' attitudes towards humanistic science education', *International Journal of Science Education*, **15**, pp. 95–106.

NELSON, L. H. (1990) *Who Knows? From Quine to Feminist Empiricism*, Philadelphia, PA, Temple University Press.

ROSE, H. (1983) 'Hand, brain and heart: A feminist epistemology for the natural sciences', *Signs: Journal of Women in Culture and Society*, **9**, pp. 73–90.

THOMAS, K. (1990) *Gender and Subject in Higher Education*, Milton Keynes, Open University Press.

THOMPSON, J. (Ed) (1980) *Adult Education for a Change*, London, Hutchinson.

THOMPSON, J. (1988) 'Adult education and the women's movement', in LOVETT, T. (Ed) *Radical Approaches to Adult Education*, London, Routledge, pp. 181–201.

WEIL, S. W. (1988) 'From the language of observation to a language of experience: Studying the perspectives of diverse adults in higher education' *Journal Access Studies*, **3**, 1, pp. 17–43.

WYNNE, B. (1992) 'Misunderstood misunderstanding: Social identity and the public uptake of science', *Public Understanding of Science*, **1**, pp. 281–304.

Chapter 6

Science and Technology: Friends or Enemies of Women?

Cecilia Ng Choon Sim and Rohini Hensman

Introduction

Two powerful newspaper images: in one, women in Bangladesh pray fervently with hands clasped that the river which has already destroyed their homes will not wreak more damage, in the second, a child vainly tries to suck water from an empty pipe in Dhaka, a city of 7 000 000 people which gets only half the 60 million litres of water required daily. The same country, the same time, two opposite problems associated with water. And it is women in their role as homemakers who bear the main burden of reconstructing homes washed away by floods, just as they are burdened with the responsibility for walking miles or spending hours fetching water sufficient for drinking, cooking, washing and bathing.

These images illustrate how startlingly *little* science and technology have affected the lives of millions of women and children. Five hundred million people in Asia, Africa and Latin America still live in absolute poverty today, and two-thirds of them are female; one-third of the world's children are malnourished. Women are still plagued by ancient problems of flood and drought, just as they have yet to find a completely safe and effective means of controlling their own fertility. Indeed, scientific and technological progress has in many cases resulted in further depriving them of control over their lives and environments through such processes as the unfettered use of water for modern industry and agriculture which further depletes the water available for domestic purposes, destruction of forests which provided essential means of livelihood, and deadly pollution from pesticides and industrial waste.

It would be easy to conclude – as some women have done – that modern science and technology as such are inherently inimical to the welfare of women and ought to be opposed. However, this impressionistic conclusion needs to be examined in the light of a more concrete investigation of actual situations.

Before going on to examine the situations, it would be useful to be clear about the categories we are using. Women are divided by class, ethnicity, nationality, religion, age and many other factors; it cannot be assumed that science and technology affect all sections of women in the same way or even similar ways. Any sweeping generalizations are sure to be wrong because they ignore this complexity. In this chapter, we are concerned with working women in the Third World, but even within this more restricted group, situations vary considerably, and general statements can be unhelpful if not positively misleading.

The meaning of *science and technology* is likewise not as obvious as it might seem. We have to make a conceptual separation between scientific and technological developments on the one hand, and the way in which they, as embedded in specific structures, are used by those who have control over them. Thus, for example, mechanization and automation of industrial processes, which actually reduce the physical effort required for a particular operation, can nevertheless result in increased workloads due to managerial practices such as speed-ups or the assignment of several different operations to one person.

At the same time, there is an even more subtle and difficult distinction to be made between the *potential* technological applications of scientific discoveries and innovations and the *actual* applications which serve the economic and political purposes of those in power. Thus, for example, we might surmise that the scientific sophistication which can create technology capable of blowing up the earth several times over or sending people into outer space, would be quite capable of solving relatively simple problems of water control or safe and effective contraception, if only the same kind of resources were devoted to research and development for these purposes.

The complexity of the issues involved becomes clear when we look at concrete ways in which science and technology have affected the lives of Third World women. The following sections discuss the impact on women of various developments in industrial, office, agricultural, military and reproductive technology. This is followed by an examination of women's access to educational and employment opportunities in the field of science and technology and ends with a conclusion and recommendations based on the discussion of these issues.

New Technology in Industry and in the Office

Ever since the Industrial Revolution there has been an ongoing debate about the impact of technology on society. Today's technocentrics are euphoric over the second industrial revolution – the use of information technology – which combines radical innovations based primarily on computers, micro-electronics and telecommunications. This new technology has certainly had a significant impact on the lives of working women. The most important new technologies today are information technology, biotechnology, materials technology, space technology and nuclear technology. Information technology is by far the most pervasive in that its range of applications is so wide that it affects the entire economic system. Computer-aided or information technology refers to systems of storage, processing and retrieving information that include micro-electronic control as well as transmission systems. A good example of the application of information technology is in CAD/CAM where the information embodied in design (Computer-Aided Design or CAD) is used to control processes that manufacture the design (Computer-Aided Manufacture or CAM).

Computer-aided technology not only results in automation, but also allows important flexibilities in production, for example through modular production of components in different locations. It thus opens up new possibilities of decentralizing production within and across countries. With the inclusion of telecommunications, factory and office production can be totally revolutionized, altering the organization and location as well as the nature and volume of work.

The impact of computer-aided technologies on women's work is complex and contradictory. Digital automation and robotic technologies, by replacing feminized labour-intensive work, reduce the scope of employment opportunities for women. This is already happening in the electronics industry, where men are taking over the more skilled, capital-intensive operations. Yet computer-aided technologies also create new forms of employment which demand multiple and cognitive skills from women, although these skills are seldom acknowledged in job classification schemes. Computer-aided technology has the potential for reducing hard physical work, but it also contributes to the possibilities of stricter supervision, intensification of work-rhythms, and stress-related hazards.[1]

The impact of new technology on women workers and the way it is structured by other social relations can be seen in both the factory and the office. We discuss here two examples, from the pharmaceutical industry in India and the office sector in Malaysia.

A Case Study in the Pharmaceutical Industry

A case study of modernization of the packing lines in the pharmaceutical industry in Bombay illustrates both the differential impact of technology on the lives of different strata of women and the distinction between technology as such and the use of it by those who control it. It also demonstrates how difficult it is to separate the impact of technology from other social relationships which affect the lives of women.

A large number of young unmarried women were recruited to work on packing lines in the pharmaceutical industry in the 1950s and 1960s when this industry was expanding in Bombay. Employers tended to regard them as cheap, flexible and docile labour, easily dismissed when they married. But these decades were to see this particular image of women workers completely shattered. Women workers, along with men, formed unions and fought for job security and equal pay, as well as for facilities which would enable them to combine industrial work with family life, such as protection from night work, paid maternity leave, and workplace crèche facilities. In some ways, these women seemed to have got the best of both worlds, although in other ways, they still suffered the double burden of industrial and domestic labour as well as different forms of discrimination at work.

However, the situation changed rapidly when competitive pressures led to technological modernization and financial cost-cutting from the 1970s. (In some cases, this process began even earlier.) Given that women were concentrated in the most labour-intensive tasks, mechanization and automation would in any case have resulted in a greater loss of women's jobs than of men's jobs. But even in the smaller number of jobs which remained, women were often replaced by men. One reason was that employers wished to use the expensive new machinery on a shift basis, and the exemption of women from night work was a hindrance; moreover, women often put up more resistance to the increase in workloads through speed-ups, reduced staffing ratios, and the compulsion to handle more than one operation or machine at a time.

Second, the cost of maternity benefits and especially of maintaining a crèche with qualified childcarers was seen as an unnecessary expense which could easily be cut by gradually reducing the number of women in the workforce. Thus employers in the organized sector tended to cease recruiting women, seeing them as less flexible and more expensive than men. The number and proportion of women employed in the large-scale sector of the pharmaceutical industry, having earlier risen steadily, began to decline (cf. Hensman, 1991).

Two observations are relevant at this point. One is that there was no prejudice against employing women as such, because although women's employment declined in the organized sector, it continued to expand in the small-scale unorganized sector, partly through the subcontracting of jobs from large-scale industry. The other is that a similar process had earlier occurred in the textile industry. Both these observations suggest that while women are readily employed – and possibly even preferred – so long as they are unorganized and can be treated as cheap, flexible and docile labour, they are no longer welcome once they become unionized and demand not only equal pay but also extra facilities which makes allowances for their domestic responsibilities.

The impact of technology in this case is differentiated, and clearly subservient to the needs of capitalist profit-making. For some women, automation reduced the physical effort required for their work, although the effort of concentration might be greater. For others, both physical effort and concentration increased. But these women were all able to suggest ways in which their work could be reorganized so as to make it lighter and more pleasant; thus the adverse effects were not intrinsic to the technology as such, but were a product of the way in which it was manipulated by those who had control over it.

Second, women in the organized sector lost jobs while women in the unorganized sector gained jobs, but this too was not an inevitable result of the technology employed. It is true that new technology would tend to result in a greater volume of production with a smaller amount of labour; but this need not result in a loss of employment if a) production is expanded and diversified in order to satisfy some of the unmet needs which are especially evident in the Third World; and b) working hours are reduced. It is certainly not necessary that new technology should result in the loss of relatively well-paid jobs and the proliferation of badly-paid ones!

Finally, the differential impact of new technology on women and men is a consequence of other social relationships such as a gender division of labour which assigns women the sole or major responsibility for childcare and housework. In other words, the industrial impact of technology is shaped overwhelmingly by relationships in the workplace, the home and society as a whole.

Office Automation and Employment

The increased use of computer technology in the office has led to a growing body of literature on its impact on female employment, since a large number of office workers are women. Issues discussed pertain to the opportunities and risks in employment, skills, changes in work organization, and health and safety.

Computerization in the office has led to the rise of a new group of white-collar workers who perform a wide range of tasks from data-entry work to high-powered software programming. The potential job losses compared to jobs gained has been difficult to measure, as evidence has been contradictory. Nonetheless, it is fair to conclude that the expansion in employment and the creation of new jobs are unlikely to compensate for those eliminated by this new technology. An example is the telecommunications industry in Malaysia which has witnessed dramatic growth in the last five years; yet, as the Executive Director himself admitted, the expansion of the customer base and the substantial profits were achieved without any increase in the number of employees.

Office automation has led to a gender polarization of skills whereby the less skilled jobs, offering few rewards, few opportunities and little control over work, are allotted to women. For example, the data entry workers employed by a public agency and by the telecommunications company in Malaysia are required to perform 10 000 to 15 000 keystrokes per hour. These workers face highly intensified and pressurized work situations as their daily productivity report is posted on the wall for public viewing.

Highly skilled jobs as computer operators, systems analysts, computer programmers and EDP (Electronic Data Processing) executives are usually taken by men. Although there are now more and more women entering this field, these new jobs will not absorb women at the same rate as men due to several inhibiting factors such as socialization, streaming in schools, differential skills development and gender discrimination in the labour market.

The increased flexibility resulting from computerization allows for decentralization of data-entry work, leading to the emergence of teleworking and offshore offices. It is now possible for a hidden pool of workers – mainly women – to combine employment and home responsibilities by keying in data at home. This is already being done by the suburban housewife in the developed countries and the off-shore worker in several countries of the Third World (Pearson, 1991). Thus teleworking offers women a means of flexible work scheduling, but also the possibility of an increase in workloads, as well as exploitation in pay and benefits.

A new set of health hazards has appeared with the computerization of office work, much of it related to work with visual display units (VDUs). Some of the hazards computer workers face are musculo-skeletal disorders (such as repetitive strain injury or RSI, neck, shoulder or back aches), eyestrain and visual problems, stress and fatigue, skin complaints and reproductive disorders. In a study of a government agency in Malaysia, it was found that 10 out of 42 data-entry operators had spontaneous abortions within their first five years of working. Although it is still unproven that VDU radiation can be a direct cause of spontaneous abortions, it is likely that these abortions are related to the work itself as well as the stress and tension at work, where productivity is the key to promotion and success (Fauziah, Yusoff and Cardoza, 1993).

As in the case of industry, new technology in the office sector creates new opportunities as well as risks for women workers. It has made possible the upgrading of skills, while at the same time precarious employment, health hazards, and work intensification and pressure are growing sources of concern. The results of these investigations confirm the point that any discussion of the impact of science and technology has to be related to other social factors such as the gender and social division of labour and the power structure within organizations undergoing technological change.[2]

Agricultural Modernization, Class and Gender Differentiation

Much has been written about the success of the Green Revolution in increasing productivity and raising farm incomes of millions of peasants in the Third World. Recently, however, there have been questions pertaining to these success claims and achievements. One of the issues highlighted is the impact of modern technology, in particular rice technology, on rural female labour.

While the introduction of biotechnological and chemical inputs (for example, high-yielding variety or HYV seeds and chemical fertilizers) might in the short-term increase the use of labour, the widespread use of mechanization (for example, seed sprayers, combine harvesters, rice mills) has substantially reduced labour, especially female labour. Studies undertaken in Japan, the Philippines and Malaysia point to a general reduction, if not elimination, of female labour from poor households in particular, as a result of technological innovation in rice production. In addition, the introduction of machines has led to men taking over labour processes which were once the domain of women, particularly in transplanting and harvesting.

However, the impact of technology on female labour should not be seen in isolation from the agrarian relations determining its ownership and access to the income it generates. It is often the case that the beneficiaries of technological change are those who have access to and control over agricultural resources such as land. In Malaysia, for example, agricultural mechanization has benefited the large farmers who claimed back land from their previous tenants. Consequently, women from households with large landholdings have benefited at the expense of women from poor and landless households (Ng, 1991). Moreover, alternatives in other agricultural or non-agricultural employment are usually limited; hence young women and men migrate to towns to seek other sources of income. Thus while the introduction of new technology in rice production has increased productivity, it has also further accentuated gender and class differences in the countryside.[3]

Military Technology and Women

Militarization is an example of a case where antagonistic intranational and international relations have created a technology which is wholly destructive. It is destructive even before it is ever used, because the enormous expenditure of resources on military research, production and purchases, especially by Third World countries, inevitably results in the neglect of basic needs for food, water, clothing, shelter, health care and education. The occasional technological spin-off which feeds into civilian life in no way changes the fact that military expenditure is overall a massive loss to civilian welfare. And of course when the military hardware is actually used, that loss is much greater.

The civil war in Sri Lanka, which has left almost 100 000 dead, many more disabled, and over 1 500 000 people displaced, is a striking example. In terms of loss of life, men have suffered more, although many women have also been killed. Women have suffered most from the drop in the standard of living, which has left them struggling to care for their families on impossibly small incomes. The death and disablement of tens of thousands of men has enormously multiplied the number of female-headed, poverty-stricken families. For many women, there is a crushing sense of loss of control over their own lives, of being at the mercy of malevolent forces which are not natural and inevitable, but yet are beyond their control. A feeling of hopelessness at the destruction of all that they have worked so hard to create, not only with their domestic labour but also with their wage labour, is very widespread. Women refugees are on the whole clearer than men that the war can have nothing but negative consequences. And it is interesting to note that while women *have* participated in the armed struggle, it has only been in a subordinate capacity, whereas they have been in the forefront of the peace movement (Hensman, 1992).

Militarization is an example of a tragically misdirected development of science and technology. Massive sums are invested in research for and production of means of destruction. Once produced, there is a compulsion to sell them, thus fuelling conflict, and the conflicts in turn create fresh demand for military hardware. While more men than women may get killed, it is often women who *feel* the impact in a more devastating way, because the lives which are destroyed are largely a product of their love and labour, and they survive to mourn the loss of those whose absence leaves a terrible emptiness in their own lives.

Thus women are, very often, the motive force in peace movements. This is not a matter of biological determinism, but a reflection of the fact that the social role of women in caring for people and nurturing life gives them a unique perspective on the purely destructive rationality of militarism. All that can be said about this branch of technology from the standpoint of the vast majority of women is that it should be scrapped entirely, and the economic resources currently wasted on it should be put to more life-affirming uses.

Reproductive Technology

Reproductive technology is perhaps the branch of science and technology with the biggest potential for changing specifically women's lives for the better. Given that pregnancy and breast-feeding are biologically female functions, the ability to decide when to have children and avoid unwanted pregnancies is obviously desirable from the standpoint of most women. And advances in this direction *have* been made, giving women considerably more control over their bodies and their lives.

Yet even here there have been developments which have had a seriously negative impact on women. Oral, injectible and implanted contraceptives have been used on women without being sufficiently tested for potential hazards to life and health; on some occasions, governments and international institutions have collaborated in employing various degrees of coercion to induce women to use these (Akhter, 1992). Once again, this illustrates the importance of *who* controls science and technology, for what purposes, and what underlying values are associated with its usage. If contraceptive technology is controlled by pharmaceutical companies interested only in making a profit out of it, or governments and international institutions interested only in population control (often with a racist twist to it), then it is unlikely to benefit women.

On the other hand, we also have to recognize that there are many more immediate factors which make it difficult for women to take control themselves, such as the attitudes of families, male partners, in-laws and religious leaders. For example, a women who does not want to have a child may be prevented by any of these from using contraceptives or terminating a pregnancy. Conversely a male partner, by refusing to take any responsibility for contraception himself, may force a woman to use contraceptives she would prefer not to use.

Perhaps the most striking example of turning reproductive technology against women is the use of amniocentesis, initially intended as a method of detecting fetal malformations, to identify and selectively abort female fetuses. In India, according to a BBC report, it has been estimated that 3000 female fetuses are selectively aborted every day, contributing to an excess of 25 million males over females in the population. In China, another BBC report estimated that as a result of amniocentesis and the selective abortion of female fetuses, there are 113 boys born for every 100 girls. Thus modern technology has been harnessed in the interests of the very ancient preoccupation with having a son; women may have to go through repeated abortions to eliminate daughters whom they might even want themselves, and social misogyny finds one more lethal expression thanks to modern science. So here too, there is a need to combat social factors which prevent women from controlling technology and using it in their own interests.

Women in Science and Technology[4]

Across Asia, there is scattered evidence of women making inroads into the traditionally male-dominated field of science and technology. In the area of education and training, several countries have displayed improvements in women's enrolment in science and technical courses. For example in India, female participation in science courses grew from 7.1 per cent in 1950–51 to 27.5 per cent in 1978–79. In Malaysia, statistics on enrolment show the number of female entrants in science courses growing from 36.3 per cent in 1980 to 44.7 per cent in 1990. Similarly, the percentage of female entrants in technical courses rose from 27.1 per cent to 35 per cent for the same period, although the women were a dismal 4.5 per cent of the total final year engineering students in 1990.[5] Data from Sri Lanka shows the percentage of women students admitted to the biological science courses rising rapidly from 44.3 per cent in 1983 to 55.41 per cent in 1990. However, a similar increase was not seen in the physical sciences over this same period.

Other countries like China, Vietnam, Singapore, Thailand and the Philippines boast similar experiences. In these cases, they claim that women's access to and participation in education and training has been facilitated by an expansion of educational opportunities, which in turn have been the result of national policies to integrate women into the development process.

While the picture above shows that the situation of women in science and technology, specifically where training and education are concerned, has changed over the last decade, it is also apparent that in real terms these figures are still low. Not only are women still under-represented, but their participation is also clustered in certain areas. For example, women are still found more in courses centering on the behavioural and health sciences, while their participation in the physical sciences is still minimal.

There are several reasons for these observations. By and large, traditional socio-cultural notions which subtly stress that women should not participate fully in education still prevail. The low social status ascribed to women coincides with the view that women are the weaker sex. Boys are seen as assets and future breadwinners, girls as liabilities with little economic importance. Financial constraints often combine with existing beliefs about women to favour boys when it comes to pursuing education, especially higher education.

Tradition also dictates that a woman's place is in the home – as housewife and mother – and that she is solely responsible for household matters. Although not all women are forced into early marriages, the long duration of science and technical courses often means that women students marry while pursuing their studies, and then familial obligations like childbearing and raising result in the abandonment of their education. Hence even in countries that profess to have equal opportunities in education and employment, societal values do not permit women to maximize this opportunity.

Against this background, women wishing to gain access to the fields of science and technology have to work at least twice as hard to receive education and training. Already conditioned not to pursue higher education, women tend to shy away from these fields which are considered to be male areas. If they do pursue higher education, it is more likely that they will opt for fields traditionally dominated by women, such as the arts, home economics, education and nursing.

The situation of women employed in science and technology mirrors that experienced at the education and training levels, with some inroads having been made across the region. For instance in China, statistics in 1989 indicate that 30.6 per cent of the 9.66 million scientific and technical personnel were women. Further, in the medical and public health spheres, women scientists and technicians make up 59.6 per cent of the total workforce. In less than ten years, the number of female scientists in the Philippines grew tenfold – from 106 in 1975 to 1060 in 1983; in its national agency for science and technology development, 68 per cent of the technical positions are occupied by women. Statistics from Indonesia also show women penetrating six national science and technology research institutes.

Though it cannot be denied that Asian women have increased their employment rates in science and technology over the last decade, a closer analysis of the data available reveals some causes for concern. For one, the absolute numbers of women employed in these fields are still small. They are also mainly employed in the lower and middle echelons of the occupational hierarchy, and their absence in decision-making positions is conspicuous.

There are several reasons for this situation. First, because of women's underrepresentation in science and technical courses, only a small number end up qualified as scientists. Second, the role of housewife and mother which hinders women's participation in higher education has a similar effect on women seeking employment in this field. Moreover, in a field where changes are taking place so rapidly, women who take time out to be with their families find it difficult to keep up with the latest developments which have taken place in their absence, and as a result find themselves lagging behind. Even in the case of women who do not actually take time out for family reasons, the *expectation* on the part of employers that they will do so sometimes acts as a bar to recruitment into or promotion to the higher levels.

Conclusion and Recommendations

We conclude that science and technology have tremendous *potential* to transform the lives of women in a positive way, freeing them from excessive childbearing and long hours of unpleasant drudgery. In fact, this has not taken place for the vast majority of women in the world, and for many of them living conditions have deteriorated and control over their lives decreased as a result of technological advance. In our opinion, however, this does not mean that modern technology as such should be opposed in the interests of women.

It is certainly true that *some* technological developments – most notably military technology – have nothing but adverse consequences, not only for women but for human beings in general, animal and plant life, and the planet itself. But this is a consequence of the purposes for which it has been developed and the people who control it; the conclusion is not that *all* new technology is opposed to the interests of the majority of Third World women, but that they need to gain control over it and use it for life-enhancing purposes. We do not subscribe to the somewhat mystical view that technology and science are in themselves a masculine way of relating to the world, as opposed to a more intuitive feminine mode, but feel that both the scientific and intuitive modes of relating to the world are universal, and can be positive provided that the *purpose* is to nurture and conserve.

Several recommendations are in line here. In terms of education and training, an equal opportunities policy should be formulated and campaigned for, to enable women and girls to have equal access to education and (re)training in (new) technology skills at all levels and in all fields. These skills should be recognized in job classification schemes and rewarded accordingly. Women should also have equal access to employment, decisionmaking, scholarships and research funds in the field of science and technology.

To maintain their participation, programmes and facilities should be implemented to take account of, as well as combat, the gender division of labour and gender ideology of women's role in the family. Equalizing the gender division should include demands such as adequate paternity leave, crèche facilities for the children of men as well as women employees, and drastically shortening the working day of both men and women so as to leave sufficient time for housework and childcare, to name but a few measures.

Any introduction of technology should entail broad-based discussion by those who will be affected by it, either at the community level or at the workplace. Technology agreements should be drawn up so that workers can codetermine the implementation, development and direction of any new technology introduced. In this context, policies should be formulated to protect (women) workers from possible health and safety hazards. Regular assessments should be undertaken to evaluate the social, economic, political and health implications of technology policies.

Support networks should be created to encourage women in the field of science and technology and solve the problems they face at the workplace and at home. For example, the recent establishment of a Third World Organization of Women Scientists to enable women scientists to share experiences and knowledge is laudable. A VDT (Visual Display Terminal) Coalition comprised of office and factory workers involved in VDT work has been set up in California to enable workers to demand better and healthier working conditions as well as increase their skills in this new technology. Another example, an all-women laboratory headed by a progressive feminist at a university in Penang, Malaysia, provides a fascinating model for training young women scientists in virology and immunology.[6]

Women activists can also link up with women scientists and science and technology institutions to discuss joint projects and promote a better understanding of the various issues faced by working women. The overall aim would be to influence science and technology policies and programmes so that they promote social justice, a peaceful environment, and the welfare of working women.

Finally, a word about appropriate technology. It is clear from what we have said so far that some forms of technology are *not* appropriate, inasmuch as they are destructive; but this does not mean that some technologies are appropriate for the Third World while others are suitable only for rich countries. If a technology contributes to an overall improvement in the conditions of life and work, then it is appropriate anywhere in the world. Conversely, if a technology is wasteful of the earth's resources or in some way destructive, then it is inappropriate anywhere in the world. In this case, as in any other, there is no need for double standards!

Notes

1 The intensification of work in the electronics industry as a result of the introduction of automation and to the detriment of women workers is discussed in Chee Heng Leng and Cecilia Ng, 'Economic restructuring in an NIC (Newly Industrializing Country): Implications for women workers', paper presented at the Conference on Insecurity in the 1990s: Gender and Social Policy in an International Perspective, 5–6 April 1993, London School of Economics, Britain.

2 For a discussion of the impact of new technologies on women's industrial and office work in other parts of the world, including Europe, North America and Australia, see Goodman, S. (1987) 'The implications of computerization and microelectronics on women's employment in South-East Asia', in Ng, C. (Ed) *Technology and Gender* (Kuala Lumpur, UPH and Malaysian Social Science Association).

3 By contrast, mechanization of wheat farming in India had not, in the early 1990s, led to a significant displacement of female labour, although the introduction of combine harvesters was expected to lead to such a result. See Agarwal, B. (1991) 'Agricultural mechanization and labour use: A disaggregated approach', in Afshar, H. (Ed) *Women, Development and Survival in the Third World*, London, Longman, pp. 174–87.

4 We are grateful to Being Hui for drafting this section using data taken from a report by APPROTECH-ASIA and WISE-Thailand entitled 'Mainstreaming women in science and technology'.

5 The majority of the vocational students were in home science, where women constituted 100 per cent of the class, and commerce (78 per cent).

6 According to the group leader, Dr Jane Cardosa, this feminist laboratory set up in 1985 aims to train a generation of women scientists who are confident, can hold their own, are willing to learn, and can work with others in a spirit of cooperation rather than an atmosphere of 'male competition'. These values are important to ensure the success of the work and the character of the people who 'graduate' from there (personal communication).

References

AKHTER, F. (1992) *Depopulating Bangladesh: Essays on the Politics of Fertility*, Narigrantha Prabarthana, Bangladesh.

FAUZIAH, W., YUSOFF, W. and CARDOSA, M. (1993) Office Workers, Computers and Health: A Malaysian Case Study, paper presented at the Conference on Computers and Office Workers: Social and Health Implications, 2–3 November 1993, Serdang, Malaysia.

HENSMAN, R. P. (1991) Women Workers in Manufacturing Industry: Problems and Possibilities, in AFSHAR, H. (Ed) *Women, Development and Survival in the Third World*, Longman, London and New York.

HENSMAN, R. (1992) 'Women and ethnic nationalism in Sri Lanka', *Journal of Gender Studies*, **1**, 4, pp. 500–509.

NG, C. (1991) 'Malay women and rice production in West Malaysia', in AFSHAR, H. (Ed) *Women, Development and Survival in the Third World*, Longman, London and New York.

PEARSON, R. (1991) 'Gender and new technology for women: New work for women?', paper presented at the international workshop of Women Organizing in the Process of Industrialization, 15–26 April, 1991, The Hague, The Netherlands.

Chapter 7

The Knowledge in our Bones: Standpoint Theory, Alternative Health and the Quantum Model of the Body

Anne Scott

Introduction

Second-wave feminism emerged from a practice – consciousness raising – which was grounded in embodied experience; this has been one of its strengths. Within the last few years, however, feminist theory has come up against some thorny problems relating to experience and essentialism. In attempting to avoid the traps created by essentialism, false universalism and biological reductionism, many feminists have enclosed the concept of experience within a grid of discourse. Taken to its logical extreme, this position leads to an epistemology which has been emptied of both embodied experience and active agency. It is, in fact, one expression of a wider idealism, which denies an independent reality to nature in general. The critiques of this perspective as politically disabling are telling; a new approach is needed.

In this chapter, I will argue that extreme social constructionist positions are attractive to feminists because the Cartesian understanding of the body has not been adequately challenged within feminist theory. I will discuss an alternative conception of the body which has emerged from various alternative health practices. From the perspective of these alternative sciences, it is possible to conceptualize nature as fluid, intentional and transformative; such a nature cannot ground the politics of biological reductionism. I will finish this chapter with some suggestions relating to the integration of the quantum model of the body into standpoint theory. I will be arguing that once we have been released from the pitfalls of biological reductionism, we can confidently return to a non-essentialistic use of bodily experience in the creation of feminist theory.

In splitting human beings into the diametrically opposed substances of mind and body, René Descartes contributed to the inauguration of the modern era.[1] Although scientists later substituted a monistic materialism for his dualism, the Cartesian understanding of the body as a biochemical machine has survived.[2] The Cartesian body is, essentially, a mechanism, without purposes – or intelligence – of its own. It is understood as a limiting structure – a fleshy shell which houses and constrains the mind. It becomes ill due to assault from outside forces, and it is repaired through the technical expertise of the physician. It is a *resource*, which belongs to its owner – the subject as disembodied mind.[3] Although most western intellectuals now claim an adherence to some form of monism, the continuing influence of the Cartesian world-view is reflected throughout both institutional structures and everyday language. We say, for example, 'I *have* a body', not 'I *am* a body'. Feminist theorists have devoted a great deal of effort to the reintegration of mind and body; it is my argument, however, that these efforts have only been partially successful.

During the late 1960s and the early 1970s, naturalistic models of the body were very powerful, and were widely used to provide a natural justification for female subordination.[4] Rather than challenging these models directly, many feminist thinkers attempted to carve out a space for social theory by limiting the biological body's scope; they differentiated *sex*, the province of the biological body, from *gender*, a supplementary, social concept. Once this new form of the Cartesian division was accepted, feminists could struggle for a greater share of the body's territory to be ceded to gender, but they had to accept that the body did have a biological core which was effectively abandoned to mechanistic conceptualizations. In a memorable metaphor, Linda Nicholson (1994) has described this as the 'coatrack' conception of the body – personality, behaviour and other cultural artifacts are thrown across a body which is, in the end, just part of the furniture.

She has not been alone in decrying the consequences of this view. As the diversity among women has become more visible, it has become apparent that female experience is always historically specific; there are very few constants in the structuring of womens' lives. With a belief that the body has a pre-social, biological core, it is thus difficult to make any generalizations across the category of *women* without becoming vulnerable to charges of essentialism or biological reductionism. Donna Haraway (1987) is one of several theorists who have challenged the uncritical use of experience as 'a prior resource'. There is no such thing as 'raw' experience, she argues; experiences are constructed within social occasions, discourses and material practices (1987: 113). Marnia Lazreg (1994) argues further that a dependence on experience makes it impossible for feminists to escape 'the "problématique" of the body' (1994: 50); reliance on bodily experience, she claims, makes some form of feminine essentialism almost inevitable. Clearly, references to the biological body can generate a great deal of anxiety among some feminists:

> announcing that reality's substance is of no matter uncovers a lingering belief that it matters too much. Such an announcement evidences an unshaken faith in patriarchy's foundational truths, for what we have located here is something believed to be essentialism's superlative – what is most essential, most incontrovertibly real, and most decidedly significant. The anatomical body remains reality's harshest truth at precisely that moment when we determine to banish its substance . . . (Kirby, 1991: 8).

The linguistic turn in feminist theory has been, at least partially, a response to these difficulties. Many feminists have turned to Foucault, Lacan, and other post-structuralist thinkers to articulate a notion of the body which is wholly socially constructed. Beginning with the argument that bodily experience is accessible only through social meanings, they have gone on to completely subsume the biological body into social discourse.[5] As Linda Nicholson suggests:

> one could give up the idea of the [coat]rack altogether. Here, biology, rather than being construed as that which all societies share in common, would be viewed as a culturally specific *set of ideas*, [my italics] that might or might not be translatable into somewhat related ideas in other societies ... (1994: 90).

The social constructionist body is an idealist production.[6] It is a mental construction in which, as Canning notes, 'languages or discourses "position subjects and *produce* their experiences"' (1994: 376). Many deconstructionists seriously question the idea that bodies have *any* a priori needs, functions or desires. As Gatens notes, the question is no longer 'How is the body taken up within culture?', but rather, 'How does culture construct the body so it is understood as biologically given?' (1988: 62).

This conception of the body seems to be dramatically opposed to the Cartesian understanding. I would argue, however, that it does not so much *transcend* the Cartesian dualism as *hide* from it. The social constructionist body is too abstract to pose a direct challenge to the mechanistic understanding of the body. Instead, it avoids the difficulties attached to the Cartesian conception of the material body by jumping over to the other pole of the dualism. From the *mental* side of the Cartesian divide, it cannot directly confront the *materialist* understanding of the biological body which continues to shape most of the western discourse on the subject.[7]

Within the less sophisticated articulations of the social constructionist postion, both embodied experience and personal agency can easily be lost.[8] The body is understood as an effect – as a cultural construction – rather than as an agent in its own right. If subjects are caught within a web of determining discourses and social practices, it is unclear how they may transform those discourses through reliance on their own experiences and the meanings they may extract from them. As Canning argues, 'experience, as the rendering of meaning, is inextricably entwined with the notion of agency, with a vision of historical subjects as actors ...' (1994: 37). To abandon embodied experience in this way, simply in order to avoid the dangers of biological essentialism is, I would argue, both politically and epistemologically unwise.[9]

I would like to suggest an alternative course of action. We can challenge – directly – the Cartesian understanding of the body as an unintelligent, static, constraining and passive mechanism. As it is these characteristics which enable the body to be continually employed as an essentialist and reductionist resource, their direct revisioning will open the way to the creation of a feminist theory which is both non-essentialistic and materially based.[10] A non-Cartesian model of the body is already in widespread use within various alternative and complementary health practices; it can, potentially, be used productively within feminist theory.[11]

The Quantum Body

Although holistic health practices have existed for thousands of years, the model of the quantum body[12] is quite new, having gradually emerged within the last 15 to 20 years. This model draws on long-standing mystical and esoteric beliefs and on the practices of a number of alternative therapies.[13] It also, however, draws on the holograph as a metaphor, and on the 'new' sciences of quantum physics, chaos theory, systems theory, and ecology, as well as some recent developments within endocrinology, developmental biology, immunology, orthopedics, and other disciplines allied to clinical biomedicine.[14] As a result, proponents of the quantum model have a great deal of confidence that their work is at the cutting edge of an 'emerging paradigm' and is in advance of, rather than in opposition to, mainstream scientific research. This is, historically, a rare position for adherents to the occult sciences to be in, and harks back to the confidence of the 'new vitalists' during the late eighteenth and early nineteenth centuries.

Endocrinology has, as a discipline, been a focus of interest for those interested in fundamentally rethinking the body.[15] Deepak Chopra, an endocrinologist who is now practicing ayurvedic medicine, argues (1989) that recent discoveries regarding the neuro-peptides[16] make the argument for a sharp division between the body and the mind increasingly hard to maintain. These diverse messenger molecules are both manufactured and received in cells throughout the body; the whole process seems to follow the stream of consciousness in an extraordinarily flexible manner. Through the neuro-peptides, Chopra claims, intelligence permeates the entire body,[17] but he follows this observation with a crucial question. How is the leap from non-material thought to neuro-peptide made? This problem haunts the Cartesian view of the body, even in its most sophisticated guises. If the mind is radically different from the body, how are the two connected? By what mechanism do they affect each other?

Chopra's solution, which derives from a mixture of ayurvedic medicine and quantum theory, is shared in its broad outlines by many of the other alternative medical practices. His approach abandons any attempt to find a *causal* link between mind and body. Thoughts do not create neuro-peptides and neuro-peptides do not cause thoughts; they are, rather, different aspects of the same thing. Chopra's model of the body has its metaphorical base in quantum theory. Light may be expressed either as energy (a wave) or matter (a photon), but it's underlying reality lies in the quantum field.[18] He argues that 'the quantum mechanical human body' is analogous, and draws on Bohmian interpretations of quantum theory which suggest that the quantum field is, essentially, a field of consciousness which can manifest either mentally or materially.[19] The neuro-peptide is not caused by the thought; it simply *is* the thought in a material form. Chopra concludes that the human body, literally, has its source in consciousness. His approach to medicine thus draws on Indian philosophical traditions which explore a fourth state of consciousness,[20] said to exist in the silent gap between our thoughts.

> The ancient doctors of India were also great sages, and their cardinal belief was that the body is created out of consciousness. A great yogi or swami would have believed the same thing. Therefore, theirs was a medicine of consciousness . . . (Chopra, 1989: 5).

Within this fourth state of consciousness, likened by Chopra to the quantum field which grounds both matter and energy, he believes both body and mind to have their source. Chopra teaches his patients meditative techniques to access this state of consciousness, and claims to have witnessed many dramatic cures. At this level the body is extremely malleable, he states, and may be, literally, remade.

The invisible basis of material reality is found in the quantum *field*, according to modern physics, and it is through this concept of a *field*, or an organising pattern, that proponents of the *quantum body* connect consciousness and the physical body.

> To be like the quantum, the body does not have to banish its molecules to another dimension; it has only to learn to re-form them into new chemical patterns. It is these patterns that jump in and out of existence, paralleling what happened in Benveniste's[21] test tubes (Chopra 1989: 130).

The concept of morphogenetic fields, which organize and control the development of the fetus, is widely used within developmental biology, although they are generally considered to be merely useful abstractions. Rupert Sheldrake (1989) has argued that these fields have a literal reality as quantum type fields, and are a subset of a wider class of *morphic fields* which organize all natural phenomena.[22] His ideas have generated a good deal of interest among practitioners of the holistic therapies.[23] One prominent homoeopath speculates that, during the process of dilution and succession,[24] homoeopathic remedies become carriers of the original substance's morphic field:

> This morphogenetic field of the remedy is then brought into contact with the morphogenetic field of the patient and there is resonant attraction between them, which draws the distorted energies of the patient towards the complete energies of the substance. The remedy

is like a template laid over the energies of the patient (Handley, 1992: 15).

The belief that the body has an associated energy field, which controls growth and the healing process, is found in varying forms within many types of complementary and alternative medicine.[25] This field is usually believed to exist at the border between consciousness and physically perceivable energy. The Chinese concept of *chi*, for example, may be defined as '. . . matter on the verge of becoming energy, or energy on the point of materialising' (Kaptchuk, 1983: 35); this description brings to mind the quantum description of light, manifesting either as matter or energy. Within traditional Chinese medicine, the acupuncture meridians are considered to be pathways for the flow of *chi* through the energetic body. Interestingly, major intersections of these meridians correspond to the most important chakras within the chakric model of the energetic body (Goodison, 1992: 146).[26] The major chakras, in turn, have been connected with the endocrine system within the physiological body (Roney-Dougal, 1991). Spiritual healers work with the aura, which is believed to have several levels, corresponding to a series of *subtle*, or energetic, *bodies* (West, 1988).[27]

It is clear that, while Chopra's account is unusual in the clarity with which it connects quantum theory, modern biomedicine and his alternative, ayurvedic practice, his general understanding of the body is shared by many practitioners of alternative and complementary medicine. There are striking parallels, for example, between his conception of the quantum body, and the homoeopathic understanding of the 'vital force' – often described by homoeopaths as 'a dynamic blueprint', or an organizing, intentional, energetic field – which grounds the bodymind.[28] Several therapies and philosophies which work with altered or transpersonal levels of consciousness are prominent within contemporary British homoeopathy.[29] Their practitioners believe that it is at this deeper level of consciousness that health and illness are created, and it is to this state of consciousness that their treatments are directed. The therapeutic systems based on the quantum model of the body integrate physical healing and personal transformation.

The esoteric belief that the body is created by, and grounded in, consciousness is not new. It is only recently, however, that this belief has received enough support from within the mainstream of science to allow its elaboration as a recognizable model. In the remainder of this chapter, I will explore some implications which the adoption of this model might have in relation to the problems discussed in the introductory section of this chapter.

Body Talk: The Body as a Natural Symbol

The alternative health model of a quantum body directly challenges the Cartesian conception. Those naturalistic models of the body which have spoken of essential, biological, characteristics have understood these characteristics to be static and impossible to change. In the quantum model, by contrast, the biological body is characterized by mobility, intelligence and the capacity for transformation. If there is such a thing as a biological essence, the *vital force* – the dynamic, organizing field which grounds body and mind – is where you would look for it. But the vital force is as far removed from a coat rack as it is possible to get. It is a *force* — a form of energy; it cannot be static. If the body is forming a fixed and limited structure, the vital force has a problem; when people are healthy, their vital forces are, according to the quantum body model, creating a maximum of mobility and social/environmental responsiveness. Second, it cannot be contained within the skin of an individual.[30] Within the quantum body model, the biological body can only be understood within its social and environmental context.

The Cartesian model is further challenged by the notion that this vital force is actually an expression of consciousness; the body is thus permeated by agency and intelligence. Homoeopaths, for example, believe that the vital force, operating through the bodymind, is the primary epistemological and healing agent. The remedies are there to support it, to confront it with a metaphorical mirror of itself, to enter into *dialogue* with it in some way . . . but they are supporting actors. The unconscious, bodily based, vital force, which connects the physical body with the deeper consciousness in which it has its source, is the central agent within the healing process.

If we conceive of the body in this way, it follows that our bodily experience can become the ground for a critical social understanding. For example, Adrienne Rich had a severe allergic reaction to her first pregnancy. Her later attempts to understand this experience led her to produce a powerful, critical analysis of the institution of motherhood.[31] Working within the model of the quantum body, we would understand Adrienne Rich's allergic reaction to her first pregnancy as a particularly creative symptom – produced by her vital force – to communicate with her conscious mind and to create the conditions necessary for her to regain her mental and emotional health. It may be possible to argue that Rich's physical reaction to her pregnancy was wholly generated by a lived conflict between the social discourses surrounding motherhood and those surrounding liberal individualism. But if this allergic reaction was simply a passive effect, it was an original and strikingly effective one. It catalysed a train of awareness which ultimately changed the way Adrienne Rich lived her life. I believe a better case can be made that this outlaw reaction, unexpected and, at the time, wholly unsupported, was actively chosen by her bodyself. Rich's body may have been acted upon, but it was certainly an actor as well. Neither a naturalistic model of the body, nor a thorough-going social constructionism, can theorize this kind of reciprocal action.

If a deeper level of consciousness is operating intelligently through such bodily expressions as physical symptoms, emotional reactions and the dream life, the biological body must be, at least to some extent, a symbolic creation of that consciousness. It may thus be understood as a *natural symbol*, creating itself in a form of discourse which cannot be contained within the conventional codes of language and social practice.[32] Many homoeopaths, for example, understand the process of remedy selection as a form of dialogue with the body:

> I'm fascinated by the way the body will ask for a particular remedy, and if not given that remedy, it will just go on producing symptoms of the same remedy, until you go 'Oh! It's Arsenicum!' And it's like the vital force will act in a particular way, and . . . keep on nudging, until you get the remedy right (British homoeopath, 1995).[33]

If we accept that the body is producing itself, in a material form of symbolic discourse, we cannot argue that experience is produced, exclusively, within language. Although bodily experience must, inevitably, be *interpreted* through social discourse, it will always maintain a fullness which overflows these limits. There always remains the possibility that we may 'see through the cracks' of our socially shaped world-view, gaining access to the alternative form of consciousness which is expressed within our embodied selves.

Therapists working with the quantum body model believe that the body can produce a discourse of astonishing complexity, in which individual symptoms embody traumatic or oppressive experiences, emotional postures and social relationships in a very precise form of symbolic language. Lucy Goodison, for example, is an intuitive massage therapist who attempts to help her patients make complex and ambiguous bodily knowledge explicit, where it can become a resource for healing and social action.[34] She offers this account of her work with one patient, a Jewish exile from Hitler's Germany, who had also survived childhood sexual abuse.

> When Peggy first came for massage, she described her body as 'in pieces': she experienced some parts as too numb to feel anything and others as too excruciatingly tender to bear being touched. She had chronic back trouble. She suffered from asthma, breathed shallowly, and was unusually troubled by her reaction to body smells like sweat. Living alone, she found it hard to cook adequately for herself. She was also anxious about penetration (Goodison, 1992: 208).

Goodison treated her with a mixture of therapy and massage. Peggy would talk about the images and symbols which Goodison's touch brought up for her; they would then become subjects for more traditional therapy. In a very dense, sensitive account, Goodison describes how Peggy had internalized her oppression within her body: 'her [sexually abusive] brother in her right side, her father in her stomach and sexuality, the Holocaust in her sense of smell, the migration in her missing legs . . .' (1992: 222). Her asthma was linked to an association of breathing with her father's death, and to a fear of violation from anything entering her body. Her hatred of her own Jewishness had led to a revulsion for food, bodily odours and sexuality. Over the course of her treatment, Peggy

> gradually reached a state where there was power in a quiet place inside her which could reach in a positive way out into the world . . . she gave the impression of slowly finding a peace within herself which could almost be described as spiritual. Contrary to conventional views of spirituality, this quality had started at her feet. I am hesitant ever to use the term, 'cure', but this hard-won reclaiming of her inner landscape was accompanied by many concrete changes in her everyday living, all reflecting a growing ability to engage with human life: to stand up for herself and to move towards others (1992: 224).

Peggy's understanding of her own oppression was richly embedded within her body, with a bodily symbolism which was deeply particular. Goodison's attentive touch had gradually evoked her bodily understanding of the Holocaust, and of the nationalism, exile, sexual abuse, violation and death which had shaped her life.

Peggy's experience, however, was unique, and the dialogue with her body could be created only within individual massage and therapy. As Lazreg (1994) notes, the disjunction between the individual nature of bodily experience, and the abstract, general nature of social theory has proved to be a major impediment to combining the two. Faced with the density of this bodily symbolism, it is obvious the sociological theory is impoverished, lacking a form of biopolitical discourse which is rich enough to incorporate the overwhelming complexity and particularity of bodily experience. Conversely, the meditative, intuitive and body-based practices which are generally used to access this inner knowledge are socially impoverished; they lack a grounding in sociological awareness. This leads us to a methodological problem: how are we to incorporate the body's knowledge into a critical feminist theory? In the next section, I will argue that standpoint theory may provide the beginnings of a solution.

Attending to the Quantum Body: A New Approach to Standpoint Theory

Standpoint theory offers one means to incorporate bodily experience into social theory. Embodiment is central to standpoint theory.[35] As Hartsock (1983) notes, the feminist standpoint is, necessarily, embodied; it is generated by people who are located *somewhere* and who are doing *something*. Women are engaged in caring, manual and intellectual forms of labour, and these activities generate a form of understanding. Furthermore, they are located outside the social élite, which makes possible a type of double vision. Those who employ the feminist standpoint understand the dominant social ideology but, because their own experience does not fit that ideology, can see that it *is* an ideology. Not everyone located outside the social élite develops this critical awareness; it should be noted. It is generally produced within social or political action, and with the support of a political community.[36] Experience, as embodied in the feminist standpoint, may be employed in the construction of theory but it is not theory in and of itself.

So knowledge belongs to the embodied, according to the standpoint theorists. But the question remains: can knowledge emerge *through* the body? Although standpoint theory uses the fact of embodiment to argue for the authority of feminist knowledge, its theorists have been almost as reluctant as other feminists to draw directly on bodily knowledge. Their awareness of the deep ambiguity and particularity of individual experience, and of the difficulties attached to the notion of experience in general, has presented them with a powerful obstacle. Alison Jaggar, however, has found her way through some of these difficulties to argue (1989) that knowledge often does emerge through the body and, in particular, through the emotions. Emotions, she claims, are not random storms sweeping the body – inimical to the production of rational and reliable knowledge. They are, to some degree, intentional, chosen, socially sensitive responses to particular situations, and they embody a set of values. The *outlaw* emotions – socially defined as inappropriate to a particular situation – can, she states, embody an implicitly held value system which is at odds with the prevailing ideology, and can thus contribute, in marginal groups, to its explication in the formation of an alternative, critical knowledge. This argument can easily be extended to include outlaw physical symptoms, such as Rich's allergic reaction to her first pregnancy. With this argument, Jaggar has opened the door to a potential transformation of standpoint epistemology. In this version of standpoint theory, the body can be a source of the alternative perspective which leads to a more complete and adequate understanding.

It is clear that the consciousness which grounds our bodymind within the quantum body model is not accessible, in any pure form, to our conscious awareness. In every version of this model, it is believed to lie outside our conscious awareness. When it does come to consciousness, it tends to do so in a fragmentary and symbolic form, where it is shaped and expressed through social discourse.[37] However, the model of the quantum body entails that experience *will* tend to overflow the bounds of social discourse, offering the potential for alternative understandings at the point where these social discourses have gaps and contradictions. Jaggar has described one way in which this process may be effected. Her suggestion, that our emotional reactions may be the expression of a system of values and awareness which lies beneath the level of conscious awareness, is compatible with the quantum body model. Jaggar's *outlaw emotions*, as well as *outlaw physical symptoms* may represent a form of bodily discourse, in which our bodily based consciousness can, effectively, create a disjunction between our experience and the social discourses within which we are operating. Thus the body may force a gap in the seamless web of social discourse and produce a space within which we can begin to formulate alternative understandings.

The creation of this disjunction is not sufficient to create a discourse of resistance. Embodied experiences and, particularly, various experiences of discomfort, simply create a *location* in which the articulation of an alternative understanding may begin, as well as providing the motivation to work towards understanding the source of the discomfort. It can also provide clues towards the nature of the difficulty; the body can, as a symbol, speak in a very precise way regarding the problem to be solved. The body can thus provide the necessary preconditions for the generation of a more accurate knowledge within standpoint epistemology. To make use of this bodily perspective, however, theorists must learn to attend to the discourse being generated by their bodies. The Marxists felt that the strength of labour's epistemological standpoint lay in it's immersion within the material world. Recent feminist discussions on the epistemology of care have recast this idea, pointing out that in attending to the bodily and social needs of others, women often become sensitive to the rich particularity of individual experience, and thus develop a distinctive and powerful epistemological approach. In attending to the body, a sensitivity to the knowledge of the body may be developed.[38] Although this sensitivity and attention to the body is necessary if body consciousness is to contribute to social theory, it is not sufficient.

The creation of useful, social, knowledge occurs at that point where experience meets social discourse and, as Haraway (1988: 191) emphasizes, experience can never be innocent. Standpoint theorists argue, in fact, that the 'view from below' is to be preferred precisely *because* this perspective may allow an experiencing agent to become conscious of her own lack of innocence. In theorizing from a marginal position, one tends to be critical . . . one must be alive to the tricks by which undesired realities can be obscured or denied. The natural body, located on the underside of the mind/body dualism, thus offers attentive theorists a powerful perspective from which to interrogate social reality. It is, however, just one perspective; the knowledge it provides must be acknowledged as partial and situated. With the hints and suggestions drawn from our embodied, experienced consciousness, we may enter into a supportive community and begin to deconstruct the received wisdom of our society. Our developing ideas, however, must be tested in critical social action. We must develop techniques for distinguishing, both in ourselves and others, between speech and actions which are based on the solid grounding of both critical reason and embodied consciousness, and those which float on a sea of social discourse.[39]

A legitimate epistemology must draw on the triple resources of social discourse, critical reason and embodied experience, but the fear of biological reductionism has prevented feminists from fully employing the final member of this triad. The new model of the body which is emerging within several alternative therapeutic systems may address this problem. The quantum body is fluid; it is capable of intentionality and transformation. This model of the natural body cannot ground a politics of biological reductionism. By discarding our essentialist anxieties and reconceptualizing the biological body as dynamic and aware, we may be able to solve some of the problems hindering the development of an effective feminist epistemology.

Notes

1 Descartes used radical scepticism to develop a philosophy which would be, he believed, of guaranteed reliability. He claimed that his bodily experiences could all be questioned, but his consciousness provided certain knowledge. In locating the person within a rational, unitary consciousness which was radically separated from the body, Descartes inaugurated the modern philosophical era. See Descartes (1968).

2 Monistic materialists maintain the Cartesian conception of the body, but discard his conception of the mind; they attempt to explain *all* phenomena mechanistically. There is now a large literature which criticizes this worldview. Kirkmayer (1988), Leder (1984), McKee (1988) and Scheper-Hughes and Lock (1987) specifically focus their critiques on the Cartesian understanding of the body and its expression within biomedicine and the social sciences.

3 See Plumwood (1993) for an interesting discussion regarding the logical structure of dualism. She argues that dualism is structured by a 'logic of colonisation'; the two terms are mutually constructed in a hierarchical relationship, so as to make 'equality and mutuality literally unthinkable' (1993: 47). This structural relationship naturalizes the appropriation of the 'colonised' by the 'master'.

4 Although the hierarchical split between the body and the mind is as old as western culture itself, the idea that human nature may be defined and understood by the study of the body is actually quite modern; it has been employed in a systematic way only since the decline of religious belief in the mid-nineteenth century (Schilling 1993: 42). See Tuana (1993) for a study of this topic.

5 Prominent feminists working with this conception of the body include Judith Butler (1990), Judith Lorber (1994) and Linda Nicholson (1994). See Schilling's critique (1993) of the Foucaldian view of the body.

6 As such, it is part of a broader tendency, within post-structuralist thought, to deny the independent reality of the object (nature) pole of the subject–object spectrum; both Kirby (1991) and Latour (1992) discuss this issue. A radically relativist epistemology may be one of the consequences of this position; in such an epistemology, there is no way to challenge coherent knowledge perspectives. The consequences of such an epistemology can be devastating for feminists who are trying to achieve practical social change with arguments based on empirical fact and appeals to reason. Fricker (1994), Hartsock (1990) and Rose (1994) discuss this issue more fully.

7 See Bigwood (1991) on this point.

8 A few post-structuralists have constructively addressed these issues, looking in particular at ways in which a social constructionist position may be reconciled with the maintenance of agency. See Hollway (1989) and Mahoney and Yngvesson (1992) for two interesting explorations of this problem.

9 Even this gain is suspect. Social constructionism does make it easier to avoid biological essentialism, but Martin (1994) argues that it replaces it with a methodological essentialism. As Fuss's in-depth exploration (1989) of the problem makes clear, essentialism is a slippery concept; it regularly shows up in unexpected places, including within the most rigorous post-structuralist theories.

10 A great deal of recent feminist work might contribute to such a project. See, for example, Haraway's discussion of recent feminist primatology (1989); in these accounts, the female body can become agent, rather than resource, and 'sex' can seem to be very close to 'mind'. In 'Situated knowledges' (1988), Haraway discusses the implications of this position for feminist epistemology. Gatens (1988) draws on Spinoza's philosophy to construct a feminist model of the body, while Scheper-Hughes and Lock (1987) outline their model of a 'mindful body'. See also Adam (1995), Bigwood (1991), and Goodison (1992) for accounts which treat the biological body as an agent.

11 I do not claim that the model I am proposing here is true in any absolute sense. I claim only that it is compatible with a great deal of empirical evidence, and that its adoption will enable feminist theory to find its way out of some difficult theoretical problems. *How* compatible with the empirical evidence it may be is a question which is beyond the scope of this chapter. I do not intend to enter the heated debate on whether the holistic therapies work. It is also beyond the scope of this chapter to discuss the social implications of the growth in holistic medicine. They have been called individualistic, essentialistic and romantic by, among others, Berliner and Salmon (1980), Coward (1989), and Kopelman and Moskop (1981), while Goodison (1992) and McKee (1988) defend them on these points. This debate is largely irrelevant to the theoretical arguments outlined in this chapter.

12 The model I have called the *quantum model of the body*, has been variously formulated, and named, in recent years. See Dossey's highly influential discussion (1985); Gerber's account (1988) describes an *etheric body*. Mindell's discussion of the *dreambody* (1990) draws on esoteric philosophy, yoga, fairy tales, contemporary physics and his own work with dreams and with body-based therapies. See Zohar (1990) for a related discussion of *quantum* psychology.

13 A distinction needs to be drawn between holistic medicine, complementary medicine and alternative medicine. Holistic medicine includes both biomedical and alternative therapies, practiced from a perspective which

integrates physical, emotional, mental and, sometimes, social issues. The holistic health practices are widely divergent, and have no shared model of the body. Complementary medicine is similar in meaning to holistic medicine, although it specifically excludes mainstream biomedical practices. The complementary practices are often used alongside biomedicine, redressing its characteristic weaknesses. Although some of these practices employ an alternative understanding of the body, many do not. My arguments within this chapter are primarily referring to those therapies which are complete medical systems in their own right, and are thus *alternative*, rather than *complementary*, to clinical biomedicine. These therapeutic systems, by definition, operate with an alternative conceptualization of the body. In the West, traditional Chinese medicine (which includes both acupuncture and Chinese herbalism), homoeopathy, naturopathy and Ayurvedic medicine (classical Indian medicine, including herbal and dietary treatments, the yogic practices, chakra work and meditation) are widely known sytems of this description. See Kaptchuk (1983) on traditional Chinese medicine, Power (1984) on naturopathy, Thakkur (1974) on Ayurvedic medicine and Vithoulkas (1986) on homoeopathy. Grossinger's anthropological account (1980) discusses all of these systems.

14 As Benton (1991) notes, biology and biomedicine are far from monolithic; they contain a few disciplines and researchers with holistic, or even vitalistic, approaches.

15 See, for example, the work of Serena Roney-Dougal (1991), on the relationship between the pineal gland and various psychic capacities and experiences.

16 Neuro-peptides are a class of messenger molecules connecting thoughts with physiological action.

17 Dossey (1985) also argues that the capacity for consciousness and thought may be found throughout the body. He points out (1985: 219) that our resistance to the idea that other organs may be co-equal with the brain has sociopolitical parallels in western culture's belief that every social organization must have a head; something, or somebody, must be in charge.

18 The quantum field is a theoretical construction developed in response to problems presented by Bell's theorem. This theorem holds that the universe *must* operate non-locally. Matter reacts to changes in connected matter instantaneously; information can thus travel faster than the speed of light. Since the laws of classical physics render such transmission speeds impossible, some physicists speculate that there must be a connecting field which lies outside the normal laws of space and time. David Bohm claims that the quantum field is an information field from which material events emerge. See Bohm (1980).

19 See Zohar's discussion of this point (1990: 41).

20 The first three are waking, sleeping and dreaming. It is important to note that the *consciousness* which Chopra is referring to is, ordinarily, *unconscious*. It is NOT the rational, conscious thought of modern philosophy;

this fact distinguishes the alternative health/quantum model from standard philosophical idealism.

21 Jacques Benveniste conducted a series of experiments which provided evidence that the homoeopathic principle of treatment with microdoses may have a basis in material reality. He found that extreme dilution, when it was combined with succession (shaking), did not reduce the effectiveness of an antigen exposed to IgE. The allergic reaction was triggered even after the antigen had been diluted beyond the point at which a single molecule might remain. Benveniste suggested that the dilutant may retain a pattern, or imprint, of the molecules which once were within it. The hostile treatment Benveniste received from the editor of *Nature* triggered a major controversy.

22 Some embryologists have proposed that embryo development is organized by morphogenetic fields which create an invisible pattern structuring the developmental process and offering a means to correct errors. Although these fields are theoretically very useful, embryologists tend not to believe in their literal existence. Sheldrake claims they do exist, as a kind of pooled, species-wide memory. They have rhythmic patterns of activity, he claims, imparting information through a form of rhythmic, non-energetic, resonance. These fields belong to a wider class of 'morphic' fields, Sheldrake claims, which operate through the accumulation of connected events into a resonant pattern, and organize all natural phenomena. Sheldrake's claims are dismissed by most scientists.

23 At a recent talk Sheldrake gave in Leeds (Schumacher College Series, University of Leeds, November 1994), a substantial minority of the audi-
.   ence turned out to be homoeopaths or other alternative practitioners, and a large number of questions relating to the connections between his work and homoeopathic theory were asked.

24 Homoeopathic remedies are made by diluting a medicinal substance and then vigorously shaking (successing) it. This process is then repeated, with the remedy's potency representing the number of times it has been diluted and successed.

25 It is also gaining credence within clinical biomedicine, although research here tends to be restricted to the effects of electro-magnetic fields. See Becker and Selden (1985) for an account of Becker's orthopedic research into the implications of these fields.

26 The chakric model of the body has its origins in Ayurvedic medicine, although many other therapeutic systems have analogous models. The chakras are believed to be reservoirs and activating centres for *prana*, the Ayurvedic life energy (*prana* is almost identical in meaning to *chi*). There are seven major chakras and numerous minor ones. See Tansley (1980) on 'subtle anatomy'.

27 A model of *subtle bodies* is employed by many alternative and complementary healers, including some homoeopaths. Within this model, the anatomical and physical body is considered the most material manifestation of

a series of interlocked, increasingly subtle, bodies, in which it has its source. See Masters (1981) for a discussion of the Egyptian version of this system; Goodison (1992) and West (1988) describe the model of subtle bodies which is actually used by most western healers. This model's adherents believe the subtle bodies can be perceived directly, as auras, and worked with through the chakra system, the acupuncture points, intuitive massage and certain psychotherapies.

28 Homoeopathy is an indigenous European vitalistic medicine of late eighteenth century origin. It is based on the principle that 'like treats like'. Homoeopaths give their patients minute amounts of a 'potentized' remedy which will, in a healthy person, create the complex of physical, mental and emotional symptoms and traits which the patient is exhibiting. They do not attempt to directly diagnose or treat diseases. Rather, they believe that their remedies will stimulate and support the patient's vital force in its own, chosen means of healing. See Vithoulkas (1986) and Grossinger (1980) on homoeopathic theory.

29 These include Jungian therapy (Whitmont, 1980), psychosynthesis, Druidism, and anthrosophosy. See Sharma (1992) and MacEoin (1993) on the extensive New Age influence in professional homoeopathy in Britain.

30 Dossey (1985: 143) uses modern physics to claim that our belief in separate, isolated, bodies is based on an illusion. If bodies are not fully separate, he argues, health, disease, and therapy cannot be understood in individualistic terms.

31 Rich (1977). I agree with Kaufman-Osborn (1993) that Rich's story indicates the importance of leaving a role for bodily experience within feminist epistemology.

32 See Halton's (1992) discussion of dreaming, which makes a similar argument. The application of the term *natural symbol* to the body was, of course, first made by Mary Douglas (1970); my use of the expression, however, differs from hers.

33 This quote is from an interview conducted as part of my thesis research.

34 The technique she uses has close similarities to the *active imagination* technique used within some dreamwork and bodywork based therapies. See Mindell, 1990: 69–72.

35 Hartsock (1983) and Rose (1983) offered important early accounts of the feminist standpoint. For more recent work, which takes greater account of the multiplicity of feminist standpoints, see Harding (1991) and Collins (1989). Rose (1994) provides a clear overview of the ongoing debate between the standpoint theorists and the post-structuralists within feminist philosophy of science.

36 Collins (1989) makes this point with great clarity.

37 This fact, alone, can explain the astonishing claims often made within 'mystical' literature, as well as their diversity of form and doctrine. A refusal to acknowledge that 'mystical' productions must be produced at the point where unconscious awareness and social discourse meet can lead

directly to all the dangers of a 'politics of illumination' – which include religious bigotry, intolerance, fanaticism and fascisim.

38 See Rose (1994) and Ruddick (1989) on the epistemology of care. This attention to the body may also take a more direct form. At a grassroots level, many feminists are employing meditation, transpersonal psychology, bodywork, nature-based religious practices, and holistic health therapies to gain access to a bodily based consciousness.

39 Adopting the ethics of caring and personal accountability, which are used as epistemological criteria within Afrocentric feminist thought (Collins, 1989) might make an excellent starting point. Gandhi's technique of '*satyagraha*' (literally, 'experiments with truth') is another candidate. He claims 'passive resistance' as an epistemological technique, stating that when one is willing to place oneself at risk in pursuit of one's beliefs, *without* physically threatening or harming one's opponent, and to maintain this position in the face of conflict or opposition, there is strong evidence that one's beliefs are well grounded.

References

ADAM, B. (1995) *Timewatch: The Social Analysis of Time*, Cambridge, Polity.

BECKER, R. and SELDEN, G. (1985) *The Body Electric: Electromagnetism and the Foundation of Life*, New York, William Morrow.

BENTON, T. (1991) 'Biology and social science: Why the return of the repressed should be given a (cautious) welcome', *Sociology*, **25**, 1, pp. 1–29.

BERLINER, H. and SALMON, J. (1980) 'The holistic alternative to scientific medicine: history and analysis', *International Journal of Health Services*, **10**, pp. 133–47.

BIGWOOD, C. (1991) 'Renaturalizing the body (with the help of Merleau-Ponty)', *Hypatia*, **6**, 3, pp. 54–73.

BOHM, D. (1980) *Wholeness and the Implicate Order*, London, Routledge & Kegan Paul.

BUTLER, J. (1990) *Gender Trouble: Feminism and the Subversion of Identity*, London, Routledge.

CANNING, K. (1994) 'Feminist history after the linguistic turn: Historicizing discourse and experience', *Signs*, **19**, 2, pp. 368–404.

CHOPRA, D. (1989) *Quantum Healing: Exploring the Frontiers of Mind/Body Medicine*, New York, Bantam Books.

COLLINS, P. H. (1989) 'The social construction of black feminist thought', *Signs*, **14**, 4, pp. 745–73.

COWARD, R. (1989) *The Whole Truth: The Myth of Alternative Health*, London, Faber & Faber.

DESCARTES, R. (1968) *Discourse on Method* (1637) and *Meditations* (1641), SUTCLIFFE, F. E. (trans.), Harmondsworth, Penguin.

DOSSEY, L. (1985) *Space, Time and Medicine*, Boston, MA, Shambhala.

DOUGLAS, M. (1970) *Natural Symbols: Explorations in Cosmology*, London, Cresset Press.

FRICKER, M. (1994) 'Knowledge as construct: Theorizing the role of gender in knowledge', in LENNON, K. and WHITFORD, M. (Eds) *Knowing the Difference: Feminist Perspectives in Epistemology*, London, Routledge.

FUSS, D. (1989) *Essentially Speaking: Feminism, Nature and Difference*, London, Routledge.

GATENS, M. (1988) 'Towards a feminist philosophy of the body', in CAINE, B., GROSZ, E. A. and DE LEPEVANCHE, M. (Eds) *Crossing Boundaries: Feminisms and the Critique of Knowledges*, London, Allen & Unwin.

GERBER, R. (1988) *Vibrational Medicine*, Santa Fe, NM, Bear & Co.

GOODISON, L. (1992) *Moving Heaven and Earth: Sexuality, Spirituality and Social Change*, London, HarperCollins.

GROSSINGER, R. (1980) *Planet Medicine: From Stone Age Shamanism to Post-Industrial Healing*, Berkeley, CA, North Atlantic Books.

HALTON, E. (1992) 'The reality of dreaming', *Theory, Culture, and Society*, **9**, 4, pp. 119–40.

HANDLEY, R. (1992) 'Homoeopathy and psychosynthesis: Remedy types, archetypes and stereotypes', presentation at the Women in Homoeopathy Conference, Nottingham.

HARAWAY, D. (1987) 'Reading Buchi Emecheta: Contests for "women's experience" in women's studies', in HARAWAY, D. (1991) *Simians, Cyborgs and Women: The Reinvention of Nature*, London, Free Association Books.

HARAWAY, D. (1988) 'Situated knowgedges: The science question in feminism and the privilege of partial perspective', in HARAWAY, D. (1991) *Simians, Cyborgs and Women: The Reinvention of Nature*, London, Free Association Books.

HARAWAY, D. (1989) *Primate Visions: Gender, Race and Nature in the World of Modern Science*, London, Routledge.

HARDING, S. (1991) *Whose Science? Whose Knowledge?*, Buckingham, Open University Press.

HARTSOCK, N. (1983) *Money, Sex and Power: Toward a Feminist Historical Materialism*, London, Longman.

HARTSOCK, N. (1990) 'Foucault on power: A theory for women?', in NICHOLSON, L. (Ed) *Feminism/Postmodernism*, London, Routledge.

HOLLWAY, W. (1989) *Subjectivity and Method in Psychology: Gender, Meaning and Science*, London, Sage.

JAGGAR, A. (1989) 'Love and knowledge: Emotion in feminist epistemology', in JAGGAR, A. and BORDO, S. (Eds) *Gender/Body/Knowledge: Feminist Reconstructions of Being and Knowing*, New Brunswick, NJ, Rutgers University Press.

KAPTCHUK, T. (1983) *Chinese Medicine: The Web that has no Weaver*, London, Rider.

KAUFMAN-OSBORN, T. (1993) 'Teasing feminist sense from experience', *Hypatia*, **8**, 2, pp. 124–44.

KIRBY, V. (1991) 'Corporeal habits: addressing essentialism differently', *Hypatia*, **6**, 3, pp. 4–24.

KIRKMAYER, L. (1988) 'Mind and body as metaphors: Hidden values in bio-medicine', in LOCK, M. and GORDON, D. (Eds) *Biomedicine Examined*, London, Kluwer.

KOPELMAN, L. and MOSKOP, J. (1981) 'The holistic health movement: a survey and critique', *Journal of Medical Philosophy*, **6**, pp. 209–35.

LATOUR, B. (1992) 'One more turn after the social turn . . .', in McMULLLIN, E. (Ed) *The Social Dimensions of Science*, Notre Dame, IN, University of Notre Dame Press.

LAZREG, M. (1994) 'Women's experience and feminist epistemology: A critical, neo-rationalist approach', in LENNON, K. and WHITFORD, M. (Eds) *Knowing the Difference: Feminist Perspectives in Epistemology*, London, Routledge.

LEDER, D. (1984) 'Medicine and paradigms of embodiment', *Journal of Medicine and Philosophy*, **9**, pp. 29–43.

LORBER, J. (1994) *Paradoxes of Gender*, New Haven, CT, Yale University Press.

MACEOIN, D. (1993) 'The choice of homoeopathic models: The patient's dilemma', *The Homoeopath*, **51**, pp. 108–14.

McKEE, J. (1988) 'Holistic health and the critique of western medicine', *Social Science and Medicine*, **26**, 8, pp. 775–84.

MAHONEY, M. and YNGVESSON, B. (1992) 'The construction of subjectivity and the paradox of resistance: Reintegrating feminist anthropology and psychology', *Signs*, **18**, 1, pp. 44–73.

MARTIN, J. R. (1994) 'Methodological essentialism, false difference and other dangerous traps', *Signs*, **19**, 3, pp. 630–57.

MASTERS, R. (1981) 'The way of the five bodies', *Dromenon*, **3**, 2, pp. 16–25.

MINDELL, A. (1990) *Dreambody: The Body's Role in Revealing the Self*, London, Arkana.

NICHOLSON, L. (1994) 'Interpreting gender', *Signs*, **20**, 1, pp. 79–105.

PLUMWOOD, V. (1993) *Feminism and the Mastery of Nature*, London, Routledge.

POWER, R. (1984) 'Naturopathy', *Self and Society*, **12**, 1, pp. 6–9.

RICH, A. (1977) *Of Woman Born: Motherhood as Experience and Institution*, London, Virago.

RONEY-DOUGAL, S. (1991) *Where Science and Magic Meet*, Shaftesbury, Dorset, Element Books.

ROSE, H. (1983) 'Hand, brain and heart: Towards a feminist epistemology for the natural sciences', *Signs*, **9**, 1, pp. 73–96.

ROSE, H. (1994) *Love, Power and Knowledge: Towards a Feminist Transformation of the Sciences*, Cambridge, Polity Press.

RUDDICK, S. (1989) *Maternal Thinking: Towards a Politics of Peace*, Boston, MA, Beacon Press.

SCHEPER-HUGHES, N. and LOCK, M. (1987) 'The mindful body: A prolegomenon to future work in medical anthropology', *Medical Anthropology Quarterly*, **1**, pp. 6–41.

SCHILLING, C. (1993) *The Body and Social Theory*, London, Sage.

SHARMA, U. (1992) *Complementary Medicine Today: Practitioners and Patients*, London, Routledge.

SHELDRAKE, R. (1989) *The Presence of the Past: Morphic Resonance and the Habits of Nature*, New York, Vintage Books.

TANSLEY, D. (1980) *Radionics and the Subtle Anatomy of Man*, Essex, UK, Health Science Press.

THAKKUR, C. (1974) *Ayurveda: The Indian Art and Science of Medicine*, New York, ASI Publishers.

TUANA, N. (1993) *The Less Noble Sex: Scientific, Religious and Philosophical Conceptions of Women's Nature*, Bloomington, IN, Indiana University Press.

VITHOULKAS, G. (1986) *The Science of Homoeopathy*, Wellingborough, Thorsons.

WEST, W. (1988) *Amethyst Days: Some Notes on Healing and Psychic Development*, Leeds, privately published.

WHITMONT, E. (1980) *Psyche and Substance: Some Essays on Homoeopathy in the Light of Jungian Psychology*, Berkeley, CA, North Atlantic Books.

ZOHAR, D. (1990) *The Quantum Self*, London, Flamingo.

Chapter 8

Technologies of Reproduction: Why Women's Issues Make a Difference

Pat Spallone

From the outset it must be acknowledged that many people come to the subject of reproductive technologies with particular expectations and priorities, and that it is a subject which touches on so many precious and complex beliefs and values – about motherhood, rationality, the sanctity of life; about paternity, sex, and the origins of humanity – that it is impossible in one chapter to address all of the concerns which it raises. Further, as a place where motherhood meets science, and where reproductive rights become a more challenging concept and reality, it can hardly be discussed without offending someone's sensibilities. I find myself bruising my own sensibilities at times.

This chapter focuses on developments in reproductive technology with which I have been particularly interested, and which I have chosen to discuss here because they help illustrate the importance of a gender-sensitive analysis of reproductive technologies. Rather than outline the organization of the chapter at this point, I do so after discussing some of the central terms and techniques which come under the umbrella of reproductive technology; this discussion is made in order to give a feel for the scope of the subject, and to raise some initial points which inform the rest of the chapter. I shall also in this chapter identify several strategies for research in feminist science studies which resonate with my concerns.

Terms

The term *new reproductive technologies* covers a whole range of techniques.[1] In the 1980s, the phrase became associated largely with *in vitro* fertilization (IVF) and human embryo research. In IVF, an egg from a woman and sperm from a man are fertilized in a laboratory dish. The resulting embryo is placed into the woman's womb, either the same woman from whom the egg came, or a different woman. To achieve egg removal, most women are given a regimen of fertility and hormonal drugs to regulate the menstrual cycle and stimulate the ovaries to produce many eggs during the cycle. *In vitro*, literally 'in glass', is a term of science used to denote biological processes which are made to occur outside the living organism and under laboratory conditions.

IVF defined the newness of the new reproductive technologies technologically and socially. Removing women's eggs is the prerequisite for many other new reproductive technologies such as human embryo research, genetic screening of embryos, and the prospect of gene therapy (genetic engineering) of human embryos. In these methods and their terminology, there is an element of technological innovation, but as well there is embedded in them a strong social element. For one, definitions of motherhood are changing. The certainty of biological motherhood no longer holds, because now that eggs can be removed from one woman and placed into another, the question arises, 'Who is the biological mother? The woman from whom the egg came, or the woman who gave birth?'

There are other innovations of reproductive technology which do not entail IVF, such as GIFT, *gamete intrafallopian transfer*, whereby an unfertilized egg and sperm are placed in the woman's fallopian tube, where hopefully fertilization will take place; *fetal therapy* which entails carrying out medical procedures on a fetus in the womb during pregnancy; and the *use of fetal tissues* for medical therapies to treat conditions such as Parkinson's disease. All of these may come under the term *new reproductive technology*. However, in another sense, these developments are not totally new, but a continuation of what has gone before. Thus reproductive technology has come to mean almost any modern technique of fertility or infertility control. It may include 'old' contraceptives such as birth control pills and relatively recent ones such as anti-pregnancy vaccines; the term might also include the use of various hormonal drugs for infertility treatment and for treating symptoms of menopause (hormone replacement therapy, HRT).

Many of the disciplines in science studies recognize the importance of definitions of terms and how the notion of science is used. Certainly, the terminology of reproductive technology raises similar considerations. The notion of *technology* here is neither straightforward nor self-explanatory. The term is doing a lot of hidden work, including projecting social meaning onto the methods. For instance, included in the term reproductive technology are two methods, donor insemination and surrogacy, which are arguably 'low-tech' and 'no tech' respectively. Neither requires advanced medical scientific knowledge and expertise as does IVF, so why the association with technology and what are the effects of it?

Insemination or donor insemination, formerly known as artificial insemination by donor, is the placing of sperm inside the woman's vagina as close to the cervix as possible, with the aim of achieving pregnancy. Insemination does not require medical or scientific knowledge, nor the kind of expertize which is associated with IVF or which is embodied in a contraceptive pill. A woman may, and some do, inseminate themselves, without the help of clinics or health professionals. (Others of course seek assistance, for a variety of reasons.) The common ground between insemination and IVF is that both are conception – getting pregnant – without sexual intercourse; this is a socially defined conflation. Insemination has been controversial because, among other things, it challenges a traditional norm about how babies are conceived. It was interesting to notice during the early controversy over IVF (between 1978 when the first baby was born from IVF conception into the early 1980s) that by associating insemination with IVF as non-coital reproduction, it became contained in its medical definition as infertility treatment as did IVF; and it came to be restricted under the same medical and legal authorities put in place to regulate and control IVF, a procedure which is much more complex and with a whole unique set of repercussions (such as the existence of frozen eggs and embryos). The language of technology here not only suggested the assisted nature of insemination but also allowed a measure of social control of the procedure. I am suggesting that the language of technology works in subtle ways. I shall return to the subject of words and their meaning in the second half of this chapter.

Similarly, surrogacy, whereby a woman bears a child for another person or couple, does not require expert medical or scientific expertize, at least when the woman who will bear the child becomes pregnant through sexual intercourse or insemination. This kind of surrogacy is not self-evidently medical, although it may be defined as such for infertility treatment. The recognition of the social possibilities of its use, and a wider practice of it (especially in the USA), occurred with development of IVF. Surrogacy became associated with new innovations in reproductive technology not because it is new nor a technological process, but because it challenged norms about the exclusivity of marriage and the relations between heterosexual couples as a family unit. The association of surrogacy with IVF is now firmly entrenched, as there is a variation of surrogacy which uses IVF, whereby the woman who will bear the child becomes pregnant with an IVF embryo, possibly from the couple who will receive the child. The boundaries between these other ways of getting pregnant are changing and blurring with time and development.

While the term reproductive technology may not seem the most appropriate anymore, all of the above considerations suggest that the meaning of technology in the term reproductive technology does not simply define the nature of the techniques involved; nor does it mean a particular category of expertize and knowledge. There is a strong element of social definition at play in the usage and meanings of technology. There is a strong element of a social norm at work in this term, including norms about where babies (naturally) come from, or at least the modern and twentieth-century view of where babies come from.

The methods I have been discussing as *new* sound rather old now, as each year witnesses further developments. In 1993 in Britain, much attention was paid to pre-conception sex selection due to the opening of the London Gender Clinic, a private concern which offered the technique for separating boy-producing sperm from girl-producing sperm. The procedure reportedly cost around £1000, and eligibility was limited to couples who already had a child. Success rates are known to be low. Eventually, the use of the procedure for non-medical reasons (that is, when there is no known risk of passing on a sex-linked heritable disease) was judged unacceptable by the British Medical Association and the Human Fertilisation and Embryology Authority (HFEA, 1993), the statutory body which oversees regulation of many of the new reproductive technologies, although it does not have jurisdiction over sperm separation procedures. More recently, reports of new developments include a US clinic's sales campaign in Britain to sell human eggs to couples seeking infertility treatment (Freedland, 1994); the real possibility of male pregnancy (Teresi, 1994); and a unique news report of a urologist who extracted sperm from a corpse of a man whose wife asked if it were possible, because she wanted to have the children they had been planning using her late husband's sperm (Freedland, 1995).

On Research Interests and Strategies

These developments raise a host of questions about maternity and paternity, sex stereotypes, the status of women, the changing profile of reproductive choice, questions such as 'what counts as medicine?', 'is being a boy or girl an illness?', or 'are children being seen as commodities?' These sorts of questions and the issues they raise are important, but they are not the subject of this chapter. Rather, I am going to address the question of how ideas and practices in reproductive technology have acquired power, and how they are gendered. This focus may at first seem a far cry from the immediately gripping issues and troubling ethical dilemmas which come to bear, but the themes which concern this chapter, I would argue, inform those very issues and dilemmas by helping us understand how and why certain issues are raised (or not raised), how decisions are made about them, and how science operates within these contexts.

This brings me to the title of this chapter, which is half serious and half tongue in cheek. I sometimes am asked to talk about important women's issues or feminist issues which are raised by reproductive technologies. My knee-jerk response is that all of the issues at stake are women's issues, the point being that women's issues are not reducible to a sub-set of concerns of a special interest group, such as feminists, or women seeking infertility treatment. There is no static set of women's issues, and those issues which have been addressed by feminist workers, researchers, ethicists and writers have emerged in particular times and places, that is, in a socio-cultural context; they are issues which relate to other aspects of societies in which women live and work.[2]

In saying this I do not intend to diminish the importance of taking gender seriously. Many of the issues which have been of interest to feminist researchers are responses to social and political circumstances such as women's experiences of infertility, and new kinds of regulation and control of reproductive practices which have repercussions for women. It is important to recognize women as subjects whose lives are different in many respects to men's. Much of my early work and interest, and that of others, focused on female fertility as an object of medical and scientific knowledge; this interest resonates with one of the research strategies within feminist studies: *How science has theorized female fertility.*

With the above thoughts in mind, the next section of this chapter illustrates some of the ways in which reproductive technologies look different when seen through the lens of gender, especially the recognition of women as creative human subjects of human procreation, that is, as the person who gets pregnant and gives birth. After that discussion, I relate in some detail an episode during the height of public controversy about new reproductive technologies, namely, the way in which a brand-new word, pre-embryo, was introduced into language as a means of redefining the embryo at the height of public controversy over developments in reproductive technology in Britain, a controversy which became focused on human embryo research to a great extent. The case of the pre-embryo illustrates among other things that natural facts do not speak for themselves; they are spoken for, by many different speakers, and who gets to do the speaking and be heard makes a difference. Both of these discussions illustrate wider research strategies. The first strategy concerns the status of scientific theories and ideas. I am concerned here with *embryology*, a division of research biological science. Embryology is the study of the developing embryo. Creating human embryos *in vitro* – outside the women's body and in a laboratory dish – is one important method by which contemporary embryologists study embryo development. Embryology is a research discipline, and embryo research is used to learn about physiological, biochemical and genetic mechanisms in order to advance knowledge. Brought to a clinical setting, human IVF and human embryo research have medical purposes, but after all human embryology is the study of pregnancy, of what goes on in women's bodies. Embryology is the study of female reproductive capacities. The second research strategy addresses how practices of science get into everyday life. By what mechanism is scientific authority established? The case study of the pre-embryo is a strong example of the way in which a controversial scientific innovation, human embryo research, came to be accepted rather than rejected.

Women as Subjects

By the early 1980s, IVF changed the course of obstetrics and gynaecology. It changed possibilities and conceptions of what is normal: that is, what boundaries could be traversed biologically and socially. For one, as I mentioned above, now that eggs can be removed from women, the question arises, 'Who is the biological mother, the woman who bears a child or the woman from whom the egg came?' In modern views of procreation, motherhood was a certainty; fatherhood was not. This is no longer the case.

Remarkably, this aspect of IVF innovation did not provoke the same level of attention as did others such as freezing eggs or embryos. For example, in the

Warnock Report, the influential report of the British Government's Committee of Inquiry on Human Fertilisation and Embryology (1984), there was little discussion of the matter, except to acknowledge that the question of legal motherhood was now open and that the committee considered that the woman who gives birth is the mother in law, no matter where the egg comes from. The opportunity to discuss the social relations of motherhood and its definitions was not recognized. The obvious death knell to the certainty of biological motherhood in modern times was not considered as important to ponder as, say, the morality of freezing embryos, another boundary-breaking innovation of reproductive technology but one which was given to much discussion in the report and elsewhere in the professional public debate. The lack of discussion of changing dimensions of biological motherhood, not to mention other kin relationships, does make some sense in the logic of the professional debates over reproductive technologies. The debate 'for' or 'against' developments so often reduced to disembodied eggs or embryos, hardly recognizing where human eggs and embryos come from and develop. The female role in human procreation was often either reduced, relegated to the margins of discussion, or left unrecognized. At other times, women's role and interests were acknowledged, but not wholly. Sarah Franklin (1993) argues that women's needs and desires were selectively represented in public and Parliamentary debates on assisted conception in Britain. In my own experience of bioethics meetings and work on this subject, women's identity in human reproduction was often called upon to support moral positions for or against medical and scientific perspectives on eggs and embryos, but hardly otherwise.

Let me give a particular example of the way in which female experience and identity was inadequately recognized. Human embryo research in the early 1980s was the most controversial development of new reproductive technologies, and it was also the linchpin of the scientific developments. Advocates of the science had to present a favourable case over and over again. An editorial arguing the need for human embryo research in the science journal *Nature* raised an often-used argument which equated removing a woman's eggs with procuring a man's sperm, saying, 'uneasiness that the ova [eggs] are obtained artificially by a relatively simple procedure is understandable but indefensibly irrational, given the widespread and apparently acceptable practice of artificial insemination with husband's sperm' (*Nature*, 1982).

The logic ignored the obviously different processes involved in procuring eggs and sperm. Sperm removal is usually a non-medical act. For the woman, removing eggs is always one. The logic also ignored the fact of the new question which arose with scientific capabilities, 'Who is the biological mother?' The logic reduced the female role to that of the male, gamete provider. Sperm provider, egg provider, what's the difference? The argument may be rational in a model of fertility which ignores everything else but the isolated act of fertilization, but if you recognize the different processes involved in getting to it, the logic is faulty.

I want to make clear two things. First, we cannot make too much of any one example, but the above quotation from *Nature* was not the only place where such arguments were made. In addition, you can see the fallout from this kind of thinking in so many reports from governments, working parties and ethical committees from the 1980s (see Spallone, 1989), and more recently in the report of the British Government's Committee on the Ethics of Gene Therapy Report (1992). The Clothier Report, as it is called, did not recognize that IVF is the precondition for gene therapy of embryos (to accomplish gene therapy on an embryo, the embryo must be located outside the woman's body). Never once in a report which was laying the foundation for a rationale of human gene therapy was it acknowledged that the innovation of embryo gene therapy expands the reasons why women might choose to get pregnant by IVF and what this entails; the issue was never recognized as part of the ethical discussion and assessment of the worth of embryo gene therapy.

Second, looking at the situation in a different way – as in the way I have suggested – does not mean that you necessarily get a different answer to the question, 'Is it acceptable to remove female eggs from ovaries and experiment on them?' than did the Warnock Report or the journal *Nature*. You might or might not, but you would be coming to the answer from a different place. This can make a difference to what counts as rational; what counts as a proper ethical perspective and what counts as good science.

The Pre-embryo

In 1985 at the height of controversy in Britain over human embryo research, a new term, *pre-embryo*, appeared to mean the human embryo from fertilization to 14 days later. The renaming of the early human embryo was at once an act of science and an act of politics, and so I shall track and analyse the appearance and use of the term in some detail to characterize the relationship between the two.[3]

A radical redefinition of the embryo was first offered to the public in April 1985 in the pages of a popular science weekly, *New Scientist*, by the president of the Royal Society, physiologist Sir Andrew Huxley. Sir Andrew did not speak of pre-embryos (the word had not yet been coined), but he did redefine the human embryo as it never had been defined before:

> Unfortunately, the public debate . . . is taking place against a back-ground of widespread ignorance about the earliest stages of develop-ment of the fertilised egg . . . This ignorance causes much confusion, which is made worse by an unfortunate ambiguity in the word 'em-bryo' . . . The ambiguity arises because the word 'embryo' is also used to denote the whole of the collection of cells formed by re-peated division of the fertilised egg during the first weeks or so,

although only a few per cent of these cells are destined to become the embryo proper; by far the greater number of them will turn into extra-embryonic tissue and ultimately into the structures that are discarded as the afterbirth ... The embryo proper is first recognisable at about the fifteenth day after fertilisation, when a specialised region of cells called the 'primitive streak' [the emergent spinal column] first appears. Before that stage, it cannot be said that a definitive embryo exists (Huxley, 1985).

The distinctions '*embryo*' (with inverted commas), *embryo proper* and *definitive embryo* had not been made before. Why now, and why this particular redefinition?

Promoters of the new definition emphasized that people were ignorant or confused about the scientific facts of embryology; there was a deficit of knowledge among the uninitiated. For example, there was one assumption that some people still thought of the embryo as a homunculus, a fully formed human being with hands and feet, and this was why these people found embryo research repugnant. Hence people needed technical information on which to base moral judgments about human embryo research. (On hindsight, this position might be called the deficit model of the 'public understanding of science', a phrase which is presently used in Britain to denote an area of concern to the scientific establishment among others.)

But the explanation offered hardly does justice to another fact, namely, that the new definition of the embryo coincided exactly with a 14-day time limit which was placed on human embryo research in 1984 by the Committee of Inquiry into Human Fertilisation and Embryology. The report of this committee, known as the Warnock Report after the chairperson philosopher Mary Warnock, recommended in 1984 that embryo research should be allowed, but only up to 14 days after fertilization. The new definition of the embryo conveniently reflected this demarcation line; and so did the new term *pre-embryo* which was soon to follow.

Although a redefinition of the embryo was perfectly in line with scientific knowledge, the idea of a 'beginning of an embryo' at the fifteenth day after fertilization was not inevitable from the facts. The 14-day limit on embryo research was only one of many options put forward by scientists. There was no consensus in the scientific community that the facts upheld a 14-day limit. There were other considered opinions. The Council for Science and Society (1984) recommended a six-week time limit, based on arguments about neural development and the assessment of when an embryo could feel pain. The Royal Society (1983) recommended a flexible or open-ended time limit. While in the state of Victoria, Australia, the government placed a 24-hour time limit on embryo research based on genetic arguments.

So why did the Warnock Committee decide on a 14-day limit? Mary Warnock explained in an interview,

I persuaded my colleagues not to use the criterion of the fetus feeling pain used by the British Medical Association because I was afraid some smart surgeon would come along and say, 'My embryo doesn't feel pain because I've anaesthetised it.' The genetic composition of the resulting child isn't determined for 14 days. Therefore you might say that continuity with your past begins at 14 days. This seems to me to be the important point, rather than when the embryo is alive (quoted in Dunn, 1984).

Thus the setting of a 14-day limit was in line with technical facts about embryos, but it also indicates that technical knowledge is mediated by social and cultural ideas (such as 'continuity with your past'). This was also the case for arguments put forward by scientists such as Huxley. In his explanation, the destiny of the majority of cells is seen to define the embryo, rather than the destiny of the small percentage which become the embryo proper. With the publication of the Warnock Report, there was no indication that anyone wanted to redefine the embryo. On the contrary, the scientific body which was eventually to initiate a redefinition – the Medical Research Council – seemed perfectly at ease with the old definition. They stated as much in their official response to the Warnock Report; they thought of the embryo as 'a viable conceptus developed from a fertilised egg' (Medical Research Council, 1985: 5). The point is that there was no indication that the Medical Research Council felt it necessary to redefine the embryo, nor did any other scientific spokespersons. This was soon to change. It changed because in Parliament, shortly after publication of the Warnock Report, MP Enoch Powell introduced a Private Members Bill banning all human embryo research. It was called the Unborn Children (Protection) Bill. It won a large majority after its second reading in February 1985. It was supported by the same mixture of political alliances which occur during Parliamentary proceedings on abortion: that is the objection to embryo research was made based on ideas and beliefs about the sanctity of life of the fertilized egg. The possibility that the Bill could actually win in a final vote was real. More than at any other time, ignorance among the uninitiated was perceived to be causing much misunderstanding about embryo research.

At this juncture, the redefinition of the embryo appears. The Medical Research Council's wish to redefine the embryo was first voiced in March 1985 (Clarke, 1985), and at the same time they announced the formation of a new regulatory body to oversee IVF and embryo research. The new body was called the Voluntary Licensing Authority. The Medical Research Council helped set it up, and handed over the task of redefining the embryo to it. A month after this announcement, the redefinition of the embryo by Huxley appeared in the *New Scientist*. Two months after that, in June 1985, a new term, *pre-embryo* appeared in a pamphlet of guidelines for clinicians and researchers from the Voluntary Licensing Authority.

After that, the term pre-embryo was promoted mostly for strategic purposes, that is, to enrol support for a controversial innovation, human embryo research. It was promoted most vigorously between 1985 and 1989, especially in *New Scientist*, as well as in various other magazines and journals, by a pro-research lobby group in Britain called Progress, and by various working parties and committees dealing with issues of regulation of research. The term was picked up and promoted in several other countries (see Spallone, 1995; 1996).

The need for technical information and for understanding of scientific concepts is certainly real, but there is something far more complex going on here, and it raises the question of how and where science may be used as a moral guide. Science was certainly used as a moral guide throughout the debate on human embryo research. The implicit message was that scientific facts help dispel cultural myths about embryos. But the pre-embryo had its own mythologies. Various embellishments were given to the explanation of the redefined embryo to the public. Two expanded explanations, for example, reflected on the meaning of maternity. These were both by women, and it is perhaps not surprising that female commentators would rightly wish to make connections to women's experience of pregnancy explicitly and concretely. One of these explanations appeared in a newspaper article by a journalist who specializes in women's issues; she located the 'life of the pre-embryo' as roughly 'between around day 14 of a woman's cycle and the date she misses her first period' (Ironside, 1985). The other was an explanatory note prepared by Dr Penelope Leach, a well-known writer and psychologist, which appeared as an annex in the first report of the Voluntary Licensing Authority (1986). It described the development of the early embryo in similar terms to Huxley's, and it too stressed that only very new scientific knowledge has brought us to this understanding, but it is particularly interesting on its unique commentary on pregnancy. Leach not only located the beginning of an embryo, but the beginning of a baby and pregnancy as well. She wrote, 'common parlance terms the moment of fertilisation "conception", calls a woman who has conceived "pregnant" and defines pregnancy as "carrying a baby". This is a vitally important over-simplification . . . fertilisation does not start an individual baby but merely sets in motion a train of events which can lead to such a beginning' (Voluntary Licensing Authority, 1986: 39). Pregnancy only begins, then, when the cells of the fertilized egg (pre-embryo) begin to differentiate into different sorts of specialized cells.

These examples begin to suggest that far from being neutral, the conceptual framework which privileges scientific findings over other kinds of understandings of pregnancy makes demands on women's relationships to pregnancy. The examples also illustrate that if you simply add women to the picture, you do not necessarily do justice to women's identity and role in human procreation, or widen understanding. Moreover, the Leach explanation especially shows how science can create its own mythologies of reproduction while at the same time relying on already existing cultural ideas about embryos and pregnancy. Why interpret the technical events of embryo development to say that pregnancy begins with differentiation of cells? Is this not a new mythology or at least a judgment beyond the scope of scientific fact? Why accept in scientific explanations the common idea that pregnancy begins when the embryo begins, rather than assume that pregnancy begins at some other stage? This is what I mean in saying that far from dispelling cultural myths, science both creates and relies on cultural ideas. The point is not that it is wrong, but that this is the way science operates, and it is difficult to imagine how it could operate otherwise. Scientific knowledge does not exist in a vacuum but in a culture and society. The situation challenges the assumption that scientific facts are uncluttered by cultural values, and that they therefore provide superior objective knowledge about embryos which can be used as a moral guide.

Although the word pre-embryo was used in the late 1980s by many different speakers in many different forums, the term was not universally accepted by medical and scientific spokespersons in Britain. The *British Medical Journal* did not use the word in their promotion of human embryo research. The journal *Nature* eventually dropped it, calling the usage a 'cop-out, a way of pretending that the public conflict about IVF and other innovations in human embryology can be made to go away by means of an appropriate nomenclature' (*Nature*, 1987: 87). Yet, in 1989, the term was listed for the first time in *Henderson's Dictionary of Biological Terms* 10th edition: 'pre-embryo (n.) in mammals name sometimes given to the fertilised ovum and its cleavage stages up to blastocyst formation and the specification of the cells of the inner cell mass that will develop into the embryo proper.' Thus, a word coined to mean human embryos in specific circumstances now appeared as a technical term for the whole of the mammalian community. It became a natural fact. The social circumstances of its coinage were erased.

The new word, pre-embryo, and its new definition, defined the embryo of embryo research. Yet it is clearly not simply a product of scientific utility. It is a construct which was aimed at the 'the public understanding of science' in order to make an impact on the debate on human embryo research. Having said that, I am not implying that the coining of the term was a cynical act. It was promoted by people devoted to the idea of imparting knowledge, as well as fighting a political battle. I am interested here in the double process. The coining of pre-embryo was an astute (conscious) political move; but it also reflects the more subtle (unconscious?) processes. I shall discuss each of these in succession.

First, the coining of the pre-embryo was an astute, conscious, political manoeuvre in the face of powerful anti-research forces. David Davies, a former editor of *Nature*, wrote,

> If research on embryos were an uncontentious matter, and if scientists were generally of the opinion that the new terminology helped their understanding, nobody would have many qualms at the name change. But those who are introducing 'pre-embryo' into the vocabu-

lary know full well that the research is indeed contentious and that fundamental issues have yet to be resolved. They complain, with justification, when embryos are described as 'unborn children' in hostile parliamentary bills, but they are themselves manipulating words to polarise an ethical discussion (Davies, 1986: 208).

The polarization of the debate is an important point, and it illustrates the general point that the terms of science have become polarized between fear and glamour: science as our enemy or our salvation; science as bad or science as good. Such a polarization in the debate on new reproductive technologies left little room to actually talk about developments in ways which recognized their complexity, such as the complicated nature of informed consent and choice, or issues important to women's health or motherhood. It might be concluded that this situation was the unfortunate consequence of the power of the anti-research Parliamentary lobby. While the lobby certainly was a strong factor, there were other political forces which shaped the terms of the debate over embryo research.

This brings me to the second point, that the pre-embryo does not simply represent a conscious political act. There is also something far more subtle at work. A theoretical insight may help here: we are socialized into an essentialist way of thinking, scientism, which privileges objects and events over relationships and processes. The insight helps explain why the formation of the primitive streak at around the fifteenth day after fertilization had a life of its own after it was named as a significant event of embryo development. Once the fact of it, and its interpretation, were accepted, its politics could be wilfully ignored.

Let me reiterate in a different way. The pre-embryo was accepted among those who used the term as if it has a self-evident power: the scientific facts stand up for it. But the scientific facts of embryology do not have self-evident power. Rather they were empowered, last but not least by the Warnock Committee which recommended that the Government set a 14-day limit on human embryo research. If the Committee had decided on, say, a 6-week limit as recommended by the Council for Science and Society, then the redefinition of the embryo would not have occurred, or it would have looked very different. The argument coming from promoters of the term pre-embryo was that it clarified issues. But rather than clarify the issues, the term pre-embryo obscured them. It obscured the history of the decision about the 14-day limit. It made it appear to those unfamiliar with the history *or* the science that the decision was inevitable, as if embryos have never really existed until 14 days after fertilization.

Did the coining of the term pre-embryo succeed? In one very concrete sense, it certainly did. Evidence of this comes from Michael Mulkay's work on the Parliamentary debates on embryo research. Although the pre-embryo was never used universally, it did work to change the minds of many Parliamentarians who had previously opposed the research. By 1989, when it came to the vote, a majority of Parliamentarians voted in favour of embryo research in conjunction with the Government's Human Fertilisation and Embryology Bill (Mulkay, 1994). The pre-embryo was meant to enrol support for a contested innovation, human embryo research, and it did.

The power of the pre-embryo was that it allowed that nothing need change ideologically while great changes were underfoot. Society could have its embryo, and all that that means, while science could experiment on early embryos by calling them pre-embryos. I implied at the beginning of this chapter that women and science is an expansive area of inquiry, and the direction my work took in regards to the pre-embryo is an example of what I meant. My earliest concern with the term was its emergence as an act of politics rather than an act of good science; and the ways in which it allowed the ancient and problematic dichotomy of woman/embryo to remain. Then it became necessary to address the pre-embryo as an act of good science too (where by *good science* I mean that the scientific facts or findings in embryo development reliably fit the new definition even if value judgments are made about the meaning of those findings).

The episode of the pre-embryo might end here, but there is much that the story standing alone cannot show. At this point, I would like to reflect further on its implications in regards to human relationships and human knowledge. I mentioned earlier that there was a perception among some advocates of human embryo research that many people 'out there' (the uninitiated public) thought of the embryo as a fully-formed human being. There was no recognition of the worth of other kinds of thinking about fertilized eggs and embryos, except to say that they were opinions, not knowledge, about embryos. By contrast, a study done by social anthropologist Jeanette Edwards (1993) suggests otherwise, providing a counterpoise to the pre-embryo, its assumptions, and the misplaced role of science as a moral guide.

Jeanette Edward interviewed people in a town in the north-west of England, which she calls Alltown, about their concerns. They articulated in depth concerns and ideas about eggs, sperm and embryos in terms of (among other things) the new family relationships and relatedness which were implicated: Who is responsible for the resulting child of a frozen embryo? What is the relationship of donors of gametes to resulting child? The study showed that far from being ignorant, people were expert about changes in kinship which were implicated, although it is important to add that there was no one opinion or perspective expressed. Edwards concluded that the people whom she interviewed had a 'relational view of human existence' (Edwards, 1993: 11).

When this relational view of human existence is compared to the professional discussion about the social and ethical implications of new reproductive technologies – where embryos and pre-embryos were being played out – a contradiction is outstanding. The pre-embryo of embryology is related to no one. In this sense, the promotion of the pre-embryo may be seen as a process of objectifying embryos, whereas the people in Alltown were subjectifying them. Jeanette Edwards concluded,

People interpret what they see as the implications of new reproductive technologies not through what they know of the techniques and philosophies of reproductive medicine, but through what they know about the practice and predictabilities of kinship. They do not, in other words, have to be technologically literate in the methods of new reproductive technologies in order to think about the implications of certain reproductive possibilities for the social relationships they create and/or influence. The Alltown people whose views are presented here ground their ideas about new reproductive technologies in what they already know and, indeed, in what they are expert at (Edwards, 1993: 63).

The comparison helps show that no terms in this discussion are free of ambiguity, not because we do not understand embryology well enough, but because the subject is complicated. A term such as embryo is ambiguous because it has multiple meanings and values. This is not a matter of some people having one viewpoint and others having a different one. The terms themselves have multiple meanings for each of us (including embryologists). It is true that we need to understand scientific findings, information and knowledge. The problem in the deficit model of the public understanding of science of the pre-embryo is that we actually do not get to understand the complexity of the information very well. The *in vitro* human embryo is a work of both science and culture: the embryo has a material reality and material conditions of living but it is far more than that. An important question is, 'why the particular conjunction of meanings which have emerged?', as not all ideas about embryos (not to mention women's experience of fertility and having babies) are equally powerful.

These aspects of new reproductive technologies have epistemological implications, policy implications and personal ones, for our everyday relationships to ourselves and having babies, for our relationships to ourselves as both objects and subjects of natural knowledge, for the public understanding of science, for the scientific understanding of the public, and for what gets counted as an ethical issue. This is what I meant when I said at the beginning of this chapter that the immediate ethical and political questions which come to bear in reproductive technology can be informed by analysing how ideas and practices of reproduction acquire power. Tracking the emergence and use of the pre-embryo in particular suggests that *the technical* and *the social* are not wholly separable, and that to treat them as such in making decisions about regulation and control of technologies is a political choice, not a necessity. The attempt to keep separate the technical and social or moral aspects of individual practices such as IVF, insemination, surrogacy, the use of fetal tissue for transplants, and so on, is precisely the problem because it allows the wider social practices (scientific theorizing and research, clinical practices, social regulation of reproduction and other medicalized practices) to be understood and developed in restricted, sometimes oppressive ways. Thus my reference at the beginning of this chapter that 'women and science' is an expansive area of inquiry, whose agenda includes informing the operation of science in society and society in science.

Notes

1 The utility of the term reproductive technology is itself open to debate. See McNeil, 1993 and Spallone, 1994: 62. It might be helpful to add here that many of the discussions in this chapter are shortened versions of previously published work (Spallone, 1989; 1994; 1995; 1996), but I have taken the opportunity here to expand on some points and to make some new ones.
2 I am indebted to Lewin and Olesen (1985: 6) for their discussion of the nature of women's health issues. Their articulation rings true for my subject area of women and science as well.
3 My discussion of the pre-embryo in this chapter is a shortened version of one which appears in Spallone, 1996, although, as I stated above, I have taken the opportunity of this chapter to think in some different directions.

References

Reports

Committee of Inquiry on Human Fertilisation and Embryology Report (Warnock Report) (1984) London, HMSO.
Committee on the Ethics of Gene Therapy Report (The Clothier Report) (1992) London, HMSO.
COUNCIL FOR SCIENCE AND SOCIETY (1984) *Human Procreation*, London.
MEDICAL RESEARCH COUNCIL (1985) *Report of Inquiry on Human Fertilisation and Embryology*, Medical Research Council Response, London.
VOLUNTARY LICENSING AUTHORITY FOR HUMAN IN VITRO FERTILISATION AND EMBRYOLOGY (1985) *Guidelines for Both Clinical and Research Applications of Human In Vitro Fertilisation*, London.
VOLUNTARY LICENSING AUTHORITY FOR HUMAN IN VITRO FERTILISATION AND EMBRYOLOGY (1986) *The First Report of the Voluntary Licensing Authority For Human In Vitro Fertilisation and Embryology*, London.
THE ROYAL SOCIETY (1983) *Human Fertilisation and Embryology*, submission to the Department of Health and Social Security Committee of Inquiry, London.

Books and other Texts

CLARKE, M. (1985) 'Voluntary authority set up', *Nature*, **314**, p. 397.
DAVIES, D. (correspondence to the editor) (1986) *Nature*, **320**, p. 208.

DUNN, E. (1984) 'Meddling with the conception', *The Sunday Times* (London), 25 November.

EDWARDS, J. (1993) 'Explicit connections: Ethnographic enquiry in north-west England', in EDWARDS, J., FRANKLIN, S., HIRSCH, E., PRICE, F. and STRATHERN, M. (Eds) *Technologies of Procreation: Kinship in the Age of Assisted Conception*, Manchester and New York: Manchester University Press.

FRANKLIN, S. (1993) 'Making representations: The parliamentary debate on the Human Fertilisation and Embryology Act', in EDWARDS, J. *et al.*, *Technologies of Procreation: Kinship in the Age of Assisted Conception*, Manchester and New York, Manchester University Press.

FREEDLAND, J. (1994) 'US clinic's sales campaign for human eggs "foundering"', *The Guardian* (London), 25 August.

FREEDLAND, J. (1995) 'Sperm extracted from corpse in world first', *The Guardian* (London), 21 January.

Henderson's Dictionary of Biological Terms (1989) 10th edition, London, Longman Scientific, pp. 426–7.

HFEA (HUMAN FERTILISATION AND EMBRYOLOGY AUTHORITY) (1993) Press Release, 20 July.

HUXLEY, A. (1985) 'Research and the embryo', *New Scientist*, 11 April, p. 2.

IRONSIDE, V. (1985) 'How to breed healthy babies', *The Guardian* (London), November 18.

LEWIN, E. and OLESEN, V. (Eds) (1985) *Women, Health and Healing: Toward a New Perspective*, London, Tavistock.

McNEIL, M. (1993) 'New reproductive technologies: Dreams and broken promises', *Science as Culture*, **3**, 17, pp. 483–506.

MULKAY, M. (1994) 'Changing minds about embryo research', *Public Understanding of Science*, **3**, pp. 195–213.

Nature (1982) 'The future of the test-tube baby', *299*, p. 475.

Nature (1987) 'IVF remains in legal limbo', *327*, p. 87.

SPALLONE, P. (1989) *Beyond Conception: The New Politics of Reproduction*, London, Macmillan, Massachusetts, Bergin and Garvey.

SPALLONE, P. (1994) 'Reproductive health and reproductive technology', in WILKINSON, S. and KITZINGER, C. (Eds) *Women and Health: Feminist Perspectives*, London, Taylor & Francis.

SPALLONE, P. (1995) 'Bad conscience and collective unconscious: Science, discourse and the new reproductive technologies', in ROSENBECK, B. and SCHOTT, R. (Eds) *Forplantning, Køn øg Teknologi*, Copenhagen, Museum Tusculanums Forlag.

SPALLONE, P. (1996) 'The salutary tale of the pre-embryo', in LYKKE, N. and BRAIDOTTI, R. (Eds) *Between Monsters, Goddesses and Cyborgs: Feminist Confrontations with Science, Medicine and Cyberspace*, London, Zed Press.

TERESI, D. (1994) 'Your father's having a baby', *The Observer (London) Life Magazine*, 11 December, p. 91.

Chapter 9

Reproductive Technologies and Lesbian Parents: An Unnatural Alliance?

Elizabeth Sourbut

Introduction

This chapter explores the borderlands between 'natural' and 'unnatural' forms of procreation. Advances in techniques of assisted reproduction over the past three decades have provided new challenges to the traditional equation of marriage, heterosexual sex and procreation. Legislation has been introduced, fertility clinics offer their services to limited sections of the population, and debates about family values are prominent in political manoeuvrings. Lesbian parents are marginalized within all of these discourses, even though (or perhaps because) lesbians who wish to have children without heterosexual sex have to use some form of assisted reproduction in order to do so.

My central argument is that procreation is a culturally constructed activity, but that part of the construction is to view it as a *natural* process. Conception, pregnancy, birth and childcare are all viewed as private matters, ideally situated within the confines of a heterosexual nuclear family (Warnock, 1984). Although, in the late twentieth century, such families are increasingly rare, nevertheless the *ideal* is still a powerful force in political debate and in the formulation of social policy.

Reproductive technologies cause problems because they bring procreation out of the private domain of the family and into the public world of laboratories and hospitals. New and difficult questions are raised; new parenting arrangements become possible, challenging the status quo. Arguments that certain forms of procreation – such as in vitro fertilization (IVF), or lesbian parents using donor insemination (DI) – are unnatural become difficult to sustain in a world where, increasingly, all pregnancies are monitored and medical intervention has become routine. This is not an argument for the indiscriminate use of reproductive technologies, but it does suggest that the terms of the debate must change, and the reasons for allowing or discouraging certain forms of assisted reproduction must be re-evaluated.

Reproductive technologies hold out interesting possibilities for lesbians, and for all women. In my exploration of the borderlands between natural and unnatural, human and machine, reality and fiction, I will look at an as yet theoretical example of technological intervention – gynogenesis (Edwards, 1990). Gynogenesis is the technique of fusing two ova to form a female embryo with two biological mothers and no father. I stress that as yet this is not a practical reality, and it may never become so. Nevertheless, as an idea it challenges preconceptions about who can benefit from reproductive technologies, and who has power and control.

I do not wish to ignore the dangers inherent in these technologies, which have been explored by many feminist writers (see Arditti, Klein and Minden, 1984; Corea, 1988; Spallone, 1989). Ideas of what is natural and unnatural are deep-seated and will be difficult to change. Within the current paradigm, women have a great deal to lose. However, I suggest that there are also possibilities, especially for lesbians.

I begin by looking at current debates around the family in relation to reproductive technologies, and the attempts which have been made to contain these new technologies within the framework of the traditional heterosexual nuclear family.

Then I move on to look at Carole Pateman's discussion of the sexual contract in liberal political theory in order to explore the question of why, in a society which values individualism so highly, the family should hold such a key ideological place. I then briefly consider five science fiction novels which offer alternative visions of childbirth and family groupings. In conclusion, I look at Donna Haraway's metaphor of the cyborg, and my own metaphor of gynogenesis, to explore possible alternative social groupings within our own present reality, and alternative ways of viewing procreation which transcend the natural/unnatural dichotomy.

Reproductive Technologies and the Family

There are several reasons for beginning with a discussion of the debates around the family in relation to reproductive technologies. First, these debates highlight the ways in which the heterosexual nuclear family has been naturalized. Reproductive technologies are seen as artificial and as creating artificial families (Warnock, 1985). But not all the methods grouped under the umbrella term *reproductive technologies* are new, or technology based. In particular, alternative insemination is included in most discussions of reproductive technologies, even though the method has been known for centuries, and is very simple. So-called *surrogate motherhood*, in which a woman contracts to bear a child for someone else, is also not necessarily technology based. A consideration of the reasoning behind which procedures are included in official debates reveals attempts on the part of the state and the scientific/medical establishment to police women's reproductive capacities (Spallone, 1989: 155–6).

Second, lesbians who wish to start families outside of heterosexual relationships (as opposed to those who have children from previous relationships with men) generally use donor insemination through a clinic or self insemination. They are, therefore, affected by legislation regulating these technologies and by public opinion relating to them.

Third, the theoretical possibility of gynogenesis, the conception of children with two genetic mothers and no genetic father, would involve most of the available techniques in reproductive medicine. Official attitudes towards what is and is not acceptable intervention, and the reasoning behind those decisions, is highly relevant to this discussion. Fourth, debates around natural and unnatural families are relevant to the families of lesbians even where alternative insemination has not been used. The use of reproductive technologies to strengthen the patriarchal institution of the heterosexual nuclear family is of relevance to everyone seeking to experiment with alternative family forms.

Since the birth of Louise Brown, the world's first test-tube baby, in 1978, reproductive technologies have been highly visible. The public sphere activities of technology and politics have become entangled with the quintessentially private activities of sexuality and reproduction. This has led to considerable concern over the ethics and social consequences of the applications of these technologies. As Maureen McNeil writes:

Some of the concern about the new reproductive technologies undoubtedly results from the prospect of technologies impinging on what have been regarded as very private domains. Heterosexual intercourse is 'private' in three ways: sexually, in its connections with procreation, and with ownership (patriarchal property rights) (McNeil, 1990: 9).

Marriage, heterosexuality and procreation no longer come in one neat package. Reproductive technologies have opened up all kinds of possibilities for variations in relationships between biological and social parents and the children conceived through use of these technologies. Official responses have centred on two sets of issues: those relating to the technologies themselves: success rates, risks to the foetus, etc; and ethical issues around the extent to which it is appropriate to interfere with the natural processes of procreation.

Reproductive technologies were developed within a particular political and social milieu, and the techniques reflect a particular view of the world. They have remained largely within a medical discourse and are presented as treatments for infertility. Debate around these technologies has been structured within official studies and reports, and regulations have been developed within a medical context. What aspects of the family are being defended by official bodies when they put forward recommendations about applications of reproductive technologies?

In 1982, Dame Mary Warnock, now Baroness Warnock, chaired a government inquiry into the new reproductive technologies. The findings of the committee were published in 1984 in a document entitled: *Report of the Committee of Inquiry into Human Fertilisation and Embryology* (Warnock, 1984), generally referred to as the Warnock Report.

The Committee was established 'to examine the social, ethical and legal implications of recent, and potential developments in the field of human assisted reproduction' (Warnock, 1984: iv). The members of the committee were drawn from a wide range of backgrounds, as were those who gave evidence, and their feelings about the issues raised were diverse:

> Some members have a clear perception of the family and its role within society; in considering the various techniques before us their focus has been on the primacy of the interests of the child, and on upholding family values. Other members have felt equally strongly about the rights of the individual within society (Warnock, 1984: 1).

These groupings of the rights of the child, family values and the rights of the individual are not as inclusive as they may seem. The individual is defined in masculine terms (see the next section), and the interests of women as *women* do not appear at all in the Report. The Committee considered the issues in two ways: first as methods of alleviating infertility, and second as the pursuit of knowledge 'designed to benefit society at large' (Warnock, 1984: 5).

The Report states that 'infertility is a condition meriting treatment' (Warnock, 1984: 10). Indeed, because of the way it is presented, without this conclusion there would be no need for a report at all. The terms of the debate are primarily a discussion as to how far technological intervention into infertility can go before it begins to weaken social and familial ties. The question of reproductive choice, of separating out marriage, sexuality and procreation is never addressed. I suggest that such outcomes are exactly the possibilities against which the Report aims to set barriers and raise limits (Warnock, 1984: 2).

The Report discusses treatment for infertility in terms of couples, who are taken to be 'a heterosexual couple living together in a stable relationship, whether married or not' (Warnock, 1984: 19). The Committee considered representations from lesbian, gay and single parent groups, but stated: 'we believe that as a general rule it is better for children to be born into a two-parent family, with both father and mother' (Warnock, 1984: 11). No reasons are given for this preference.

In general terms, infertility treatment is recommended to be undertaken with the supervision of a registered medical practitioner; anonymity should be maintained between the donors of eggs, sperm, embryos or wombs (surrogate mothers) and the receiving couple; counselling should be available; and no treatment should take place without fully informed consent of all the parties involved.

Regulation is an important recurring theme in the Report. Even in the case of artificial insemination by husband (AIH), which the Report acknowledges is a very simple procedure, and which involves no donation from a third party, the recommendation is made that a medical practitioner performs or supervises the procedure. There is no good medical reason for this recommendation.

Legal recommendations around the provision of artificial insemination by donor (AID), in vitro fertilization (IVF), egg and embryo donation, and surrogacy are aimed at maintaining nuclear family structures and the primacy of the relationship between husband and wife. Concern is expressed at the stigma of illegitimacy which may attach to a child. This problem no longer applies, as the Children Act of 1989 abolishes illegitimacy as a legal concept (Saffron, 1994: 144–5). The other major concern is to amend legislation to establish the husband and wife as legal parents of children conceived through the use of reproductive technologies.

In an article written in 1985, Mary Warnock expands upon her own views of the topics covered by the Warnock Report. She takes as her baseline 'the accepted norm of the family, as depicted in the cornflakes advertisements. Such families consist of mother, father, and children who are genetically related to both parents, and who were conceived in the usual way, by sexual intercourse' (Warnock, 1985: 138). She could add, although she does not, that the cornflakes family is white and middle-class and without apparent disabilities. She repeats this appeal to generalized ideas which 'most people' have about the family later in the paper: '[P]eople . . . think of the family as mother, father, and children, all genetically bound to one another, as well as to aunts, uncles, and grandparents. They are aware that there are many other patterns of family life . . . but they still regard the traditional family as ideal' (Warnock, 1985: 149).

In considering AID, IVF and surrogate motherhood, Warnock's ethical concerns spring principally from the degree to which the traditional family form is usurped, rather than from the degree of technological intervention into the mother's reproductive cycles. IVF is considered, on the whole, to be unproblematic, despite the need for surgical and hormonal intervention, when the child is genetically related to both parents. Intrusion by the medical practitioner into the marital relationship is not perceived; in fact in the Warnock Report such intrusion is recommended, even in the case of AH, as described above. AID, on the other hand, although physically non-invasive, is considered problematic, 'a third figure, (albeit a shadowy and anonymous figure) has been introduced into what ought to be the two-person relation of marriage . . .' (Warnock, 1985: 143). The logic which perceives the donation of sperm as more invasive than repeated uses of the laparoscope, the speculum and the surgeon's knife stands in need of explanation. Just what is being invaded? The marital relation, it seems, is more sacrosanct than the wife's body.

Erica Haimes (1990) suggests that the Warnock Report divides up available reproductive technologies into three groups:

1 'Simple cases', where the wife's and the husband's gametes are used to conceive a child with technological assistance. These cases are considered quite acceptable.

2 Applications of the technologies which involve donors to enable stable heterosexual couples to conceive. 'Ultimately, the form is acceptable, it is argued, because it represents the opportunity for couples to have a family, at least partly genetically related' (Haimes, 1990: 163).

3 Applications which are technically possible, but considered socially undesirable, such as surrogacy and assisted conception for single parents.

Haimes comments that, 'it is evident that there are different elements which make up the notion of "the family" as it is being used here. These apparently have different degrees of importance in relation to each other' (Haimes, 1990: 163). She identifies three elements: *the ideological component*, which polices the inherent worth of families and the values they display; *the structural dimension*, of two parent, plus children; and *genetic composition*, the children being related to both parents. A 'normal family' is posited with reference to these elements, and 'artificial families' (Warnock, 1985) are evaluated according to how closely they resemble this 'normal family'.

Haimes further argues that the ideological component is most important, closely followed by the structural component. Questions of genetic relatedness are not considered unless the ideological and structural components are uncontentious.

So how has this ideological construction of the family come about, and why is it so central to official views of the stability of society as a whole? In an attempt to find an answer, I turn to liberal political theory, and the story of the social contract.

Liberal Political Theory

Liberal political theory posits that *'all men are by nature free and equal'* (Lessnoff, 1990: 3, italics in original). This replaces older notions of status, where people are born into their place in the world, and kings rule by divine right. Under liberal theory, government is justifiable only if those who are to be governed consent to the authority of the ruler. Political theorists have to explain why an individual would consent to a restriction on his freedom. Classic theorists constructed an origins story in which civil society is brought into being by an original contract. Before the contract was made, people lived in a state of nature in which there was no law, or only natural law, or in some accounts the law of the patriarchal father. The social contract was made between free and equal individuals who agreed to live together peacefully under a chosen ruler. The rule of the father, by right of his procreative powers, was overthrown. In metaphorical terms, the sons slew their father and shared his power amongst themselves.

There have been many feminist critiques of contract theory, one of the earliest being Mary Wollstonecraft's *A Vindication of the Rights of Woman* (1792, 1992[1]). More recently, writers such as Jean Bethke Elshtain (1981),

Anne Phillips (1993) and Iris Marion Young (1990) have brought a variety of perspectives to questions of women's position within liberal democracy. However, I will be focusing here on Carole Pateman's book *The sexual contract* (1988).

Pateman argues that modern theorists tell only half the story. 'We hear an enormous amount about the *social* contract; a deep silence is maintained about the *sexual* contract' (Pateman, 1988: 1, italics in original). Pateman argues that in the story of the social contract *men* means exactly what it says. Women were not born free. Women in fact are the subject of the social contract, which is partly about orderly sexual access for all men to women. Women are not seen as having the attributes of individuals, and did not take part in the original contract. The free and equal individuals living in the state of nature were in fact male heads of households. Families already existed, and are seen as non-political institutions. According to Pateman, the sexual contract – by which she means a heterosexual contract – preceded the social contract.

The term *civil society* is ambiguous. Where it is contrasted with the state of nature, it refers to the whole of the modern, contractual state. But this state is divided into two spheres, the public and the private, and civil society is also used to mean just the public sphere.

> The civil sphere gains its universal meaning in opposition to the private sphere of natural subjection and womanly capacities. The 'civil individual' is constituted within the sexual division of social life created through the original contract. The civil individual and the public realm appear universal only in relation to and in opposition to the private sphere, the *natural* foundation of civil life. Similarly, the meaning of civil liberty and equality, secured and distributed impartially to all 'individuals' through the civil law, can be understood only in opposition to *natural* subjection (of women) in the private sphere (Pateman, 1988: 113–4, my italics).

Liberal society is still patriarchal, but not in the classical sense of the term. The original, literal, meaning of the word is the power of the father, and in the seventeenth century the monarch was seen as being a father to his people; his power was legitimated through this familial analogy. Pateman argues that: 'Modern patriarchy is fraternal, contractual, and structures capitalist civil society' (1988: 25). That is, modern patriarchy is based on the rights of men as men, and as husbands over their wives. 'The "individual" is a man who makes use of a woman's body (sexual property)' (Pateman, 1988: 185).

So the individual of liberal theory is by definition masculine, the head of a family and able to exercise sex-right over women. He is free and able to enter into contracts with other individuals. He is also an owner, owning in John Locke's words, 'property in his own person': 'Though the Earth, and all inferior creatures be common to all Men, yet every Man has a *Property* in his own *Person*. This no Body has any Right to but himself. The *Labour* of his Body, and the *Work* of his hands, we may say, are properly his (Locke, 1690, 1967: 305–6, italics in original).

Property in the person implies that a man stands in the same external relation to his body and abilities as he does to his material property. The individual is seen as existing prior to relationships with others, and his capacities and attributes owe nothing to anyone else, they are his alone. Individuals will only enter into relationships if they can ensure the safety of their property in doing so. By entering into contracts, the two parties recognize each other as equals and as property owners. They exchange use of their property for mutual gain. In the case of exchanges of property in the person, contracts involve an exchange of obedience for protection (Pateman, 1988: 58–9).

Many feminists have argued that women do possess property in their own persons, in the same way as men. But Pateman claims that in doing so, they are accepting the patriarchal concept of the individual. Property in the person is a political fiction. People are related internally to their bodies and abilities, not externally. We are all engaged in non-contractual relationships with others, and our attributes and abilities grow and develop over time, in large part due to our reciprocal ties with others. The individual with his impermeable boundaries is also a political fiction, and this becomes apparent when trying to fit women into the mould:

> The body of the 'individual' is very different from women's bodies. His body is tightly enclosed within boundaries, but women's bodies are permeable, their contours change shape and they are subject to cyclical processes. All these differences are summed up in the natural bodily process of birth. Physical birth symbolises everything that makes women incapable of entering the original contract and transforming themselves into civil individuals who uphold its terms (Pateman, 1988: 96).

If we accept property in the person as a concept, and simply try to extend it to women, we cannot fully understand the difficulties around three contracts specifically involving women *as women*. These three contracts are: the marriage contract, the prostitution contract and the surrogacy contract. The last two are seen as forms of the employment contract, but they are very specific forms.

In each of these contracts, men are contracting for the specific use of women's bodies and sexual or reproductive capacities. Of particular relevance here is the surrogacy contract, which concerns women's right to contract out the use of their wombs to create children for somebody else. Pateman sees surrogacy as a new form of access to and use of women's bodies by men. It highlights the contradictions for women in the connected liberal ideas of property in the person inhering in a masculine individual masquerading as universal:

A woman can be a 'surrogate' mother only because her womanhood is deemed irrelevant and she is declared an 'individual' performing a service. At the same time, she can be a 'surrogate' mother only because she is a *woman*. Similarly, the relevant property of the man in the surrogacy contract can only be that of a *man*; it is the property that can make him a father (Pateman, 1988: 217, italics in original).

Feminists writing critical analyses of reproductive technologies have argued that the idea that we own our body parts opens the way to exploitation of women's bodies by medical researchers. In contrast, the women's health movement has insisted that we do not own our bodies, we *are* our bodies (Spallone, 1989: 177–8).

This is the background to the ideologies of the family and the state which stand in the way of women becoming full citizens. But women are not passive victims of such ideologies. The rest of this chapter focuses on one dissident group – lesbian parents – who are challenging notions of women's dependence on men. Lesbians are bearing children and creating families in our own right and for our own pleasure. In doing so, we face tremendous opposition. We are challenging the patriarchal basis of the family, and making our own choices about what to do with our bodies and our reproductive capacities.

Science Fiction, Utopias and Reproduction

In this section, I move into the realm of fiction to look at five feminist science fiction novels, four of them also classified as utopias. They are of interest here because they offer a fictional form of opposition to the status quo. In particular, they focus upon kinship structures and the relationships between family life and the wider life of the community. All of the novels look at reproduction, imagining ways of conceiving children which challenge our ideas of what is natural and unnatural and where the boundaries might lie between human, animal and machine.

In 1970, Shulamith Firestone wrote about the problems in creating a feminist revolution. 'I am aware of the political dangers in the peculiar failure of imagination concerning alternatives to the family . . . we haven't even a literary image of this future society; there is not even a *utopian* feminist literature yet in existence (Firestone, 1970, 1979: 211; italics in original).

The feminist utopian literature began to appear soon afterwards, inspired, at least in part, by Firestone's book (Lefanu, 1988: 57). These novels reflect a range of feminist desires (predominantly those of lesbian separatists) for changed conditions under which women, and often children, are self-determining, and free to develop fully as human beings, unfettered by patriarchal notions of female biological destiny.

In worlds where women do everything, reproduction is not separated from the rest of life and culture, what we would see as the public sphere.

Female bodies in all their diversity are *human* bodies, not inferior deviations from an idealized white, male norm. I stress that it is not my intention to interrogate these texts as though they were scientific treatises. I seek, not blueprints nor formulae, but visions of what it might mean for women to be able to live their lives free of gender oppression, in societies where parenting (though not necessarily biological motherhood) is a shared experience of almost every adult, and where the care of children is considered one of the most important tasks of all.

I will look at five science fiction novels. Four were first published in the 1970s: *The Female Man* (Joanna Russ, 1975, 1985); *Motherlines* (Suzy McKee Charnas, 1980, 1981); *Woman on the Edge of Time* (Marge Piercy, 1978, 1987); *The Wanderground: Stories of the Hill Women* (Sally Miller Gearhart, 1979, 1985). All four were published as utopias, and all except *Woman on the Edge of Time* are separatist utopias, describing women-only societies.

The fifth novel, *Ammonite* (Nicola Griffith, 1993) was written almost 20 years later, at a time when, it has been suggested (Bartkowski, 1989), it is no longer possible to write utopias in the same way. Griffith has stated that she did not intend it as a utopia, it is simply a world in which there are no men, no better nor worse than any other (Green, 1993).

Clearly, any all-women world must address the question of how to reproduce. If sperm-banks and captive males are to be rejected, some other way than that which is considered *natural* must be found. Neither parthenogenesis nor gynogenesis occur spontaneously in mammals, and so these separatist utopias must step into the realms of the *unnatural*. How the authors choose to overcome the problem reflects their general attitude towards science and technology. It is the process which is important.

I begin with Sally Miller Gearhart and *The Wanderground* (1979, 1985). Gearhart establishes a firm equation between woman and nature; man and technology. One day, the Earth rebels against male violence. Machines stop working, animals won't respond to the commands of men, and men can no longer maintain erections outside the boundaries of the cities, so they are unable to hunt down and rape the women who have taken refuge in the hills. Most of the novel takes place 70 years or so after this event. Men are confined to cities, which are presented as a dystopia. Some women also still live there and are reduced to sex objects. The Hill Women, meanwhile, have learned to commune with nature. They can do with the power of their minds most of the things which technology used to do, as well as other things, such as being able to communicate telepathically with each other and with the animals and plants around them.

Gearhart takes an extreme, radical feminist position in equating technology with men with violence. Her women have rejected all male science and technology. They do everything with their own physical, emotional, mental and spiritual powers. Women in the Wanderground are fully a part of nature and their ability to reproduce by gynogenesis is also presented as natural.

The novel describes a conception, but in a curiously distanced way. Fora has come to the Kochlias, a community living in deep caverns, to see if she wants to have her implantation ritual in the deepest cavern. During her visit, she imagines the ritual occurring, so we see it only at second hand. The event is entwined in natural substances:

> I'm already so full of mugwort and thyme that I feel like I could do it right now all by myself (Gearhart, 1985: 47).

> A long line of women surging down the path, their arms and voices linked to each other, carrying with them the oils and sweet scents, the fire, the water, the necessary green living plants (Gearhart, 1985: 49).

And in amongst this naturalness, Gearhart adds:

> and behind them Yva marched, carrying in her cradled hand the precious egg-laden liquid. Yva of all the seven sisters was past egg-producing and as a reminder of her own part in the motherhood she had balanced on top of the small vial of living ova a large and wildly painted chicken's egg, aglow with her name in gothic lettering (Gearhart, 1985: 49–50).

Attention is distracted from the scientific sounding 'small vial of living ova' by the garish chicken's egg on top. The process of conception itself is described in terms of sharp-smelling leaves and incantations. But it is not completed, Fora being harshly dragged back out of her reverie by the women who are showing her the cavern, who fear that she is becoming lost inside herself.

Gearhart's Hill Women are a part of nature, and yet have transcended nature with their still-developing mental powers. She offers us a vision of entirely non-invasive ways of knowing, not dependent in any way upon technological artefacts. And yet, the division she has made between female and male knowledge and female and male behaviours, means that her women are almost too gentle. By maintaining a rigid dichotomy, she ends up with a book which has sometimes been dismissed as escapism, a snug, happy, loving world containing no real danger or even discomfort. It is a harmonious, never-never land in which the women are barely differentiated from each other and there is no real conflict (Lefanu, 1988: 65).

A more rounded description of women appears in Joanna Russ's *The Female Man* (1975, 1985). Her heroine from Whileaway, Janet Evason, tells us in the first chapter that she killed a wolf single-handed at the age of 13 and that she has fought four duels, and killed four times. She is loving, generous, impatient, and completely independent. She has been chosen to time travel because she is not particularly special, and can be easily spared.

Russ is more robust about science and technology than Gearhart. Whileaway is a technological utopia, there are colonies on the Moon and Mars, and mining on Jupiter, but everything possible is recycled, and most people walk when they want to go somewhere. The invention of the induction helmet allows one woman to do the work of thousands at a distance. However, the narrator of Chapter VIII (Janet?) speculates: 'Whileaway is so pastoral that at times one wonders whether the ultimate sophistication may not take us all back to some pre-Paleolithic dawn age, a garden without any artifacts except what we would call miracles' (Russ, 1985: 14).

Outwardly, then, a similar goal to that of Gearhart, but in Russ's utopia humanity is very much in control. A garden, after all, is not natural. Reproduction is quite clearly carried out by technological means:

'Humanity is unnatural!' exclaimed the philosopher Dunyasha Bernadetteson (A.C. 344–426) who suffered all her life from the slip of a genetic surgeon's hand which had given her one mother's jaw and the other mother's teeth . . . Katharina Lucyson Ansky (A.C. 201–282) was also responsible for the principles that made genetic surgery possible. (The merging of ova had been practiced for the previous century and a half.) (Russ, 1985: 12).

In Charnas's *Motherlines* (1980) too, women's reproduction began in the lab. The Riding Women of the plains in this post-holocaust world bear children who are genetically identical to their mothers. They are descendants of experiments before the Wasting, as they call the nuclear war which devastated Earth. Scientists were looking for mind powers, which tended to manifest more in women than in men. To simplify their task, the scientists bred women with a double set of traits from their mother and no father. 'That way their offspring were daughters just like their mothers, and fertile – if they didn't die right away of bad traits in double doses . . . the change of trait doubling was bred into the daughters, to be passed on ever since . . . The lab men used a certain fluid to start this growth. So do we' (Charnas, 1980: 273–4).

Because the Riding Women's ancestors knew that the Wasting was coming, and that there would be no labs afterwards, they adapted their process of conception so that it would work without technical input. The fluid which the Riding Women use to trigger the division of their eggs is horse semen. In an elaborate sex-ritual, the young women are mated with the smallest of the stallions at the annual Gather when all the tribes meet to celebrate. The horse doesn't provide any genetic material, its semen simply acts as the necessary medium within which the eggs will begin to divide to form an embryo.

Marge Piercy's *Woman on the Edge of Time* (1978, 1987) is the only one of these books which deals with a mixed-sex society. In her utopian community of Mattapoisett, both women and men 'mother' children. Gender has been done away with entirely, and biological sex difference is only a matter of different genitalia, no more important than differences in height or bulk. Racism has also been abolished, although cultural differences and diversity are encouraged. Bee, a native of Mattapoisett, tells Connie, the traveller from our own time, that their society has broken the bonds between genes and culture (Piercy, 1987: 104). Children are not biologically related to their mothers. When they are birthed, they enter a family of three mothers, who may be any combination of women and men. Both sexes can breast-feed.

Piercy's novel is a fictional fleshing out of Shulamith Firestone's contention that only by freeing themselves from their biology, from their natures, can women be free (Firestone, 1979). Children are conceived and brought to term in brooders. Bee takes Connie to visit:

'Here embryos are growing almost ready to birth. We do that at ninemonth plus two or three weeks. Sometimes we wait tenmonth. We find that extra time gives us stronger babies.' He pressed a panel and a door slid aside, revealing seven human babies joggling slowly upside down, each in a sac of its own inside a larger fluid receptacle.

Connie gaped, her stomach also turning slowly upside down. All in a sluggish row, babies bobbed. Mother the machine. Like fish in the aquarium at Coney Island. Their eyes were closed . . . Languidly they drifted in a blind school (Piercy, 1987: 102).

Ammonite (Griffith, 1993) is not a utopia, it is a science fiction story of an anthropologist who travels to an alien world to study its inhabitants. Marghe has been paid by Company to travel to the world Jeep to test a vaccine against the virus which kills all men and 20 per cent of women exposed to it. The planet was colonized several hundred years previously by humans. The women who have survived have learned to reproduce without men, and Marghe is determined to find out how they do it. During the course of her adventures she 'goes native'. She stops taking the vaccine and falls sick with the Jeep virus. After recovering, she learns that it is the virus which allows women to reproduce. She falls in love with Thenike, a *viajera* or travelling wise woman, and together they experience the trance which allows women to reach inside one another and to start the processes of pregnancy.

The passage telling of Marghe and Thenike's trance is described in meticulous detail. It is a remarkable synthesis of mysticism and modern science:

And Marghe was standing before the cathedral that was Thenike's body and all its systems, as Thenike stood before hers. She stepped inside . . . Thenike was ovulating . . . The virus had altered everything. She saw how she could change the chromosomes, how she could rearrange the pairs of alleles on each one . . . She reached out again, and the thrumming electrum strand that was the virus coiled and flexed and the cell divided . . . Chromosomes began their stately dance, pairing and parting . . . each with slightly rearranged genetic material . . . It was like watching beads on a string rearrange themselves. Gorgeous colours, intricate steps, every bead knowing just the right distance to travel (Griffith, 1993: 267–8).

In her language, Griffith takes literally the descriptions of modern science. The enhanced images of stained cell samples, showing *chromosomes* (so-called because they take dye easily) as seen through powerful microscopes are here used as the basis for a description of direct spiritual experience.

These novels offer a range of images of childbearing which do not oppress women. In doing so, they challenge the parameters of the heterosexual nuclear family, imagining totally different constellations of relationships both between adults and children, and between adults and adults. They also, in different ways, blur the boundaries set up in modern, western culture between human, animal and machine. Within these five novels, conception variously involves: interactions with plant life (herbs), infection with a virus, trance states and direct spiritual/emotional experience of manipulating genes, sex with horses, genetic surgery and complete ectogenesis – gestation outside the human body.

Within these science fiction texts, the dichotomy of nature/culture no longer exists. Procreation as a natural process has been replaced by a variety of processes, none of them involving sexual intercourse in the heterosexual sense. These processes bring procreation fully into the realms of culture or socially constructed activity. And, because they are controlled by women, they also bring women and women's embodiment into the realms of culture. In the cases of *Motherlines* (Charnas, 1980) and *The Wanderground* (Gearhart, 1985) conception itself is a public act, an event at the centre of general celebration.

This is in contrast to the current medical model of reproduction, which sees reproductive technologies as a series of scientific interventions into natural processes, designed to control, manipulate and improve upon those processes. The site of these interventions is that part of nature which is the body of women (Arditti *et al.*, 1984; Corea, 1988; Spallone, 1989).

Piercy presents a world in which women can only become free by denying the female specificity of their own bodies. However, this is not simply a case of women having to imitate the supposedly gender-neutral individual. Aspects of female experience have been retained and universalized to all adults, in that both women and men breast-feed.

All the other books involve some form of parthenogenesis or gynogenesis. Women's bodies are still the site of conception and pregnancy, but the boundaries have become permeable, allowing the incorporation of elements from plants, viruses and animals as well as machines.

Cyborgs and Gynogenesis

Similar ideas to those appearing in these utopias have also been incorporated into feminist theory. Donna Haraway, in her article 'A manifesto for cyborgs', uses the metaphor of the cyborg – cybernetic organism, part human, part machine – to explore the borderlands between human, animal and machine:

> I am making an argument for the cyborg as a fiction mapping our social and bodily reality and as an imaginative resource suggesting some very fruitful couplings . . . [T]he relation between organism and machine has been a border war. The stakes in the border war have been the territories of production, reproduction and imagination (Haraway, 1990: 191).

Haraway argues that 'the cyborg is a creature in a postgender world' (Haraway, 1990: 192). It has no origins story of an original identification with nature, it does not 'dream of community on the model of the organic family' (Haraway, 1990: 192). She suggests that we are moving from an organic, industrial society to a polymorphous information system, in which science and technology are altering global social relations. The realities of microelectronics and highly portable cybernetic systems consisting largely of electronic signals change the forms of domination.

> The dichotomies between mind and body, animal and human, organism and machine, public and private, nature and culture, men and women, primitive and civilised are all in question ideologically. The actual situation of women is their integration/exploitation into a world system of production/reproduction and communication called the informatics of domination (Haraway, 1990: 205).

The dominant metaphor now is one of information systems. Communications and biotechnologies are the tools recrafting our bodies.

> Sexual reproduction is one kind of reproductive strategy among many, with costs and benefits as a function of the system environment. Ideologies of sexual reproduction can no longer reasonably call on notions of sex and sex role as organic aspects in natural objects like organisms and families (Haraway, 1990: 204).

In constructing a cyborg myth, Haraway acknowledges her indebtedness to science fiction writers such as Joanna Russ and others (Haraway, 1990: 215), who she describes as storytellers exploring what it means to be embodied in high-tech worlds. While radical feminist writers such as Susan Griffin (1984) and Adrienne Rich (1986) have profoundly affected our imaginations, they have restricted their definitions of the friendly body to the organic, opposing it to the technological. This is the path followed also by Gearhart in *The Wanderground* (1985). Haraway is more interested in embracing the possibilities inherent in the breakdown of distinctions between organism and machine. 'Perhaps ironically, we can learn from our fusions with animals and machines how not to be Man, the embodiment of Western logos' (Haraway, 1990: 215).

Where the cyborg is a being, albeit with fluid boundaries, often defined in terms of information flows, gynogenesis is a process, the process of reproduction. In this context, it seems to me that gynogenesis too is a fruitful metaphor for feminists seeking to explore the borderland between human and machine.

As a technology, gynogenesis involves removing the genetic material from one woman's ovum and inserting it into an ovum from a second woman. The technology of micro-injection necessary to do this already exists. The fertilized zygote can then be replaced into the uterus of one of the two donor women, or into the uterus of a third woman. It would therefore be possible to create a child with three mothers: two having provided the genetic material and a third having undertaken the pregnancy and birthing.

The problem with the process at the moment is that an embryo created in this way does not implant into the wall of the uterus, and so gestation never proceeds past the first few days (Solter, 1988). This is due to a process which geneticists call *imprinting*, in which different genes are switched on and off at different stages of embryogenesis. The genes responsible for the full development of the placenta are only switched on if they have come from the paternal genome (Solter, 1988: 130). Nobody yet understands how gene imprinting works but research continues, and at some future date it may be possible to give one of the ova a paternal pattern of imprinting before injecting it into the other. Children thus conceived would have two biological mothers, and no biological father, although the first generation would, of course have grandfathers. All such children would be girls, because the Y-chromosome necessary to create boys comes only from sperm. All ova contain X-chromosomes.

Reproduction, the ability to give birth, is described by Pateman as symbolizing everything which makes women incapable of becoming civil individuals (Pateman, 1988: 96). It is the equation of reproduction with motherhood with essential natures which forms the background for the pursuit of scientific knowledge using women's bodies as raw materials (Spallone, 1989: 84). According to Haraway:

> Up till now (once upon a time), female embodiment seemed to mean skill in mothering and its metaphorical extensions. Only by being out of place could we take intense pleasure in machines and then with excuses that this was organic activity after all, appropriate to females. Cyborgs might consider more seriously the partial, fluid and sometimes aspect of sex and sexual embodiment (Haraway, 1990: 222).

Cyborgs reproducing via gynogenesis can take intense pleasure in machines at the same time as experiencing specifically female embodiment.

I suggest that the fictional depictions of women-only reproduction are interesting because they provide us with some alternative visions of the family which Shulamith Firestone (1979) felt were so important. These utopias are dreams rather than blueprints (Moylan, 1986: 10), they do not set out to describe real futures. But in transgressing boundaries which are presented as natural by the dominant world-view, they open up a space in the imagination in which change comes to seem possible.

Specifically in the case of reproduction, they furnish us with visions of women moving beyond biological essentialism in gaining control of their own reproduction. The metaphor of gynogenesis brings technology and motherhood together in a way which has the potential to create a shift of perception away from seeing the bodies of women as passive recipients of technological intervention, and towards a vision of women as active participants in the cultural activity of reproduction.

Conclusion

There have already been a few cases in the United States of lesbian couples using IVF to create an embryo from one partner's egg and donor sperm which is then carried to term by the other partner (Martin, 1993: 358). This is clearly an unnatural way of creating a child, but it is one which allows both women to be mothers. It is a use of reproductive technologies which is designed to overcome biological difficulties which are socially rather than scientifically constructed.

The biological definition of infertility as the inability of couples to conceive together where they wish to do so could include lesbian couples. A lesbian couple cannot conceive together through their sexual relationship and to this extent, like some heterosexual couples who are reproductively incompatible (Pfeffer, 1993: 60–1), they are infertile. However, infertility has been socially constructed as an illness, which afflicts only heterosexual couples. In her discourse analysis of infertility, Sarah Franklin remarks that:

> It remains, of course, an open question as to how successful either popular representations or legislation will be in containing the transgressive potential implicit in the very existence of reproductive technologies. The contradiction between the 'unnaturalness' of test-tube conception, and the supposed 'naturalness' of the institutions these techniques are meant to perpetuate can never be resolved, but only contained (Franklin, 1990: 226).

Reproductive technologies bring procreation out of the private sphere of the family and into the public sphere of the laboratory, where infertility treatment takes place. But in the public sphere of contract and the marketplace there is no place for the couple. Only free and equal individuals can make contracts. No taint of status should adhere to such individuals, including the status of sexual difference.

But the dominant discourse reserves infertility treatment for heterosexual couples. This is where the contradictions inherent in the attempts to police reproductive technologies appear most clearly. The structures of the family have been brought into the public sphere where the tensions between the ideas of a universal individual and patriarchal sex-right are clearly revealed.

If we attempt now to explain why gynogenesis is unacceptable, the only recourse left open is an overt appeal to patriarchal sex-right. It is unacceptable because it does not involve a father. An appeal to the unnaturalness of the process, which is only a variation on standard IVF procedures, does not stand up to scrutiny.

In order to take control over our reproductive choices, women must recognize that procreation is socially constructed; whatever form it takes in the late twentieth-century western world, it is unnatural. If reproduction is seen as a social and cultural activity, then the questions we must ask about which reproductive technologies are acceptable, and who should have access to them, become different. We begin to ask about the welfare of the mother(s) and of the child, and about who should make the decisions. Reproductive technologies have profoundly changed our ideas about procreation. Women, and especially lesbians, need to encourage the process of challenging established ideas.

Note

1 Where references to texts appear with two dates, the first is the date of first publication, and the second is the edition I have used for reference. Page numbers and details in the references section refer to this later edition.

References

ARDITTI, R., KLEIN, R. D. and MINDEN, S. (1984) *Test-tube Women: What Future for Motherhood?*, London, Pandora.

BARTKOWSKI, F. (1989) *Feminist Utopias*, Omaha, NB and London, University of Nebraska Press.

CHARNAS, S. M. (1980) *Motherlines*, London, Gollanz (first published 1978, New York, Berkley).

CHARNAS, S. M. (1981) *Walk to the End of the World*, London, Hodder and Stoughton (first published 1974, New York, Ballantine).

COREA, G. (1988) *The Mother Machine: Reproductive Technologies from Artificial Insemination to Artificial Wombs*, London, The Women's Press.

EDWARDS, R. (1990) 'The choreographing of reproductive DNA', *Lesbian Ethics*, **4**, pt. 1, pp. 44–51.

ELSHTAIN, J. B. (1981) *Public Man, Private Woman: Women in Social and Political Thought*, Oxford, Martin Robertson.

FIRESTONE, S. (1979) *The Dialectic of Sex: The Case for Feminist Revolution*, London, The Women's Press (first published 1970).

FRANKLIN, S. (1990) 'Deconstructing "desperateness": the social construction of infertility in popular representations of new reproductive technologies', in MCNEIL, M., VARCOE, I. and YEARLEY, S., *The New Reproductive Technologies*, London, Macmillan, pp. 200–29.

GEARHART, S. M. (1985) *The Wanderground: Stories of the Hill Women*, London, The Women's Press (first published 1979, Watertown, MA, Persephone Press).

GREEN, C. A. (1993) 'Pretty bloody happy!: Nicola Griffith interviewed', *Vector: The Critical Journal of the BSFA*, **173**, June/July.

GRIFFIN, S. (1984) *Woman and Nature: The Roaring inside Her*, London, The Women's Press.

GRIFFITH, N. (1993) *Ammonite*, London, Grafton.

HAIMES, E. (1990) 'Recreating the family? Policy considerations relating to the "new" reproductive technologies', in MCNEIL, M., VARCOE, I. and YEARSLEY, S. (Eds) *The New Reproductive Technologies*, London, Macmillan, pp. 154–72.

HARAWAY, D. (1990) 'A manifesto for cyborgs: Science, technology and socialist feminism in the 1980s', in NICHOLSON, L. (Ed) *Feminism/postmodernism*, London, Routledge, pp. 190–23.

LEFANU, S. (1988) *In the Chinks of the World Machine: Feminism and Science Fiction*, London, The Women's Press.

LESSNOFF, M. (Ed) (1990) *Social Contract Theory*, Oxford, Blackwell.

LOCKE, J. (1967) *Two Treatises of Government* (a critical edition with an introduction and apparatus criticus by Peter Laslett), 2nd Edn, Cambridge, Cambridge University Press (first published 1690).

MARTIN, A. (1993) *The Guide to Lesbian and Gay Parenting*, London, Pandora.

MCNEIL, M. (1990) 'Reproductive technologies: a new terrain for the sociology of technology', in MCNEIL M., VARCOE, I. and YEARLEY, S. (Eds) *The New Reproductive Technologies*, London, Macmillan, pp. 1–26.

MOYLAN, T. (1986) *Demand the Impossible: Science Fiction and the Utopian Imagination*, London, Methuen.

PATEMAN, C. (1988) *The Sexual Contract*, Cambridge, Polity.

PFEFFER, N. (1993) *The Stork and the Syringe: A Political History of Reproductive Medicine*, Cambridge, Polity.

PHILLIPS, A. (1993) *Democracy and Difference*, Cambridge, Polity.

PIERCY, M. (1987) *Woman on the Edge of Time*, London, The Women's Press (first published 1978).

RICH, A. (1986) 'Compulsory heterosexuality and lesbian existence', in RICH, A. *Blood, Bread and Poetry: Selected Prose 1979–1985*, London, Virago, pp. 23–75.

RUSS, J. (1985) *The Female Man*, London, The Women's Press (first published 1975).

SAFFRON, L. (1994) *Challenging Conceptions: Pregnancy and Parenting Beyond the Traditional Family*, London, Cassell.

SOLTER, D. (1988) 'Differential imprinting and expression of maternal and paternal genomes', *Annual Review of Genetics*, **22**, pp. 127–46.

SPALLONE, P. (1989) *Beyond Conception: The New Politics of Reproduction*, London, Macmillan.

WARNOCK, M. (1984) *Report of the Committee of Inquiry into Human Fertilisation and Embryology*, London, HMSO.

WARNOCK, M. (1985) 'The artificial family', in LOCKWOOD, M. (Ed) *Moral Dilemmas in Modern Medicine*, Oxford, Oxford University Press, pp. 138–54.

WOLLSTONECRAFT, M. (1992) *A Vindication of the Rights of Woman* (edited with an introduction by Miriam Brody), Harmondsworth, Penguin (first published 1792).

YOUNG, I. M. (1990) *Throwing like a Girl and other Essays in Feminist Philosophy and Social Theory*, Bloomington and Indianapolis, IN, Indiana University Press.

Chapter 10

Rethinking Bodies and Boundaries: Science Fiction, Cyberpunk and Cyberspace

Jenny Wolmark

Science fiction, despite its tangential relationship to science and its marginal position in popular fiction, has been notable for the way in which it has sustained and promoted a belief that science will provide *the future*. In the context of postmodern culture, however, science fiction has become not only less marginal but also increasingly unable and unwilling to subscribe to such a belief. Indeed, some of the most deeply felt expressions of contemporary disaffection with the notions of *science* and *the future* have come from within science fiction itself, most notably from within cyberpunk. In addition, cyberpunk has provided one of the most original metaphors currently available to us for thinking about the new electronic spaces and places of information technology – cyberspace. It is a metaphor which not only describes a new way of conceptualizing the relations between space and place, but it has also opened up new possibilities for thinking about embodiment and gendered identity. As Scott Bukatman (1993) argues, the specific location of cyberspace within science fiction is crucial because, since the subject is denied 'a fixed site of identification' within its narratives, then the 'limits of the existing paradigms' of subjectivity are revealed (1993: 180). However, because of its refusal to engage fully with the possibilities that cyberspace offers for rethinking definitions of identity, cyberpunk has limited the ways in which it has been possible to think about the disruptive and creative possibilities of cyberspace. In a discussion of three science fiction film narratives, I will be examining the extent to which anxieties about the erosion of masculine identity are revealed through visual metaphors of spatial and bodily dislocation. Further, I will argue that, in order to prevent the threatened loss of hegemonic masculinity, cyberpunk narratives envision cyberspace as a place with determinate and known boundaries: only within cyberpunk narratives written by women are cyberpunk and cyberspace explored from a differently gendered perspective in which spatial boundaries are disrupted and gender identity can be detached from fixed definitions of masculinity and femininity. To support this contention, I will be discussing two recent science fiction novels, written respectively by Mary Rosenblum and Mary Gentle, in which a different set of relations between gender, identity and technology are proposed.

Science fiction has been described by Mary Ann Doane as 'the genre that highlights technological fetishism' (1990: 174), but the relationship between science and science fiction is more problematic than this description suggests. The historical trajectory of science fiction demonstrates that it is capable of expressing a range of different and competing attitudes towards science and technology, and it is more satisfactory, therefore, to think of the genre as providing a cultural space for the expression of complex and contradictory popular attitudes towards science and technology. At one end of the spectrum, there are the early pulp SF magazines of the 1920s and 30s such as *Science Wonder Stories*, *Amazing Stories*, and *Astounding Stories*, which are character-ized by a largely uncritical enthusiasm for science and technology. The first of such magazines, *Amazing Stories*, was, in fact, the 'first periodical in the world devoted solely to science fiction' (Carter, 1977: 4). The magazine was founded in 1926 by Hugo Gernsback, and under his editorial control it tirelessly pro-moted and popularized ideas about scientific and technological innovations. In a 1926 editorial, Gernsback explicitly celebrates both the ability of science to produce 'modern marvels' (Carter, 1977: 4) and the prophetic abilities of the science fiction writers themselves: 'There are few things written by our scientifiction writers, frankly impossible today, that may not become a reality tomorrow' (1977: 4). The predominantly male readers of these magazines were able to share in the fantasy that they were uniquely placed to endorse a future that was in the very process of being constructed, and this future was confidently based on an instrumentally rational and masculinist science. At the other end of the spectrum, there are those science fiction narratives written from the 1960s onwards, which reveal a noticeable lack of confidence in both science and scientists, and a much greater emphasis on explorations of inner space rather than outer space. Describing this shift, Gérard Klein draws a contrast between the kind of utopian science fiction, initiated by the pulp magazines, that could be thought of as being 'the bearer of a scientific messianism' (1977: 8), and science fiction which, particularly in the 1970s, was increasingly marked by a 'distrust of science and technology, and of scientists, especially in the exact or "hard" sciences of physics, chemistry, biology and genetics' (1977: 3). The production of more dystopian science fiction leads Fred Pfeil to suggest that the 'highly literary science fiction in the 1960s was itself paradoxically the sign of a certain exhaustion of content, of the bankruptcy of the utopian/dystopian dialectic on which virtually all serious SF was based for the first hundred years of its existence' (1990: 92). It is, of course, no coinci-dence that this period also saw the emergence of conflicting social and political agendas around the issues of civil rights and women's liberation, as well as the development of a huge groundswell of opposition to the military involvement of the United States in South-east Asia. The science fiction that emerged from these disputed ideological imperatives rejected the by now tenuous presump-tion that science and technology were in some way inherently progressive, and the genre became increasingly distanced from the uncritical technophilia that had been its original motivating force. The changing social, political and cultural agendas of the 1960s and 70s generated a range of oppositional stances towards the dominant discourses of power and control, and within science fiction, general anxieties about corporate and political control of science and technology coincided with the feminist critique of patriarchal structures.

Traditionally, science fiction has been marked out as a gendered cultural space occupied primarily by men, like science itself. Although women have always been involved in the writing and publishing of science fiction, their involvement was very often a covert one and the use of androgenous sounding names or male pseudonyms was fairly common; writers such as Leigh Brackett, C. L. Moore, Andre Norton, Julian May and James Tiptree, Jr. have all used these devices. In her discussion of the work of Lilith Lorraine, a less well-known woman science fiction writer who had several stories published by Gernsback, Jane Donawerth quotes Lorraine's own opinion that 'if the editors and publishers knew I was a woman they wouldn't accept more than half what they do now' (1990: 253). Since the 1970s, however, women have been writing science fiction with explicitly women-centred and feminist content, and this change is visible in landmark texts such as *The Wanderground* (1979, 1985) by Sally Miller Gearhart, *Motherlines* (1978, 1980) by Suzy McKee Charnas and *The Female Man* (1975) by Joanna Russ.[1] These texts in particular explore the utopian possibilities of separatist, women-only communities, and they have had a powerful impact on the genre as a whole because of the way in which they relocate gender as a culturally constructed phenomenon. Many more women have since entered the field, and representations of gender and gender relations have become key issues in science fiction narratives. These issues are typically addressed from within the soft social sciences, and science fiction narratives have necessarily moved away from their traditional base in hard science; at the same time, definitions of science itself have been problematized, not least by the feminist critique of the discourses of science. The cultural relocation of science fiction, from the sub-cultural marginality of pulp fiction where writers, readers and fans were predominantly young, white males, to generic respectability and a significant number of women writers, readers and fans, also acts as an external indicator of these shifts in definition and address.

The emergence of the science fiction sub-genre of cyberpunk in the mid-80s caused something of a rethink about representations of gender in science fiction generally, and in feminist SF in particular, and what became visible was a tendency in the feminist utopia to avoid confronting the high-tech realities of contemporary postmodern culture. As Joan Gordon puts it, 'Virtually every feminist SF utopia dreams of a pastoral world, fueled by organic structures rather than mechanical ones, inspired by versions of the archetypal Great Mother. And virtually every feminist SF novel, utopian or not, incorporates a longing to go forward into the idealized past of earth's earlier matriarchal nature religions' (1991: 199). Some of the narrative devices that are used in feminist science fiction to sidestep the issue of technology involve situating women-centred utopian communities in a post-apocalypse world in which the only technology that exists is both rudimentary and/or tainted, as in Sheri Tepper's *The Gate to Women's Country* (1989); or the utopian women-only society might be presented as predominantly arcadian and rural, and is then shown to be in conflict with another society that is both patriarchal and aggressively technological, as is the case in Sally Miller Gearhart's *The Wanderground* and in Suzy McKee Charnas' trilogy of novels, *Motherlines* (1980), *Walk To The End of The World* (1974, 1981), and *The Furies* (1994, 1995). Inevitably, this has helped to perpetuate the assumption that science and technology are irrevocably linked to masculinity, a link that the feminist critique of science has been concerned to deconstruct, as has feminist science fiction in its reaction against hard science fiction. Cyberpunk itself seems to be situated within hard SF because of its fascination with the new technologies of information, and thus, as Nicola Nixon argues, it could be said to have 'represented a concerted return to the (originary) purity of hard SF, apparently purged of the influence of other-worldly fantasy, and embracing technology with new fervor' (1992: 220). However, despite cyberpunk's apparently uncritical identification with science, it has nevertheless provided alternative ways of envisioning the relationships between human and machine, organic and non-organic and, ultimately, between self and other. The fictions of cyberpunk enact what Thomas Foster describes as 'a literalizing of the effects of inhabiting a postmodern communications environment' (1993: 3), and as such they have helped to generate a creative space within which identity can become ambivalent and thus problematic.

Although cyberpunk has become an umbrella term characterizing a wide range of cultural productions, including music, performance art, film and video, it was originally used to describe William Gibson's science fiction novel *Neuromancer* (1986), and the cyberpunks were a small group of SF writers whose work was drawn together into an anthology of short stories edited by Bruce Sterling, *Mirrorshades* (1988). With the exception of Pat Cadigan, all the writers in the anthology are white and male, and the main connection between their work is the fact that it draws on the counter-cultural ethos of punk and rock and roll, combined with the flirtatious world of hacking. Cyberpunk is both a celebration and a critique of the destabilizing impact of new technology and transitional corporate capitalism; it ironically collapses the distinction between the present and the future by constructing credible, technologically enhanced *near futures*. These postmodern near futures are unstable, incoherent and saturated with the problems and possibilities of information technology. They disrupt the familiar linear relationship between the present and the future, and in so doing they blur the distinction between utopia and dystopia. The unstable postmodern environment of cyberpunk is precisely the kind of environment that opens up real possibilities for rethinking representations of gender, and social and sexual relations generally. The initial excitement generated by cyberpunk has, however, declined, and its counter-cultural pretensions have not been sustained. It has become increasingly clear that the promise that cyberpunk held for new representations of gender and new social and sexual configurations would not be fully explored without the intervention of women, either as performers, directors or writers. Not only was there an almost complete absence of women writers from the first flush of cyberpunk, but cyberpunk itself has never acknowledged the clear debt that it owed to feminist science fiction in terms of both narrative construction and gender representation. The lean, mean anti-heroes of cyberpunk are reminiscent of the familiar hard-boiled urban cowboys of other popular narratives, except that instead of walking down the mean streets of Tokyo, New York or Los Angeles, these computer cowboys jack into cyberspace by means of direct neural input. Cyberpunk transforms the archetypal figure of the adolescent white, male hacker into a street-wise operator who cruises the information highways as disembodied consciousness, freed from the troublesome body, or the 'meat' as Gibson's characters contemptuously refer to it. The body was a source of continuing anguish for these cyberpunk cowboys, and in Gibson's cyberpunk novels they leave it for the new frontiers of cyberspace as fast and as often as they can; some of them, like Bobby in *Mona Lisa Overdrive* (1989), even opting to stay there. As more women have entered the field, however, the implications of information technology for the way in which we think about gender and its embodiment have been explored in increasingly interesting ways, a point to which I will return in my discussion of the work of Mary Rosenblum and Mary Gentle.

The real significance of cyberpunk is that it found a way to articulate what it means to be immersed in a technology-saturated culture. Through its fictions it has provided a conceptual vocabulary for describing this immersive experience, even as it has backed away from the implications of such an experience, particularly where definitions of identity are concerned. The new environment of immersion is cyberspace, and the word itself was invented by William Gibson to describe the 'consensual hallucination' (Gibson, 1986: 12) that constitutes the artificial spatial and temporal environment of electronic information. In an interview Gibson (Greenland, 1986) says 'I had a hunch from talking to people about computers that everyone seemed to feel at some level, without really ever saying it, that there was a space behind the screen' (1986: 7). Gibson has admitted that he knew very little about computers when he was writing *Neuromancer*, the book in which the term first appeared, and he actually wrote the book on a manual typewriter. Nevertheless, the *idea* of cyberspace, as the space/place that exists behind the computer screen, has had a tremendous impact. Nowadays both the word and the concept of cyberspace are ubiquitous – the Internet is familiarly referred to as cyberspace, as are the cybernetic environments of virtual reality. Cyberspace has moved, therefore, from being located in a science fictional possible near future, to being both a word and an environment that refers to the actualities of the present, and this move is indicative of a considerable shift in cultural expectations and outlook. It is a shift that runs parallel to, or is perhaps a consequence of, the contemporary cultural moment of postmodernism.

Postmodern theory has developed during a period of enormous change: globalization and technologies that allow the instantaneous transmission of information around the world have produced a sense of dislocation and fragmentation which has generated a climate in which many of the taken-for-granted assumptions about 'the way things are' in white, male dominated, eurocentric culture and society can be challenged. This in turn has had a profound and often progressive impact on questions of identity and positionality, and questions of self and of location. The way in which we think about space and time has inevitably undergone similar changes: the geographer David Harvey (1989), for example, describes postmodernism in terms of time–space compression and many contemporary anxieties are focused on the way in which the familiar dimensions of space and time are being compressed or even undermined. Paul Virilio refers to what he calls a postmodern 'crisis of dimension' in which speed has replaced 'the distances of space and time' (1984: 21) and in so doing has obliterated the meaning of space–time as the 'continuum of society' (1984: 26). Fredric Jameson, in his magisterial book on postmodernism, *Postmodernism, or, the Cultural Logic of Late Capitalism* (1991), argues that the temporal has been replaced by the spatial in postmodernism, and because the linear logic of the temporal has been displaced, we can, therefore, only inhabit a schizophrenic environment of unrelated present moments, all of them equally vivid and indistinguishable one from the other. Jameson presents postmodern culture as being preoccupied with media enhanced surfaces rather than with depth of meaning, and he argues that postmodern culture suffers from a loss of critical historical memory, which is why, for example, it is besotted with nostalgia and has a morbid fascination for endless movie remakes. He also recognizes that, if indeed the postmodern world is dominated by the spatial, then we have to find new ways of thinking about it, and cyberspace would seem to provide an appropriate metaphor for doing just that.

In a discussion of the effect that new concepts of chaos and randomness are having on both science and literature, Katherine Hayles describes the contemporary feeling that time has somehow flattened out, so that we experience time as a series of disconnected moments rather than as linear progression. She suggests that this leads to a 'growing sense that the future is already used up before it arrives' (1990: 279), and since 'time itself has ceased to be a useful concept around which to organise experience', then it is not only history, but time itself that appears to have become 'obsolete' (1990: 281). Jean Baudrillard has described the future as imploding into an increasingly science fictional present, which to him signifies the end of history because, as he says in the title of one of his articles, 'The year 2000 has already happened' (1988). In other words, it is no longer necessary to write science fiction, since we are already living it. For Baudrillard, the role of science fiction has changed from presenting possibilities of multiple and expansive futures to that of simply reflecting back for us the hyperreality in which we already live. For many writers on postmodernism, information technology has fatally undermined the concept of time as linear progression, which in turn has resulted in an emphasis on the spatial and on location. Since science fiction has always been about spatial and temporal dislocation, it is not surprising that it should have provided one of the most potent metaphors of recent years for exploring the confusion of spatial and temporal boundaries within postmodern culture. There have been numerous conferences and papers, drawing together a wide variety of perspectives from design, anthropology, ethnography and cultural theory, which have contrived to give the 'consensual hallucination' of cyberspace actual form, sometimes in highly celebratory terms. In one of the published papers from the auspiciously named First Conference on Cyberspace, held at the University of Texas, Austin, Texas, 1990, it was claimed that cyberspace offers the possibility of fulfilment of 'the dream of transcending the physical world, fully alive, at will, to dwell in some Beyond – to be empowered or enlightened there, alone or with others, and to return' (Benedikt, 1991: 131). Despite this heady mixture of information technology and mysticism, it seems to be the case that cyberspace does indeed describe a new spatial configuration. At present it is a conceptual space that is uncertain and open-ended because it is, as yet, neither fully colonized nor fully policed. On the one hand, cyberspace is about control, surveillance and the invasion of privacy, but on the other hand it is also about subverting boundaries, hierarchies and power structures. It contains both threat and promise in equal measure: what might be regarded as the threat of anarchy and loss of control over space, place and identity from one point of view becomes, from another point of view, the promise of new freedoms and new forms of identity and community. Although cyberspace has become more than a consensual hallucination, it clearly remains a space that is marked by its own ambivalence.

It is not only the conceptual spaces of cybernetic systems that are ambivalent: the simulated selves that become possible in those spaces are equally ambivalent. Anxieties about the disruption of existing spatial and temporal borders are paralleled by anxieties about the instability of the borders between self and other, inside and outside. Cyberspace can be thought of as a transitional or 'liminal' space, in the sense in which Sharon Zukin (1991: 28) uses the term, to mean one that exists at or between known borders and in which, therefore, the familiar spatializations of embodied social existence are disrupted. Cyberspace can therefore be thought of as signifying a complex shift in the ways in which we think of the relation of the body to space and time. In case this seems too fanciful a view of cyberspace, it is interesting to note that even the language that is used by those involved in designing the software and hardware for three dimensional computer interfaces reflects this shift. A discussion of cyberspace in the 1989 issue of the American design journal *CADalyst*, has a group of designers speculating that in cyberspace the 'conditioned notion of a unique and immutable body will give way to a far more liberated notion of "body" as something quite disposable and, generally, limiting' (Gullichsen *et al.*, 1989: 47). Their discussion ends with the question: 'Does an alternative personality, active only in cyberspace, legally constitute a person?' (Gullichsen *et al.*, 1989: 47). Indeed, questions such as these have now entered the media mainstream, as have related questions about whether or not sexual harassment, rape and adultery can take place in the Internet.

The bodily and spatial dislocation that is possible in cyberspace has the potential to throw definitions of gender into considerable disarray because it undermines the notion of the body as a privileged site, and identity thus becomes problematic. One can choose who to be when signing on the Internet, and this can have positively utopian effects, since hierarchies based on gender, ethnicity, age or disability would seem to be rendered inoperative by the simulated selves of cyberspace. But there may be some problems that need to be thought through regarding the enticing postmodern embodiment or rather, disembodiment of cyberspace. In the cyberpunk novels of William Gibson there is a continuing emphasis on the masculine, despite the presence of some striking female characters, such as the prosthetically enhanced Molly Millions in *Neuromancer*. Once in cyberspace, the body, suggests Katherine Hayles, is 'reconstituted as informational patterns in a multidimensional computer space' (1993: 81); questions of identity, positionality and embodiment, always problematic for women, are simply side-stepped as the material self is transcended and desire becomes merely a symptom of disembodied consciousness. Gender identity remains significantly intact in this disembodied form. Cyberpunk's refusal to work through the implications of cybernetic disembodiment severely limits the capacity of cyberspace to become a space of heterogeneous desire, and it is the implications of this that I will be considering in the following discussion of three specific science fiction films.

In each of the three films under discussion, *Robocop* (1987), *Total Recall* (1990) and *The Lawnmower Man* (1992), anxieties about masculinity constitute a significant narrative, and these anxieties are explored through the visual metaphors of bodily and spatial dislocation. In Paul Verhoeven's *Robocop* and *Total Recall*, these anxieties are dealt with more ironically than in many other cyberpunk narratives. Both films construct an uncomfortably familiar-looking near future and the opening section of *Robocop* establishes the central male character in familiar heroic mould: Murphy is a cop who is killed while trying to arrest a vicious drugs gang virtually single-handed. The politics of the Reagan–Bush era and the politics of cybernetics are both touched on in the film, since Murphy's death occurs partly as a result of the privatization of law enforcement, which has resulted in the drastic reduction of the police force. In addition, once Murphy is dead, the corporation that owns the police force then uses his body to effect a particularly drastic make-over, and he undergoes what is referred to in the film as a 'whole body prostheses' in which almost his entire physical body is replaced by robotic parts. As far as the corporation is concerned, Murphy has become merely product and programme, an organic machine with built-in play back facilities but without an identity. He is, therefore, effectively positioned as victim and object in the narrative, and as such he is feminized: because he is both literally and metaphorically disembodied, his cyborg status does not allow him to be unequivocally reinstated as male hero. His identity thus remains ambiguous. The only way in which Murphy can reconstruct a sense of self is by accessing data banks: memory is reconstituted as playback and embodiment depends absolutely on information circuits. General anxieties about the relationship of technology to the body become particular anxieties about the male body. As a cyborg, Murphy occupies a liminal space in which identity is unresolved – he is both self and other, feminized as victim but with a simulated masculinity. An increasingly ironic account of masculinity is developed in the narrative, as Murphy's ambiguous cyborg identity is juxtaposed against several familiar and stereotypical representations of masculinity in which, for example, Robocop prevents two men from raping a woman, Robocop busts the all-male drugs gang, and Robocop finally blows away the corrupt male chief executive. The comic book style of these encounters serves to undermine the apparently unproblematic representation of masculinity, while at the same time leaving the ambiguities of cyborg identity unresolved. These ambiguities are also present in the spatial dislocation that results from the visual playback system that is built into Murphy's vision: as viewers we are constantly placed in the position of looking with and at him, from both the inside and the outside. In western culture, the gaze is hierarchically constituted as masculine, so that the subject who looks is male and the object of the gaze is female. This is partially reversed in the film so that as viewers we look at Murphy being looked at, as the object of the gaze, but we are also placed in the position of looking back through Murphy's cybernetic vision; we therefore move between male and female narrative positions. As Judith Mayne notes in her discussion of cinema spectatorship, 'In cinematic terms, this would suggest that cinematic identification is never masculine or feminine, but rather a movement between the two. From this vantage point, positions may well be defined as masculine or feminine (or both), but they are taken up by spectators regardless of their gender or sexuality' (1993: 71). This spatial dislocation and disruption of the gaze allows us to question hierarchies of the visual as well as received judgments about subjectivity, identity and positionality.

A similar dislocation occurs in *Total Recall*, although the dominant physical presence of Arnold Schwarzenegger tends to mean that it is dealt with less subtly. As is the case in many other science fiction films, TV monitors and video screens litter the narrative, signifying surveillance and simulation but also drawing attention to the erosion of the boundaries between the real and the simulated. The proliferation of technologies of the visual is a noticeable characteristic of the genre and Garrett Stewart has commented on the extensive presence in SF films of 'banks of monitors, outsized video intercoms, x-ray display panels, hologram tubes, backlit photoscopes, aerial scanners, telescopic mirrors, illuminated computer consoles, overhead projectors, slide screens, radar scopes, whole curved walls of transmitted imagery, the retinal registers of unseen electronic eyes' (1985: 161). The narratives of science fiction films explore the erosion of the boundaries between the real and the simulated while simultaneously drawing attention to the main cause of that erosion, which in this case is the technology of special effects. Thus, the fetishization of technology that has traditionally been at the heart of science fiction is both endorsed and disparaged, which leads Garrett Stewart to suggest that the 'self-conscious allegories of science fiction talk us out of the truisms of ready identification by which we are lured to these films in the first place' (1985: 207). This self-consciousness within the genre allows identity to be deliberately confused within the narrative of *Total Recall*, and because of the presence of Schwarzenegger, this confusion inevitably gets focused onto masculine identity in particular.

In the film, which is based on a story by Philip K. Dick, first published in 1966, *We Can Remember It For You Wholesale*, Mars is ruled by a dictatorial corporation which has control of the air supply. Schwarzenegger plays Quaid, a corporate employee who has joined the rebel organization opposed to the corporation. His defection has been discovered by the corporation, however, and it has replaced his memory, and therefore his identity, with a memory implant. Ironically, Quaid discovers this when he attempts to buy recreational memories of a trip to Mars, and the process of acquiring yet another set of false memories accidentally uncovers the presence of his real memories. The obliteration of his real memories was apparently anticipated by Quaid, who recorded a videotaped message from his real self to his simulated self, in which everything is explained. Later in the narrative, the corporate chairman shows Quaid yet another video recording of himself, in which he claims that his two other simulated selves are lying, and that he is, in fact, still working for the corporation as a double agent. The technologies of viewing are here used to demonstrate in a general sense the potentially disruptive impact of simulation on identity. This disruption becomes more specifically focused on representations of masculinity by means of two striking images in the narrative which explicitly draw attention to themselves as special effects. In the first image, Quaid uses a female simulation to return to Mars undetected, and we are presented with the spectacle of Schwarzenegger's real male self gradually being revealed from within the simulated female head, in a parody of the process of giving birth. The sequence ends with Schwarzenegger removing the false head, but remaining clothed in a female body, and the knowing smile that Schwarzenegger gives to the camera acknowledges both the parody and the irony of the narrative play on representations of gender. The second image also makes clear references to the reproductive process, in that the male rebel leader is a mutant who has a second embryonic self that emerges periodically from his chest cavity and, although it looks remarkably like a new born baby, this second self is the actual leader of the rebels. Both of these images are presented as localized special effects, but, when taken together with the narrative emphasis on identity and simulation, their function is to interrogate the effects of technology on bodily limits, specifically those of the masculine body. In a general sense, the technology of special effects reveals what Andreas Huyssen has referred to as the 'male phantasm of a creation without mother' (1986: 71), in which the fantasy of complete control of the reproductive processes is also a metaphor for the desire for control over both nature and woman.

The limits of the body are explored in a slightly different way in *The Lawnmower Man*, as are the limits to the representation of the body in science fiction film. The film struggles with the problem of how to translate the interactive space of cyberspace into cinematic terms, and, despite its high-tech special effects, the narrative remains largely within the realist conventions of Hollywood precisely because it is not interactive. One consequence of the privileging of special effects is that, as Brooks Landon suggests, 'production technology has become more interesting than the stories ostensibly justifying the use of that technology' (1990: 67), and potentially interesting questions about the instability of gender identity are generally postponed in favour of the kind of technological fetishism for which the science fiction genre is noted. In the case of *The Lawnmower Man*, however, because the film does not contain a charismatic male icon, like Schwarzenegger in *Total Recall*, through which masculinity can be rendered problematic, problems of identity and representation are displaced more directly onto cyberspace. Cyberspace thus becomes a site and signifier of instability, and the technology of special effects is inevitably implicated in this instability, at least at the level of narrative structure.

The ostensible themes of the film are concerned with the ethics of corporate control of technology and the dangers of chemically and, by implication, genetically enhanced intelligence. The narrative depicts the transformation of an affable but simple neighbourhood handyman called Joe into a vindictive, superintelligent being who is able to function in both the real and the virtual world. Despite its worthy themes, the film is best known for its computer-generated cybersex sequence, at the end of which Joe's female partner is so transported by his orgasmic cybernetic prowess that she is rendered comatose and brain dead. In this film, cyberspace is completely dominated by male desire, which means that it is a space with no ambivalence and therefore no eroticism. Joe finally leaves the meat behind, just like one of William Gibson's computer cowboys, and enters cyberspace to become disembodied consciousness. This disembodied masculinity is presented as a fearful prospect in the narrative, because once in cyberspace, Joe begins to exert a malign influence over both the simulated and the real world, and the boundaries between the two become almost indistinguishable at certain points in the film. The body that is always most at risk at these points is the male body, and the ensuing string of corpses that litters the narrative suggests that the potential overlap between the real and the simulated is perceived as a threat rather than as a potential source of pleasure. The film sequences in which special effects are used to depict virtual reality are disturbing, not only because the special effects disrupt the familiar spatial and temporal relations of narrative cinema, but also because they emphasize the diffuse and fluid qualities of cyberspace. Cyberspace thus becomes a doubly threatening environment which, in Vivian Sobchak's view, 'disorients and liberates the activity of consciousness from the gravitational pull and orientation of its hitherto embodied and grounded existence' (1990: 58). The disembodiment that is possible within the immersive electronic environment of cyberspace is thus both disorientating and liberating, and in striving to provide a visual approximation of cyberspace, the special effects in *The Lawnmower Man* briefly share this ambivalence. However, the potential instability of disembodiment is not sanctioned in the narrative, and indeterminacy is rejected in favour of the known boundaries of the masculine: thus, in order to enter and possess the virtual world, Joe must defeat his arch rival, the same scientist who facilitated the development of his new powers, in a familiar reworking of the oedipal narrative.

The cultural representations of cyberspace that I have discussed so far have retained their strong connections with cyberpunk and with the boys' own world of hacking, and this is revealed particularly clearly in two final examples, both of which strikingly coalesce around masculinity and masculinization of information technology. The first example is taken from *The Hacker Crackdown* (1994), a non-fiction book, first published in 1992, by one of the original group of cyberpunk science fiction writers, Bruce Sterling. He introduces the book in the following way: 'This is a book about cops, and wild teenage whiz kids, and lawyers, and hairy-eyed anarchists, and industrial technicians, and hippies, and high-tech millionaires, and games hobbyists, and computer security experts, and Secret Service agents, and grifters, and thieves' (1994: xi). The masculine inflection of this description is unmistakable, and despite its contemporary references to the cultural environment of information technology, it is highly reminiscent of the scientific messianism that was so characteristic of the Gernsback era. The flavour of this environment is reproduced almost exactly in *Sneakers*, a film released in the same year as *The Hacker Crackdown*, which starred Robert Redford as a computer hacker. The film alludes to the radicalism of the 1960s, which was the period in which the character played by Robert Redford went underground because of his hacking activities. In an almost exact reprise of the book, the narrative features most of the kinds of characters mentioned by Bruce Sterling in *The Hacker Crackdown*, and the only significant female character in the film is given the task of retrieving information, not by using her skills as a hacker, but by seducing a stereotyped computer nerd. Since he is portrayed as a man possessing few social or sexual skills, she is unable even to claim much credit for her success in seducing him.

Although cyberspace gives every impression of being dominated by the masculine, it is also a space in which the male body and identity are in constant jeopardy, and the question of whether or not cyberspace has the potential to be a utopian space for women can be addressed in the context of this contradiction. In the popular version of cyberspace that has become familiar through the kinds of cultural representations already discussed, it is imagined and mythologized as a place, rather than a space. Places have a geography, they are associated with fixed and known boundaries, and as Doreen Massey indicates, the emotional attachment that we might feel for places depends on their construction as 'bounded, enclosed spaces defined through counterposition against the Other who is outside' (1994: 168). In mainstream popular culture, cyberspace is represented as a place to which anyone, in theory, can have access, but it is also a static place with fixed and known boundaries, and these boundaries create a space which is becoming increasingly homogeneous and repetitive, and which is absolutely opposed to the recognition of difference and heterogeneity. As such, cyberspace has the capacity to become invested with a nostalgia for origins that suggests that going 'back to the future', at least for women, may not be such a good idea after all. However, as Doreen Massey points out, the assumption that the identity of places can be known in advance and somehow frozen around a particular set of meanings is a mistaken one: The identities of places are inevitably unfixed . . . in part precisely because the social relations out of which they are constructed are themselves by their very nature dynamic and changing' (1994: 169). The identity and meaning of a place cannot be fixed any more than the identity and meaning of spaces can, because both place and space have meaning for us only in terms of what happens within them; in other words, spaces and places are constructed out of the social relations operating within them. If cyberspace was, therefore, defined as a 'site without a geography', (Bruno, 1993: 57) without boundaries, then it could be imagined as a space of diversity and difference rather than of homogenization and sameness. For those who are used to being subjugated within confined definitions of self and identity, like women, the erosion of fixed boundaries and immobilized spaces is a positive feature of cyberspace, in that it allows for recognition that identity is multiple rather than singular. It is important, therefore, to characterize cyberspace as a fluid space of proliferating and horizontal networks that people use for their own purposes, either as individuals or as groups, and a space like this will thrive on contradiction and ambiguity, rather than rationality and certainty. Since such a characterization will also entail the recognition of difference and multiplicity, then cyberspace can operate as a powerful ongoing critique of those spatial systems that do not function in this way.

The final part of this chapter will consist of a discussion of two recent science fiction novels written by women, in which the dominant male ethos of cyberpunk has been rewritten from an alternatively gendered point of view, to enable cyberspace to be presented as a space of and for difference. Although the constraints of space prevent me from discussing their work here, there are many women science fiction writers who are currently exploring the double-edged possibilities of cyberpunk conventions in order to undermine masculinist assumptions about technology. The technological fantasies of cyberpunk have largely been an expression of anxieties about the impact of technology on the male body in particular, and the boundaries of identity have, therefore, been as fixed as the imagined boundaries of cyberspace. When the hard science of cyberpunk is used instead to unfix those boundaries, a quite different set of fantasies can emerge that is to do with fluidity of identity and desire, rather than fear of female sexuality and of the erosion of the male body, with the result that cyberspace can become an imaginative environment that is no longer dominated by heterosexuality.

One of the central characters in Mary Rosenblum's *Chimera* (1993) is David Chen, a gay man who moves in and out of cyberspace, not in order to retreat from the harsh realities of the real world, but in order to find solutions to problems of difference in both dimensions. In Rosenblum's narrative, cyberspace is not described as a nostalgic place of retreat from the 'meat', as it is in the work of so many male cyberpunk writers. It is a place in which the experience of struggle over identity and difference is as live and as crucial as it is in the non-virtual world. The novel is predicated on the idea that the real and the virtual are integrated rather than separate zones, so that the events and social relations of the non-virtual world inevitably intrude into and define the virtual, and, equally, what takes place in the virtual has consequences in the real world. In the narrative, David Chen has become alienated from his wealthy but traditional family, and from his father in particular, partly because of his decision to become a virtual reality artist and partly because he has a long-term male lover, Flander. In order to become a virtual reality artist, David's whole body is wired up to the Net by means of electronic fibres, enabling him to enter cyberspace at will, as he explains: 'They inject a dividing ovum with engineered epithelial cells. The fibers are actually part of my epidermis. They grow back with the skin if I get injured ... The subdermal jewels and the primary interface chips are added later ... I carry a lot of embedded hardware here and there.' (1993: 43). David's difference is, then, both literally and metaphorically embodied, and his embodied experience as an artist and as a gay man means that the disembodiment of cyberspace is not presented in the narrative as a threat either to the male body or to identity. His sense of himself as a subject is not eroded by the virtual, in contrast to those cyberpunk narratives in which disembodiment is shown to undermine masculine identity.

The other significant character in the narrative who is marked by difference is Jewel Martina: she is one of those who cannot afford to be 'netted' and has to use 'skinthins' or external public access points in order to enter cyberspace. Jewel is from a poor white neighbourhood where 'she looked too Hispanic' (1993: 93) to be allowed to feel she belonged; she has fought her way out of poverty in order to become a medical aide, but her ambition is to become an information broker in the Net. She operates as an outsider in the financial sector because she never has enough capital to be an effective broker, and like David, her body is marked by the embodied experience of difference, not only in terms of her marginal position and her ethnicity, but also because she is, unknown to her, a clone. Jewel is the daughter/sister of Serafina, and as Serafina explains it to her, 'I thought I could find my immortality in a daughter. You're *mine*, gene for gene. I paid to have one of my gametes split and rejoined in a private lab. You're mine and no one else's' (1993: 238). The woman whom Jewel thought of as her mother was actually Serafina's lover, and she had carried the rejoined gamete as if it was a fertilized egg, eventually giving birth to Serafina's clone. Just she used her lover as a surrogate mother, Serafina also thought of Jewel as a surrogate self, a clone to whom she would eventually transfer her own memories, thus achieving a kind of immortality through bodily possession. However, as Serafina has come to recognize, Jewel's own distinct and developing sense of self refuses such a outcome, just as she refuses to be an object of desire for Serafina. Serafina's identification with and desire for Jewel becomes an appropriate metaphor for an exploration of the way the boundaries between the real and the simulated blur in the narrative. Significantly, both Jewel and Serafina have access to the Net, so that the struggle to articulate difference is situated both in real time and in cyberspace.

In contrast to the dominant cyberpunk view of cyberspace as a place in which identity is implicitly threatened with dissolution by and in the virtual, Rosenblum's novel presents cyberspace as an environment in which the real and the virtual persistently overlap and interact. As Henrietta Moore suggests, 'recent feminist critique of science . . . have pointed out that if our worlds are compartmentalized, they are only imperfectly so. The fact that we traffic back and forth across their borders means that they contaminate each other. More than this, they become not just intertwined, but interdependent' (1994: 130). Such border crossings allow diversity and difference to be accommodated rather than viewed with apprehension, as is the case in much cyberpunk fiction. As in the relationship between Jewel and Serafina, the relationship between David and his lover Flander demonstrates this interdependence, although in a slightly different way. Flander is also 'a VR artist' and 'one of the best operators in the Net. Maybe *the* best' (1994: 23), but Flander is utterly seduced by the possibility of becoming fully integrated in the Net, and his desire to 'lose the flesh' (1994: 296) increasingly alienates David and puts an intolerable strain on their relationship. In pursuit of his ambition, Flander becomes involved in a fraud involving the creation of multiple virtual selves which would enable their owner to control the Net illegally. Flander's death would ensure that scheme remained secret, and because his life is in danger, Flander prudently disappears. In order to make Flander come forward, David is kidnapped and severely beaten, but because he is 'netted' the horrific experience of his real-time torture is instantly transferred to the Net for public consumption, as is the enjoyment of his torturer, to be endlessly reviewed and experienced by anyone who wishes to look into the file. Although David is rescued, not only does his body bear the marks of his experience but the experience itself cannot be deleted, either from real or virtual memory, and in this way it serves both to mirror and to reveal the pleasure and the pain of the relationship between David and Flander. The narrative development of both sets of troubled and ultimately unresolved relationships allows Rosenblum to avoid the necessity of having to depict cyberspace in either utopian or dystopian terms, and with the collapse of these binary oppositions, it becomes possible to imagine cyberspace as a dynamic and fluid space within which difference can be accommodated. Embodied identity is thus not threatened with dissolution by the erosion of the boundaries between the real and the simulated.

Mary Gentle's novel, *Left to his Own Devices* (1994), combines the politics of cyberspace and the politics of female desire in a witty critique of contemporary panics about both information technology and definitions of gender identity. The narrative employs the familiar cyberpunk device of suggesting a near future world that is recognizably based on the contemporary, in this case, enervating heat indicative of climatic damage, war in Europe, and a sealed-off, gridlocked London in which tourists and middle-class refugees from the war mingle. There are plenty of other references to cyberpunk fiction, including its tendency towards dystopia, but the narrative significantly refuses to present technology in either wholly utopian or dystopian terms. As a result, the novel cannot be framed within the binary opposition between *technophobia*, and *technomania* suggested by Carol Stabile, whereby 'feminists have either withdrawn into reactionary essentialist formations [what I describe as *technophobia*] or equally problematic political strategies framed around fragmentary and destabilized theories of identity [*technomania*]' (1994: 1). Gentle is more concerned to explore the ways in which such binaries can be subverted, and she uses the conceptual vocabulary and technological determinism of cyberpunk ironically, in order to undermine the somewhat over-familiar distinction between technophobia and technomania.

The two main characters in the novel, Valentine Branwen and Baltazar Casaubon, display the kind of daunting technological expertize that most characters in cyberpunk narratives seem to possess, but their differences from such characters are sufficiently noticeable to suggest that Gentle is parodying those narratives. Thus, Valentine Branwen once worked as a programmer of simulation war games for the US Defence Department, 'I flew virtual F16s. Or, should I say, I *wrote* virtual F16s. And virtual M1 Abrams tanks, Apache helicopter gunships, aircraft carriers, satellite submarine detectors, cruise missiles . . . And I wrote the landscapes for wars' (Gentle, 1994: 25). Valentine's characterization is not wholly defined by the technology, however, and it is equally important to the narrative that she is bisexual, married to a bigamist, and currently makes a living as a sword fighter and fight instructor who takes part in battle re-enactments. Baltazar Casaubon, her husband and the father of her two children, similarly undermines the familiar image of a street-wise, narrow-hipped computer cowboy: although he, too, has recently been employed to create software for the US military, he is also a six foot four, immensely fat bigamist who appears to have a food fetish. Both Valentine and Baltazar have independently been prompted to stop working for the military because each made a crucial advance within their particular fields in information technology, and the narrative explores their agreed decision to release the two developments simultaneously into the public domain, and the process by which they implement that decision. Baltazar has developed the software that makes possible the direct neural input (DNI) of data from a human memory into a computer, thus dramatically decreasing the time it takes to transfer all existing human knowledge onto data bases; Valentine has solved the decryption algorithm and released it in a virus that will have corrupted 'ninety-five per cent of global databases' within months (1994: 140).

Valentine has to explain their decision to the track-suited, trainer-wearing Pan-European Minister of Defense, who is also her mother, and says, 'I suppose you could call this data corruption. Corrupted with change. But the world always is' (1994: 140). Although the material changes that will result from all information becoming freely available are clearly going to be of some global significance, they are not explored in the narrative and are merely described somewhat summarily in Valentine's comment, 'But there *is* going to be open government, information flood, chaos. People *are* going to know what they're not supposed to' (1994: 141). The narrative emphasis lies instead on the necessity to take for granted the fact that new technology must inevitably produce change, and Gentle thus avoids the compulsion either to celebrate or to demonize technology. Rather, technology becomes situated in a cultural context within which its meanings and uses can be disputed rather than imposed, a stance which undermines the technological determinism inherent in many contemporary accounts of the impact of information technology, including cyberpunk. Valentine explains the decision to place the information in the public domain in those terms,

> It wasn't a choice between good and bad, order and anarchy. It never is. It's a choice between the good of the powerful and the welfare of the powerless . . . The choice is between things getting worse for just the powerless, or things getting worse for everybody. It's rock bottom pragmatism. I chose the option where everybody suffers, so I can include those in power. Because otherwise only the powerless suffer (Gentle, 1994: 165).

The argument put forward here is that it is in literally everyone's interests that existing structures of power should be disrupted in order to facilitate change, which is a distinct reversal of the more familiar argument for maintaining those structures in the interests of an unspecified definition of progress.

Gentle makes ironic use of the cyberpunk device of a sentient matrix in order to further undermine any tendency towards technological determinism, since what develops from the first experimental attempt to transfer information via direct neural input from a human brain into a computer is the creation of an Artificial Consciousness (AC). In sharp contrast to the dominant masculinity of cyberpunk narratives such as *Neuromancer*, in which cyberspace seems to be 'haunted by creatures just a step away from Godhood' (Delany, 1988: 33), this AC is explicitly androgenous and it 'can answer questions we haven't asked yet. It can give amoral, pragmatic solutions to political problems – but it won't give them secretly. It can't keep a secret' (Gentle, 1994: 165). In a further radical reversal of cyberpunk, this cyberspatial entity is not concerned with the possession and control of information, but with its dissemination. Baltazar describes it as the 'collective unconscious of the information age' because 'What else would you call an artificial intelligence that works randomly, on dream-logic, and can access and download any data? No conscience and all creativity' (Gentle, 1994: 140). The device of an artificial consciousness enables cyberspace to be conceptualized in the narrative as a fluid and evolving space in which memory, information and technology are no longer objectified but, rather, interact creatively. The ironic use of conventions from cyberpunk allows Mary Gentle to suggest a near future in which change can be considered to be both creative and empowering, in contrast to other cyberpunk near futures which merely replicate and reinforce existing power structures. The predominantly masculine ethos of cyberpunk is disrupted by the unexpectedly parodic characterizations in the novel, and by the suggestion that the matrix could contain an artificial consciousness that is authentically and appropriately androgenous because it is the 'collective unconscious of the information age'. The curious masculinization of data that has resulted from cyberpunk's gendered assumptions about cyberspace, artificial intelligence and technology is thus effectively undermined by Gentle's reuse of cyberpunk motifs, as is the hegemonic masculinity of cyberpunk itself.

The singular enthusiasm for science and technology for which science fiction narratives have been noted stems from an assumption that technology can in some sense both guarantee the future and at the same time ensure that it will be a recognizable if vastly improved version of the present. Although what Andrew Ross calls 'the dark imagination of technological dystopias' (1991: 135) results in narratives which demonstrate a profound mistrust of science and technology, the near futures created in the 'technological dystopias' of cyberpunk nevertheless continue to assume that technology can and must guarantee the boundaries of the known and the familiar in the interests of hegemonic masculinity. This contradictory response to technology means that science fiction itself has become an unstable and uncertain cultural space within which anxieties about boundaries are manifold. As I have argued elsewhere (1993) cyberpunk narratives suggest that these anxieties are based around fear of the dissolution of hegemonic masculinity and of the male body, and the science fiction films that I have discussed reveal a similar set of anxieties. In contrast, the science fiction narratives by Mary Rosenblum and Mary Gentle evoke near futures that are not circumscribed by the regulatory environments of cyberpunk's 'technological dystopias', and the way in which the conventions of cyberpunk are reused in order to explore difference rather than to exclude it means that the novels are far more radical both in intent and outcome than cyberpunk itself has been. It is highly significant that these narratives incorporate the metaphor of cyberspace, not as a bounded place but imagined as a borderless and inclusive environment in which gender identity is destabilized, enabling the relationship between embodiment and identity to be creatively reconceptualized. Feminist writers in science fiction have done more than simply appropriate the genre's conventions, such as those of cyberpunk, they have also implicitly challenged what Donna Haraway refers to as the 'fictions of science', (1991: 24) and with this challenge goes an expectation that science and technology must also be redefined, perhaps as a 'paradigmatic model not of closure, but of that which is contestable and contested' (1991: 23).

Note

1 Because there is often a considerable gap between US and British publication dates for science fiction, I have sometimes included two publication dates in the same bracket, and where this is the case, the first date is the date of original publication, the second is the date of the actual edition from which I have quoted in the chapter. The page numbers refer to the second date.

References

BAUDRILLARD, J. (1988) 'The year 2000 has already happened', in KROKER, A. and M. (Eds) *Body Invaders: Sexuality and The Postmodern Condition*, London, Macmillan.

BENEDIKT, M. (1991) 'Cyberspace: Some proposals', in BENEDIKT, M. (Ed) *Cyberspace: First Steps*, Cambridge, MA, MIT Press, pp. 119–225.

BRUNO, G. (1993) *Streetwalking on a Ruined Map*, Princeton, NJ, Princeton University Press.

BUKATMAN, S. (1993) *Terminal Identity: The Virtual Subject in Postmodern Science Fiction*, Durham and London, Duke University Press.

CARTER, P. A. (1977) *The Creation of Tomorrow*, New York, Columbia University Press.

CHARNAS, S. M. (1980) *Motherlines*, London, Gollanz (first published 1978, New York, Berkley).

CHARNAS, S. M. (1981) *Walk To The End of The World*, London, Hodder and Stoughton (first published 1974, New York, Ballantine).

CHARNAS, S. M. (1995) *The Furies*, London, The Women's Press (first published 1994, New York, Tom Docherty Associates).

DELANY, S. (1988) 'Is cyberpunk a good thing or a bad thing?', *Mississippi Review*, **16**, 2 and 3, pp. 28–35.

DICK, P. K. (1991) *We Can Remember It For You Wholesale*, London, Grafton.

DOANE, M. A. (1990) 'Technophilia: Technology, representation, and the feminine', in JACOBUS, M. *et al.* (Eds) *Body/Politics*, New York and London, Routledge.

DONAWERTH, J. (1990) 'Lilith Lorraine: Feminist socialist writer in the pulps', *Science Fiction Studies*, **17**, pp. 252–57.

FOSTER, T. (1993) 'Incurably informed: The pleasures and dangers of cyberpunk', *Genders*, **18**, pp. 1–10.

GEARHART, S. M. (1985) *The Wanderground Stories of the Hill Women*, London, The Women's Press (first published 1979, Watertown, MA, Persephone Press).

GENTLE, M. (1994) *Left To His Own Devices*, London, Orbit.

GIBSON, W. (1986) *Neuromancer*, London, Grafton.

GIBSON, W. (1989) *Mona Lisa Overdrive*, London, Grafton.

GORDON, J. (1991) 'Yin and Yang duke it out: Is cyberpunk feminism's new age?', in McCAFFERY, L. (Ed) *Storming the Reality Studio*, Durham, NC, and London, Duke University Press, pp. 196–202.

GREENLAND, C. (1986) 'A nod to the apocalypse: An interview with William Gibson', *Foundation*, no 36, pp. 5–9.

GULLICHSEN, E., WALSER, R. and GELBAND, P. (1989) 'Cyberspace: Experiential Computing', *CADalyst*, December, pp. 46–7.

HARAWAY, D. (1991) 'The actors are cyborg, nature is coyote, and the geography is elsewhere: Postscript to "Cyborgs at Large"', in PENLEY, C. and ROSS, A. (Eds) *Technoculture*, Minneapolis, MN, University of Minnesota Press, pp. 21–6.

HARVEY, D. (1989) *The Condition of Postmodernity*, Oxford, Basil Blackwell.

HAYLES, K. (1990) *Chaos Bound: Orderly Disorder in Contemporary Literature and Science*, Ithaca, NY, and London, Cornell University Press.

HAYLES, K. (1993) 'Virtual bodies and flickering signifiers', *OCTOBER*, **66**, pp. 69–91.

HUYSSEN, A. (1986) *After The Great Divide: Modernism, Mass Culture, Postmodernism*, Bloomington, IN, Indiana University Press.

JAMESON, F. (1991) *Postmodernism or The Cultural Logic of Late Capitalism*, London and New York, Verso.

KLEIN, G. (1977), 'Discontent in American Science fiction', *Science Fiction Studies*, **4**, Part 1, pp. 3–13.

LANDON, B. (1990) 'Rethinking science fiction film in the age of electronic (re)production: On a clear day you can see the horizon of invisibility', *Postscript*, **10**, 1, pp. 60–71.

MASSEY, D. (1994) *Space, Place and Gender*, Oxford, Polity Press.

MAYNE, J. (1993) *Cinema and Spectatorship*, London and New York, Routledge.

MOORE, H. L. (1994) *A Passion for Difference*, Cambridge, Polity Press/ Blackwell.

NIXON, N. (1992) 'Cyberpunk: Preparing the ground for revolution or keeping the boys satisfied?' *Science Fiction Studies*, **19**, pp. 219–35.

PFEIL, F. (1990) *Another Tale to Tell: Politics and Narrative in Postmodern Culture*, London, Verso.

ROSENBLUM, M. (1993) *Chimera*, New York, Ballantine.

ROSS, A. (1991) *Strange Weather: Culture, Science and Technology in the Age of Limits*, London, Verso.

RUSS, J. (1975) *The Female Man*, New York, Bantam.

SOBCHAK, V. (1990) 'Towards a phenomenology of cinematic and electronic presence: The scene of the screen', *Postscript*, **10**, 1, pp. 50–9.

STABILE, C. (1994) *Feminism and the Technological Fix*, Manchester, Manchester University Press.

STERLING, B. (Ed) (1988) *Mirrorshades*, London, Paladin.

STERLING, B. (1994) *The Hacker Crackdown*, Harmondsworth, Penguin.

STEWART, G. (1985) 'The "videology" of science fiction', in SLUSSER, G. and RABKIN, E. (Eds) *Shadows of the Magic Lamp*, Carbondale, IL, Southern Illinois University Press, pp. 159–207.

TEPPER, S. (1989) *The Gate To Women's Country*, London, Bantam.

VIRILIO, P. (1984) 'The overexposed city', *ZONE*, Part 1/2, pp. 15–31.

WOLMARK, J. (1993) *Aliens and Others: Science Fiction, Feminism and Postmodernism*, Hemel Hempstead, Harvester Wheatsheaf.

ZUKIN, S. (1991) *Landscapes of Power: From Detroit to Disney World*, Berkeley, CA, University of California Press.

Notes on Contributors

Jean Barr is a lecturer in continuing education at the University of Stirling. She has worked in adult education for 15 years, for most of the time as district secretary of the Workers' Educational Association in the West of Scotland. She has published several articles on adult education and women's education, and she teaches the philosophy and sociology of adult education. She is interested in feminism's capacity to produce 'really useful knowledge' and in pedagogical approaches which contribute to this.

Lynda Birke is in the department of continuing education at the University of Warwick, where she teaches courses in both biology and women's studies. She has had a long interest in feminism and science and is a founding member of the Brighton Women and Science Group. Her publications include *Women, Feminism and Biology: The Feminist Challenge* (1986), Harvester. She has recently set up science courses for women in Coventry, which (she hopes) are based on really useful knowledge.

Rohini Hensman is a freelance researcher and writer working with women's groups and trade unions, and the author of *To Do Something Beautiful*, a novel focusing on the lives of working women in Bombay.

Nancy J. Lane lectures and researches in the zoology department at Cambridge University, where she is also an Official Fellow at Girton College. Born in Canada and the mother of two children, she has published widely in the fields of cellular and neuro-biology. She chaired the working party on Women in Science and Technology for the Cabinet Office, which published a report, *The Rising Tide*, in 1994. This led to the instigation of a Development Unit in the OST to carry forward the recommendations and encourage greater participation of women in science and technology. Dr Lane was awarded an OBE in the 1994 Queen's Birthday Honours List.

Many Maynard has recently transfered to the department of social policy at the University of York, having previously been director of the Centre for Women's Studies there for 11 years. She has published on issues relating to feminist theory and methodology, race and ethnicity and violence towards women, and is currently developing a project on older women.

Hilary Rose is Emerita Professor in social policy at the University of Bradford, England. In 1995/6 she spent six months as a guest professor in feminist studies and science theory at the University of Göteborg. She has published widely in feminist science studies. Her most recent book is *Love, Power and Knowledge: Towards a Feminist Transformation of the Sciences* (1994), Polity. Currently she is working on the Human Genome Project and on the social shaping of research policy in the European Union.

Anne Scott is a lecturer in women's studies at the University of Bradford, where she is completing a doctorate on the historical relationship between alternative health and feminism. She has a background in philosophy and is interested in feminist epistemology and the embodiment of knowledge.

Cecilia Ng Choon Sim teaches gender and development studies at the Universiti Pertanian Malaysia where she is an associate professor. Her current research focuses on new technologies and women's employment in the services and industrial sectors. She is currently seconded as a research fellow to the United Nations University Institute for New Technologies (UNU/INTECH), the Netherlands. Cecilia is also active in women's groups in Malaysia.

Elizabeth Sourbut has a BSc in physics from the University of Durham and an MA in women's studies from the University of York. She is currently a freelance writer specializing in science fiction, and has reviewed books for, amongst others, *New Scientist, New Internationalist* and *Everywoman* magazines.

Pat Spallone formerly worked as a biochemist in medical research. In 1984 she took the MA in women's studies at the University of York where she began researching and writing about social dimensions of reproductive technologies and genetic engineering. Her most recent book is *Generation Games: Genetic Engineering and the Future of Our Lives* (1992), The Women's Press, London and Temple University Press, Philadelphia.

Ailsa Swarbrick is a senior lecturer in the Open University's Yorkshire Region, where amongst other things, she set up and was responsible for the Women in Technology (WIT) returners' scheme. A returner herself, most of her employment has been in university adult education both in the UK and overseas. Her particular interests have been in contributing to equal opportunities policies and helping translate them into practice.

Jenny Wolmark teaches cultural theory in The Hull School of Art and Design at the University of Humberside. She has published articles on science fiction, cyberpunk, and feminism, and is author of *Aliens and Others: Science Fiction, Feminism, Postmodernism* (1993), Harvester Wheatsheaf. She is currently researching the relationship between cyberspace and the post-human body. She is co-editor of *The Journal of Gender Studies*.

Index